MONEYWISE

YOUR GUIDE TO KEEPING AHEAD OF INFLATION, TAXES, AND THE DECLINING DOLLAR

To Dave Boy

Charles Knott

MONEYWISE

YOUR GUIDE TO KEEPING AHEAD OF
INFLATION, TAXES,
AND THE DECLINING DOLLAR

Charles Kraut

Tate Publishing & Enterprises

This book is designed to provide accurate and authoritative information with regard to the subject matter covered. This information is given with the understanding that neither the author nor Tate Publishing, LLC is engaged in rendering legal, professional advice. Since the details of your situation are fact dependent, you should additionally seek the services of a competent professional.

RET Elliott wave charts from elliottician.com used by permission.

The opinions expressed by the author are not necessarily those of Tate Publishing, LLC.

Published by Tate Publishing & Enterprises, LLC
127 E. Trade Center Terrace | Mustang, Oklahoma 73064 USA
1.888.361.9473 | www.tatepublishing.com

Tate Publishing is committed to excellence in the publishing industry. The company reflects the philosophy established by the founders, based on Psalm 68:11,
"The Lord gave the word and great was the company of those who published it."

Book design copyright © 2009 by Tate Publishing, LLC. All rights reserved.
Cover design by Jeff Fisher
Interior design by Cole Roberts

Published in the United States of America

ISBN: 978-1-60799-336-0
1. Business & Economics: Personal Finance: General
2. Business & Economics: Investments & Securities
09.05.28

Contents

Introduction 9

How This Book Is Organized 17

Chapter One: the Wealth Creation Way 19

Part I

Why should you manage your money? 23

Chapter Two: Why invest? 25

The importance of reducing your dependence upon government and becoming more self-reliant in financial matters, particularly retirement.

Chapter Three: Three: The Five Is 29

Part II

The Basics 43

Chapter Four: What is a "financial professional"? 45

The financial services industry is very different from most professions. Here are the reasons why millions of Americans don't get what they pay for.

Chapter Five: Guaranteed to Win: How Wall Street Takes More People for More Money Than Las Vegas Ever Will 63

Who derives the greatest benefit from creating and maintaining "free and fair capital markets?" Hint: it isn't you.

Chapter Six: What You Don't Know—How to Get The Right Amount of the Information You Need. 75

A brief overview of the myriad sources of information available to investors, with some suggestions regarding their value and usefulness.

Chapter Seven: "Do It Yourself" 81

Part III

Tools and Techniques 101

Chapter Eight: Saving More and Spending Less 103

Most Americans lack the discipline to put money aside regularly. Here are some ideas you may find useful.

Chapter Nine: Making It Grow: Stocks, Bonds, Mutual Funds, and ETFs 115

The value of opinions and the basics of common investments: stocks, mutual funds, ETFs, bonds, and options.

Chapter Ten: Making It Grow: Options and Leverage 131
Chapter Eleven: Making It Grow: Commodities.. 143
Chapter Twelve: Making it Grow: Precious Metals, Gems, Real Estate, Art, and Collectibles 147
Chapter Thirteen: SIR 169

Part IV

Risk and Reward 175
Chapter Fourteen: Understanding and Managing Risk.. 177

The nature of risk and how our investment decisions are or should be affected by it.

Chapter Fifteen: Analyzing Investments.. 183

An introduction to fundamental and technical analysis.

Chapter Sixteen: "This Time It's Different".. 193

Are there rules in investing that always apply? Were there any in the past? What's different about the world today, and how will it affect your money?

Chapter Seventeen: Keeping ahead of Inflation 199

In personal finance, the single most important risk we face is that of not increasing the purchasing power of our money.

Chapter Eighteen: How do you figure out what to buy? 213

When the financial plan is complete, investment decisions need to be made.

Chapter Nineteen: Trading and Investing.. 225

The differences between trading and investing.

Chapter Twenty: Tax Avoidance Is Legal; Tax Evasion Is Not 245
Chapter Twenty-One: Protecting Yourself.. 247

Part V

Creating a Brighter Future 251
Chapter Twenty-Two: Participating in the Global Economy 253

Gallery..259

Appendix..285

Links 287

A Brief History of Money...289

Bibliography 293

Recomended Reading...297

Index..299

Endnotes 317

Introduction

Why this book?

This book is about money. It's about what it is and what it isn't, about what it's worth, how to obtain it, and how to spend it well. Lots of books on personal finance talk about those things, but here the similarity ends. This book will help you understand how you can effectively compete against the best and brightest on Wall Street and carve your own path to financial success. In these pages you will find out how to avoid many of the traps Wall Street sets for the unwary. You will learn what constitutes a *real* rate of return. You will understand how money can work for you and why it may well have been working against you.

The Federal Reserve ("the Fed") was created by Congress in 1913 and charged with one primary mission: to preserve the value of the U.S. Dollar. Since then the Federal Reserve has slowly and systematically debased and depreciated the dollar so that today it takes a dollar to buy something that cost three cents in 1913.

That's the "good" news. The bad news is that the Fed has accelerated its efforts in recent years. The dollar you depend on for everything in your life is quickly being destroyed.

I think you ought to do something about that. This book will help if you understand what is happening and apply its lessons.

Unless you have at least $3,000,000 or more in investments (or a very large, guaranteed pension plan) don't plan on retiring anytime soon; if you are like more than half of all Americans, you probably won't be able to afford it. More and more Americans are working until they simply can't work anymore. Most of them have little choice.

That's my wake-up call for millions of Americans for whom the American dream is becoming the American nightmare. While we are being lulled into a false sense of security, the world we know is vanishing. It is being replaced by one we won't recognize, a world with great promise and tremendous peril. Financially, most of us fall into the "peril" column.

Here are some of the reasons why the future holds great promise:

- Technological advances will accelerate, offering solutions to many environmental problems.

- Medical science will develop cures to more and more illnesses, extending the length of life and helping to improve its quality.

- Access to information will increase as traditional forms of education adjust to the Internet age.

These are wonderful things, but that list does *not* include some items most of us would like to see:

- An informed and involved citizenry who actively participate in keeping our republic alive and vibrant by preserving the principles of the founders.

- An upsurge in morality, integrity, and ethical conduct.

- A federal government whose members feel bound by their oath of office to uphold and defend the Constitution of the United States.

- Elementary and secondary schools all across the United States that teach without bias or political agenda, who see it as their duty to build character and integrity in those for whom they are responsible.

And then we have the negatives that are causing our future to be imperiled:

- The presumed "fact" of global warming, with the possibilities of catastrophic climatic changes, continued desertification, loss of agricultural land, and so on.

- The end of "the American Century" as we begin what will be called "the Chinese Century."

- The gradual but accelerating decline in the available supply of crude oil.

- The increasing use of terror as a weapon.

- America's immense debt burden.

- The real threat of running out of critical natural resources.

- The desire of billions in the third world to the live a first-world standard of living.

- Overfishing in the world's oceans resulting in the loss of many "commercial" species.

- Destruction of the rain forest due to slash-and-burn agriculture.

- Growing rates of illiteracy, even in the United States; dropout rates of over 30 percent from high school.

- A negative national savings rate as cash-strapped consumers dig deep into their home equity to continue to maintain their lifestyle and live beyond their means.

- Unpredictable financial markets that deliver poor performance to a growing number of participants.

- The greatest real estate bubble in history in the American housing market, a bubble that has begun to burst.

- The systematic destruction of the U.S. dollar, the source of most of America's remaining wealth, through printing-press inflation.

- Our growing dependence on government rather than ourselves as the solution to our problems.

Why is money so important?

Why is money so important? To a great extent it defines your *potential.* It determines the quality of your life, though your net worth and your quality of life are not synonymous. If you are like most people, you want to enjoy the comforts of life and perhaps have a few luxuries. You want to have a good career earning adequate pay for doing work you enjoy. You want to own a home you can be proud of. You want to be able to provide for your family. If possible, you would like to send your children to a good school of their choice and provide some if not all of the costs of their education. Finally, you would like to be able to retire and live in comfort and dignity for the rest of your life.

Most Americans cannot afford to do these things. Forty-six percent of the American people pay no income taxes because their income does not meet the minimum threshold. There are 2.39 million millionaires (and three hundred or so billionaires) in the United States out of a population approaching three hundred million. The rest of us fall somewhere in between those who pay no taxes and those who are paying too much.

Even if you have a million dollars, it will not provide a comfortable retirement these days. That's why so many of us are dependent on welfare - which is the correct legal description of Social Security. Social Security may keep sending out checks each month for the rest of our lives, but those checks will be payable in depreciating dollars and will pay a dwindling share of our monthly expenses.

In other words, most of us fail in the most significant aspect of our lives, the one thing that affects all the others: the accumulation and management of money. We fail because we let our spending habits rule our lives instead of carefully managing our income. That's the key difference; we want what we want and will do whatever it takes to obtain it. If obtaining what we want causes us to spend more than we earn, we hope for that raise or that better job—or for a boost in housing prices so that we may sell at a profit or refinance and pull out the money we need.

Failure is not an option any of us would choose. The common wisdom—that we *deserve* the things we want, and that we don't need to think about tomorrow—is not entirely our own fault. It is pushed on us by every advertisement we see. The push is always to buy because you deserve it, as if deserving something were a valid economic criteria.

Consumption at the expense of all else—and especially at the expense of common sense—is called for not only by Madison Avenue, but by the highest levels of government. We are told that our economy will falter if we stop spending. It is, we are told, our patriotic duty to spend more money to keep the economy chugging along. For fifty years we have done just that. In that same period of time, we have gone from being the richest nation in the world to the greatest debtor nation in the world. Perhaps it's time to end our spending binge and pay more attention to the growing risks and uncertainties of life.

Crisis and Opportunity

We live in a day of great crisis and great opportunity. More millionaires and billionaires walk the planet than at any time in history, even as a million dollars buys less and less each day. There is greater hunger, disease, pestilence, war, and strife than ever before. Life has become vastly more complex, and we are inadequately prepared to deal with its complexities.

We expect to live longer than our parents, and we think we will enjoy a comfortable retirement after funding our children's college education and having kept up with the Joneses throughout our working lives. We think the government will take care of us and provide us with our health care needs as well as our income in retirement. America, the land of the free and the home of the brave, has become an empire of debt and the home of the dependent.

One book will certainly not solve our problems and set us back upon the path of self-reliance. In this volume I will not address many of these compelling issues except to show how you may work around them. What I hope to do is establish a platform upon which you may build a more secure future for yourself and your family. I want to teach you the things you need to know to be more successful in managing your personal finances. Those who learn and apply these things need not be blindsided by events, nor watch as the future goes against them.

• • •

The Available Literature

If you have read one book or many on the topic of personal finance, you may have discovered that they don't seem to be written for people like you or me. Some are written for people who already have millions to diversify into the author's favorite investments. Others are written for people who can apply a simple strategy and watch their money multiply over thirty to fifty years. A few are written for people who are willing to accept the recommendations of another on nothing more than blind faith.

That leaves out a lot of people. It leaves out those who are struggling to pay their bills, who are concerned about the security of their job, who are dreading the day when the kids go off to college, or who would like to enjoy a higher standard of living without paying much more for it.

Actually, there are books written for the latter group. They are the feel-good books written (or ghost written) by popular entertainers and motivational speakers. These books usually can be condensed into a couple of paragraphs of investment advice; the rest is fluff and bragging. Unfortunately, these books are indeed very successful, for they make a lot of money for one person in particular—the author.

I have read dozens of personal finance and self-help books over the years. I have met many of their authors. I have tried to put their ideas, strategies, and recommendations to good use but have found that each book was lacking in one area or another. No book (including this one) is meant to stand alone.

Personal finance books on the market today fall into these categories:

- Financial planning–basics of savings and investment, income taxes, retirement planning, college planning, budgeting, etc.

- Topical self-help–authoritative guides to working your way through the Medicare or Medicaid bureaucracy, for example.

- Estate planning–basics of wills and trusts, life insurance, powers of attorney, etc.

- Investment guides–basics of investing in stocks, bonds, mutual funds, ETFs, limited partnerships, and so on.

- Analytical guides–specific strategies for investing. Strategies fall into two categories, fundamental and technical, which will be discussed later in this volume.

- Specific focus investment books–dealing with one category of investment, such as rare coins, residential real estate, stocks, or others.

- Feel-good books–"Here's how I made my millions, and you can too." Don't waste your money on these. Almost all of them stretch, distort, and embellish the truth.

- Prediction books–these focus on a single upcoming event and try to build a rationale as to why it will happen and when. These books can be either negative or positive, e.g., "The Coming Crash of ____" or "Dow 36,000" (a real title, by the way).

- "Issue" books–"Voice of warning" books that make a case about how your privacy is being invaded or how the decline of the dollar will affect you in the future or why Saudi oil will run out much sooner than we expect. Some of these are well researched, well written, and very useful to certain types of investors.

- "Political" books–why the Federal Reserve is a fraud, or why Social Security will collapse just when we need it, or why the actions of Congress have prevented Americans from getting a raise in real dollars for the past thirty years.

- What is lacking in all of these books? Each usually has *something* worthwhile to offer, though digging through the fluff can be time-consuming and frustrating. None of them, however, takes into consideration all of the factors that can affect your savings and investments. Most simply ignore key issues.

- I recently read a book on exchange-traded funds (ETFs) that gave a reasonably detailed description of what an ETF was and why it was superior in some ways to a mutual fund, but it gave no clues as to how to find a specific ETF, nor how to decide when to buy it.

- I have read numerous "issue" and "political" books about America's enormous debt burden, and how in two generations we went from the world's richest nation to the greatest debtor in history. None of them adequately address the question of what to do about it, either politically or personally. Not offering a plan of action is somewhat like watching the evening news; most of us are powerless to change anything, so why bother watching?

• I would also like to provide a basic but comprehensive overview of the world in which we live as it pertains to your financial future. With the decline of the dollar and persistent inflation, there is much to be considered if you hope to make your money grow in real terms.

If you are genuinely interested in improving your financial situation I hope you will be motivated by this overview to pursue further reading in areas of interest. I will reference numerous recent books in this volume, but there are many more that can be helpful once you are on the right track. I will not attempt to dictate a specific plan or path you should follow. Rather, I hope to help you find your own successful path to financial freedom, in which you will utilize those tools and techniques that are best suited to your temperament and risk tolerance. My role is that of educator and facilitator; I teach you the basics and make available programs and investments of many different types.

• • •

This book has a fairly broad scope, but it is by no means all-inclusive. I'm not going to talk about real estate or Chinese porcelain or antique furniture because I'm not qualified to advise you on these subjects. I'm going to talk about what I know, what I have worked with daily for close to thirty years.

Keep in mind that for the majority of those who create wealth, the best path to riches is a high-paying job or, even better, their own business. Owning rental real estate, though cyclical, has been an effective path to wealth for some who knew what they were doing and whose timing was good. Owning a dry-cleaning establishment, selling real estate, being a stockbroker, or providing a valuable service has worked for others.

With over a million millionaires in the United States, you can be certain that they didn't all make their money in the stock market. Opening a medical supply store next to a brand-new hospital worked very well for a client of mine several years ago. Four mostly profitable years of operations prepared them to sell the business for a profit of several million on an investment of less than a tenth that amount.

Another client had a good business going of making private, short-term loans. Before we met he had made only one disastrous foray into what most people would call "investing." A stockbroker contacted him and got him to open an account. The client insisted upon complete safety and was given the usual reassurances by the broker. Within a few short months, the client had lost several hundred thousand dollars on an investment neither he nor the broker fully understood. The client had made an expensive venture outside his area of expertise and was victimized by a financial "professional" who was anything but.

• • •

What Most People Need and Seldom Receive

Most of us need to be pointed in the right direction. We need to get up to speed on what is really important, and we cannot afford to waste time and effort learning about things that have little value. I will help you cut to the chase. I will show you some methods that work, why they work, and how you can make them work for you.

I have been serving my clients for almost thirty years. I work with people like you and me, people who work for a living. I don't work with millionaires; I work with people who need me. This book is written primarily for those who don't yet know that they need the kind of services I provide.

The difference between me and most other people who write books on personal finance is that I take personal responsibility for my clients' money. Think about that for a moment. How many people in either the retail or the service professions do you know who actually take responsibility for ensuring that your relationship with them is successful?

That responsibility affects the way I look at things. I cannot "just" be a salesman; I must perform a great deal of research to be able to make specific recommendations to each client. If I sit across the table from a prospective client in an adversarial relationship, as is usually the case between salesman and prospect, it is unlikely I will be able to do much good. Instead, I work *for* them. They tell me what they would like to accomplish with their personal finances, and I do everything in my power to make it happen.

In this book I will try to highlight some of the techniques, strategies, traps, and pitfalls of personal finance. I will do what I can to make the material as readable and enjoyable as possible. In these pages you'll probably read things you have not heard about before; you'll see the financial markets from the point of view of one who has participated in them both as an investor and as a professional for many years. You'll find an unusual point of view. I have no axe to grind, and I do know where many of the "bodies are buried." My goal is to help you discover how you can improve your financial situation day by day. You will do this with a higher degree of safety while taking less risk, managing your risk more effectively, and enjoying a better real return than you may have experienced previously.

How This Book Is Organized

Whether you have significant investment experience or have never invested before, you will find something of value in this book. For this reason I recommend that you read it straight through. If, however, you are simply looking for the essence of my rather unique point of view, you might want to focus on the following chapters:

1. Part III, chapter thirteen.

2. Part IV, chapters fourteen through nineteen.

3. Part V, chapter twenty-two.

• • •

Part I

These chapters are designed to help you understand why actively managing your disposable income is so very important to you and your family. I always feel that we're better motivated when we know *why* we do the things that we do. In the chapter on the five *Is*, I will begin to make a detailed comparison between the truly professional financial adviser and the majority of people who call themselves financial professionals.

• • •

Part II

This section is devoted to the basics. I will describe in the financial services industry as it exists today and talk about why it generally does not work to your benefit. You'll read about Wall Street from the perspective of one who has been a part of it for over twenty-seven years. We will talk about how to obtain the right amount of high-quality information to help you make your investment decisions, and we will discuss which parts of personal financial management you ought to do yourself.

• • •

Part III

This section is devoted to the tools and techniques of financial planning and investing. We will discuss setting aside a larger portion of your disposable income in more detail than we did previously. I wish that every American could have a cushion, whether it's money in a cookie jar or a comprehensive, fully-implemented financial plan using the most sophisticated, state-of-the-art investments available today.

We will then review a lengthy list of investments and investment vehicles, which I will prioritize as I see them fitting into your financial plan. Finally, I will show you a simple way to sort out your assets to understand better how each piece fits in. I call it SIR, "Savings, Investment, Retirement."

• • •

Part IV

The chapter on understanding and managing risk is one of the most important in this book. In it you will learn about some types of risk that are generally not discussed by most financial professionals. That knowledge will help you make better investment and financial decisions.

We then discuss what you must do to be successful. I will talk about how you can apply the analytical methods I described in chapter fifteen to overcome the "triple threat" of inflation, taxes, and the declining dollar.

Now that you have a firm foundation in my view of the financial world, I will present specific strategies that I use every day with my clients. I believe this combination of strategies is unique to me, in part because I know of no other financial professionals who have the experience, the training, and the licenses to enable them to utilize all of these strategies with their clients.

Part IV concludes with brief discussions about taxes and protecting ourselves from known and unanticipated liabilities.

• • •

Part V

Finally, I will raise several issues of particular importance in our day. Some of these issues deserve further study, and I will refer you to reliable sources you might want to investigate. I do not fully discuss these issues in this book, but I am watching closely as we strive to find solutions to them.

• • •

Let's get started!

Chapter One

The Wealth Creation Way

There are millions of people in this world who call themselves financial professionals.

Most of them have opinions about the markets and how you ought to manage your money.

Most of them are wrong.

Why? Because they don't see the full picture. As you will see in chapter four, those who call themselves financial professionals are often, at best, professional *salespeople* whose job it is to make *your* money their *employer's* money. Most of them conduct their business in such a way as to fully comply with all the applicable regulations. That way they keep themselves out of trouble. What they know about the world and how they react to what is going on in the world does not necessarily translate into any benefits for their clients.

The Wealth Creation Way is different. My job is to provide you with all the education, solid research, good advice, and encouragement you need to make better financial decisions every day of your life. I will not waste our time talking about things you can read about in any financial publication. Much of what you see in the print media, on the Internet, and on TV and radio regarding investing is worthless because it's not useful to you.

You need to do three things:

1. Create a personal financial plan that will help you navigate decisions, pitfalls, and traps in personal financial management.

2. Set aside more money out of each paycheck for savings, investment, and retirement.

3. Make every dollar you have work harder and more efficiently for you.

I help people create their own personal financial plan and motivate them to set more money aside. Most people go through life without a financial plan.

The most important thing I can do for you is to make your savings and investment dollars work harder and more efficiently for you. In this I have one goal: to make sure that the return on your savings, investments, and retirement funds at least equals the combined effect of inflation, taxes, and the declining dollar.

Since most Americans seldom or never achieve that goal with their money, I have a lot of work to do. I can't do it all myself, which is why I wrote this book. I want to help Americans find out what they *really* need to know about money. You can create and implement an appropriate, meaningful, worthwhile personal financial plan only if you have the right information and know what to do with it. Knowing what you need to know will enable you to accomplish the things you really want to do in life.

• • •

A Unique Approach

Let's look at how the *Wealth Creation Way* makes it possible for people like you and me to stay ahead of inflation, taxes, and the decline of the dollar. Here is my first fundamental principle of personal money management:

> There is not today, nor is there likely to be in the future, *any* savings account, money market fund, bank certificate of deposit, or fixed annuity that will pay enough to keep ahead of inflation and taxes.

People buy these things because they are "safe." They are safe in only one sense of the word, and that is that your principal does not decline *in amount.* However, the purchasing power of that principal *does* decline every year that we have inflation. For example, if inflation is running at 6 percent per year and your CD or annuity is only paying 5 percent, you are falling behind. In other words, *most fixed products are "guaranteed" to lose money in an inflationary environment.* We are in an inflationary environment and have been for many years. It is unlikely that we shall ever enter a deflationary environment again. The last one of any great significance was the Great Depression, and our government and the Federal Reserve will do whatever is necessary to make sure that we do not repeat that event.

Having said that, think for a moment about this: what will enable your money to keep ahead of inflation, taxes, and the declining dollar? The *only* things that will—and I have come to this conclusion after many years of extensive research—are those things that are called *investments,* and they have an element of *risk.*

Risk is that four-letter word so many people hate and fear, primarily because they do not understand it. Risk can be managed and even controlled to some extent, but it takes work and discipline to do so.

The Wealth Creation Way separates the world of investments into two specific categories:

- The U.S. stock market, and

- everything else.

I make that particular distinction because stocks, and especially U.S. stocks, can be bought and sold on any day the market is open for minimal commissions. Today's technology enables money to literally fly around the world at the speed of light, and stocks are an ideal vehicle to take advantage of rapid changes in investor sentiment.

Everything else includes tangible assets that may require storage and maintenance, and which are marketable only through a less direct process of matching up buyers and sellers. If you have to search for a buyer you do not have a marketable asset.

I use a different set strategies for each category.

There is a long list of criteria an investment must meet for me to recommend it to my clients. Three of them are much more significant than the others. They are:

1. The investment must have the *potential* to provide returns in excess of the combined effect of inflation, taxes, and the declining dollar.

2. The investment must be *marketable;* it must be easily bought and sold, and there must be a relatively large pool of prospective buyers. This excludes the vast majority of investments such as antiques, art works, businesses, and individually owned real-estate properties, both commercial and residential.

3. The investment must produce a *history* of price performance. This excludes many collectibles, among other things. I don't mind if an investment has a roller-coaster history with lots of volatility; rather, I am looking for consistent trading.

Let's look briefly at each of these categories and see how the *Wealth Creation Way* deals with them.

• • •

The Stock Market

The stock market is a very important investment category. You don't buy "the market"; you buy one or more of the stocks that comprise the stock market.

• • •

Everything Else

Here's a list of the investments outside the U.S. stock market I frequently recommend for my clients:

1. Silver: one-ounce silver eagles, "junk" 90 percent silver dimes, quarters and half dollars minted before 1965, and ten- or one-hundred-ounce silver bars.

2. Natural Resources ETFs and mutual funds.

3. Foreign currency ETFs with covered call options against them.

4. Gold and silver precious metals ETFs and mutual funds.

5. High-yielding closed-end mutual funds and ETFs selling at a significant discount to their actual value.

6. Twenty-dollar gold "double eagle" coins minted by the U.S. Mint prior to 1933 and graded by either NGC or PCGS at MS-63 or higher.

7. Energy trusts that pay a large, reliable dividend.

8. Alternative energy ETFs and mutual funds.

This is a peculiar list both because of what it includes and what it excludes. Note that I say that these investments are outside the U.S. stock market, but many of them trade on those same markets. We don't have much choice in that if we are to get the marketability I insist upon. Also, these investments are primarily in commodities rather than paper securities—at least, the mutual funds and ETFs (except for number three and number five) are based in certain commodities, all of which have an intrinsic value.

• • •

In Summary

Most Americans are honest, hard-working, respectable people who work very hard and would like to get more out of life. The *Wealth Creation Way* provides a middle ground where, if you are willing to learn and do a little work, I can help you make better financial decisions and do better financially.

There is much that separates the *Wealth Creation Way* from the Wall Street herd. In the pages that follow, you will gain insights as to how and why the *Wealth Creation Way* was developed. Much of my work involves finding ways to reduce the risks in investing without sacrificing the potential for gains. I will show you several strategies that can help you do this successfully. You will lear was n how you can do this yourself.

Many financial authors confine their careers to writing about money and investing. Financial professionals usually confine themselves to selling investments and insurance. Money managers confine their activities to managing money. I do all three, and I do them every day. This gives me a unique insight that will benefit you as you read this book.

The Wealth Creation Way is not a static thing. Change is rapid and constant, and I must adapt. I have personally tested the methods and strategies you will learn about in this book, and I am constantly working on refinements and new methods. You can profit from doing what I do.

In this book you will learn how you can create real wealth for yourself and protect your family during these very uncertain times.

Part I

Why should you manage your money?

Chapter Two

Why Invest?

Each of us has twenty-four hours available to us each day. We spend most of our time meeting our needs and caring for our families. We awaken from sleep, prepare for the day, commute, exchange our time for an income, commute again, and, if we are married, try to be husbands or wives, parents, or grandparents until it is time once again to rest.

Most of us are very busy doing those things, and these days it seems we are busier than ever. The activities of daily life can leave us little time for that which is just as important. There are "labor-saving" devices that can make us more efficient in the use of our time. Some of us are set in our ways, "too busy sawing to take time to sharpen the saw" as Stephen Covey would say.

If we work for an hourly wage, we may be spending too many hours trying to earn enough to meet our basic needs. Many Americans who work for a salary put in many extra hours without additional compensation because we feel it is required of us. The economy is weak, good jobs are hard to find, and we cannot afford to be out of work, so we put in the extra time.

I advise my clients who work for a living to spend their careers doing something that is personally fulfilling, something that pays more than a wage and benefits. Since we spend so much of our time working for a living, we ought to accomplish more than getting another raise or obtaining a promotion. Work should be edifying; it should afford us opportunities for personal growth.

As an employer, I have always tried to hire people who wanted more than a job, people who were willing and able to make a positive contribution to my organization. When one of my employees is on the job, I deserve their loyalty and their best efforts each workday. I believe in a full day's work for a full day's pay. I do not want personal concerns, hobbies, or any type of distraction keeping them from giving their best each day. To that end I try to create an environment in which all can share in a sense of purpose, a place where personal contribution and effort are valued. After all, my job is to serve those who wish to work with me as my clients. The better I can serve them, the more successful they will be. I want my employees to share my commitment so that my business can be more successful.

You need to utilize some of your precious spare time to manage your finances. You don't need to be a "day trader", with one eye on the markets throughout the day. What you need is a regular, constant source of worthwhile guidance and ideas that you can incorporate into your personal financial plan.

I have spoken with many people who take time from their workday to monitor their investments. It's hard not to do because the markets are open during working hours. You shouldn't be trading your 401(k), for example on the company's time. The strategies I have developed are designed to be put into place "on your own time."

Let's say that you have looked at your financial situation and have outlined some goals for the future. These goals can only be subjective, for we have very little control over our own disposable income, the markets, Congress, the IRS, or the economy. As long as we have inflation, you will not be able to put a price tag on expenditures planned for several years from now. You want the money you have set aside to work for you and build a nest egg you can rely on.

Making any amount of money work effectively and efficiently for you requires some active investing. Investing takes time and effort. If you don't work on your investing at work or when you are asleep, you will have to steal time from those few hours that you share with family and friends.

I come back to my original question, which is "Why Invest?" The question has two parts: first, why should you set money aside for the future, and second, why should you devote the necessary time and effort to becoming competent at managing your money?

If you never set anything aside, you never need to invest. Unfortunately, far too many of us adopt that approach because we let "necessities" drain off our disposable income. As recently as thirty years ago, it was very common for men to retire in their early sixties and be dead in a year or two, in some cases because they could not adapt to having all that free time. Such people didn't really need to invest because their employer of thirty years provided a modest pension. For those who didn't receive a pension, the government invented Social Security as welfare for the destitute who had attained what was then the "extreme old age" of sixty-five.

Things are different today. Americans are living much longer, and we need to find out how we are going to pay our way after we retire. In fact, for many people retirement is becoming a more significant financial event than buying their first house.

Even if Social Security was fully solvent - and it is not - it would not provide the income you need to live comfortably in retirement. Social Security pays benefits like a defined *benefit* plan, but it is funded like a defined *contribution* plan. Defined benefit plans are required to provide benefits for life and, these days, even to survivors of retired workers. For this reason an actuary must make educated guesses each year about how much must be put into the plan. Defined contribution plans only pay benefits until the money runs out. The day of the defined benefit pension plan is over because corporations realized what government did not: giving a person an unlimited stream of income can be equated to fiscal suicide.

What we are seeing now is a major shift to defined contribution plans, even in the public sector. Defined contribution plans offered by corporations and other private employers are usually funded by the employee. The employee is motivated to do so by the understanding that his money will grow faster because the plan enjoys a favorable tax status. No taxes will be paid on contributions or growth until after he or she retires. The matching contributions made by many employers can be another motivation.

To answer the first part of the question, *we must invest because we probably will not always bring home a living wage.* We might become disabled, we might get laid off, we might retire, or we might face unanticipated financial consequences. In such circumstances our investments - or their absence - will determine the quality of our lives for some time to come. If you think that putting food on the table when you have a job is difficult, imagine what it's like when you cannot go back to work. Even if you have a comprehensive program of life, health, and disability insurance, you still need a good investment program. If you become disabled, the law permits you to receive disability benefits of no more than 60 percent of your income; your investments will have to make the difference.

The second part of the question is, why should you become competent in managing your own investments? If you are a participant in a defined contribution plan or if you own an IRA, it is up to you to manage your own funds. You *have to* make investment decisions, even if it means simply taking the lowest risk available and dumping the money into the stable income fund or fixed account. The latter happens to be a very popular choice, and it is almost always a mistake. Many people choose it because they don't want to take responsibility for that portion of their future. If you don't invest wisely or if you take the "easy way out," your retirement accounts will probably not grow enough to provide you with the income you will need in retirement.

Investing will take some of your time and some of your energy. Some of your investments will lose money. You will take risks you do not fully understand, and you will suffer from losses you could not reasonably have anticipated. Despite this, investing done properly will improve the quality of your life. It will broaden your horizons and increase your awareness of the world around you. Intelligent investing can lead to financial freedom. The purpose of this book is to show you how to do it properly.

Chapter Three

The Five *Is*

If you want to invest, you must have disposable income. Disposable income is what's left over after you have paid all of your bills. If you can't afford to pay off your credit cards in full each month, you don't *have* any disposable income[1]. Many Americans are in that situation today, but with proper planning and some discipline, you can change that.

Many times I have been introduced to someone as a financial adviser, and that person shook my hand and told me that he wished he had money to invest. Each time I wanted to reply that if you wish to have a large sum to invest you need to begin now with a small amount. You have to start somewhere. If you have to start small, start small. Any plan is worthless if it has no start date or completion date. For many, investing requires self- discipline. Unfortunately, that is a virtue many do not possess.

What about those who don't think they can afford to set money aside or for those who do not believe they have enough money available for investment to interest a true financial professional?

The answer to that is simple. If you are like many Americans, you feel that you cannot afford not to put money away on a regular basis. Our generation has convinced itself that we need to "live for today." Numerous reasons are cited for that philosophy, but most of them distill into the five *Is*:

- Inertia

- Ignorance

- Inadequate income

- Inflation

- Investment risk

• • •

Inertia

You probably remember inertia from high-school physics. It's that old law about how a body in motion tends to stay in motion, while a body at rest to tends to stay at rest. Many Americans are "at rest" when it comes to saving and investing, and they either need to find a way to overcome that inertia or find someone who can help them overcome it.

Inertia can be overcome. Most people just don't know what to do. Many people who have invested have had a bad experience—especially after the market's collapse in 2008. Investing seems to be just too much work, and if they do it at all, they would rather leave the decisions and the responsibility to someone else. In fact, most people don't know what to expect and don't know how to assess their results.

Case in point: the U.S. stock markets have made no progress since October 1998. There are three well-known primary stock market indicators: the Dow Jones Industrial Average (DJIA), the Standard & Poors 500 (S&P 500), and the NASDAQ 100 (NASDAQ). All are down significantly from their year 2000 peaks. In other words, if you bought almost any of the thousands of stock mutual funds at the 2000 peak, you are losing money.

That does not mean that there have been no opportunities to make money in the stock market during that period; it simply means that most stock funds and stock index funds haven't done you any good.

My clients have enjoyed significantly better returns by investing a portion of their money into specific market sectors, including real estate, precious metals, natural resources, energy, and energy services. This involves market timing, which many claim cannot be done. It can, and I will show you how.

Much of my clients' money that is in the stock market and *not* in the sectors named above is in vehicles that have no downside risk. These vehicles offer you the opportunity to participate in the stock market's gains but not its losses. Would you feel more comfortable about putting money away for the long term if you knew that you would at least break even every year? I have asked that question hundreds of times, and no one has ever said no.

Our inertia usually stems from our attitude. We see ourselves living from paycheck to paycheck, and we see our friends and neighbors doing the same. We convince ourselves that we are doing the best we can and that everyone we know is in the same boat. We often can't see things getting much better in the foreseeable future. We feel that if we began something now we would be very disappointed if we had to quit later on.

Many Americans have lost the initiative and drive which made this country such an economic powerhouse. Maybe we're just living too long these days, and we outlive our income. Maybe we have become too dependent upon government at all levels to support us and to bail us out when we need help. Whatever the cause, I find that most people want to have confidence in the future, in themselves, and in someone they trust to give them good advice.

I show people a better way, a proven, successful way that they should begin right away to secure their financial future. Most people are unskilled investors with limited experience and available time. Even those who enjoyed a brief fling during the "dot.com" bubble generally got burned when it burst. Few people ever invest regularly and systematically into anything that can do them much good over the long run. After all, many investments have not kept up with inflation. Why would you put your hard-earned money into something that doesn't retain your purchasing power?

The best way to overcome inertia is to *start moving*. I have never met anyone in their working years who couldn't find a way to begin a systematic program of investment. I try to provide enough education for my clients to make informed decisions. Once they have made their decisions and implemented a plan, it is up to me to ensure that the plan they have implemented is successful.

I do not expect my clients to know as much about personal finance as I do, nor do I expect them to remember all that I tell them. If I can bring them to a point where they are comfortable with the decisions they are making and are comfortable with me, we have the basis of a good working relationship.

• • •

Ignorance

Most Americans don't know a fraction of what they need to know in order to succeed with their investments. Don't feel badly; most financial professionals don't either. As is the case with many disciplines to which we are exposed from time to time—medicine, law, accounting, tax preparation, and so on—we ought to do our own homework and not rely solely on the advice of others. As a nation we have become far too complacent and dependent. Life is so complex that we have to seek the help of "experts." Throughout my career I have attempted to educate my clients so that they may make informed choices. In almost every case they have simply gone along with my recommendations. Because I know my recommendations are sound, I permit it, but that's not the way I would like it to be.

To me, it is important for a client to have the humility to acknowledge that he or she doesn't know everything there is to know. I can work with people who have that attitude. If they will work with me, most of the time I will make them more successful financially than they have been previously.

For a number of years, I gave "update" seminars for my clients and the general public. In those seminars I would try to bring people up to speed on the latest investments, programs, and techniques I was using. I would explain what I expected from each of them, and why I felt they were appropriate for my clients. I believed it was my obligation to try to provide that type of ongoing education. It didn't take too long to realize that most of my clients—and almost everyone else—were not really interested. They were too busy doing other things, and as long as they felt they could trust me they didn't think they needed to learn more.

Now, instead of trying to get my clients to come to seminars, I provide a quarterly newsletter. This way I fully discharge my responsibility to educate my clients, and my clients may learn from it as much as they wish. I also invite my clients to contact me at any time when they have specific questions about any aspect of personal finance, especially when they have questions about things we have not discussed.

I don't mind that my clients have other things to do than to listen to me. I enjoy my work because I know that I'm helping them. The research I perform on behalf of my clients enables me to meet people all over the world and gain insights and wisdom from them.

As long as my clients do not have the time or the inclination to learn more about personal financial management, I have only two concerns for them:

First, I must remain completely objective and focused upon their needs and their wishes.

Second, and perhaps more important, all of us can be susceptible to a sales pitch. Knowledge and experience can be our only defense. In chapter four we will talk about what happens in the world of investments and how it is often completely legal for people to make outrageous claims and promises for their products and services. I do what I can to protect my clients from people and products that can harm them.

When we're sick, we go to the doctor. When we get sued, we hire a lawyer. When April comes around, we find a tax preparer. When we want to do better financially, there's nothing wrong with seeking out a financial professional you feel you can trust. The doctor doesn't try to teach you everything he knows about medicine; a financial professional shouldn't feel he has to teach you all there is to know about money. We all need to rely on others in our complex world, but we should not rely *solely* on the advice of others. It's up to you to fill in the gaps in your knowledge so that you can make *informed* decisions. That knowledge will give you some additional comfort when you have to make a decision about surgery, or that little legal problem, or the investment your broker is recommending.

• • •

Inadequate Income

For many of us it seems that our income is inadequate to allow us to set money aside regularly; for some, the little we save comes from bonuses or tax refunds or just scrounging together enough on April 15 to fund an IRA for the previous year.

It is easy to believe that the necessities of life overwhelm our income. Sometimes that is the case; the gap between rich and poor has been widening for decades, and the great American middle class is rapidly shrinking. Americans' incomes have been declining in real dollars since the 1970s. One of the reasons I became a financial professional was to help address this huge problem.

In some instances, however, we have confused "needs" and "wants." These days, what we need is comprehensive, competent health care, but what we want is to obtain it for free. We think little Johnny ought to go to an Ivy League school—and we don't realize that incomes equalize five years after graduation regardless of our undergraduate school. We think we need a new car or that boat or RV or that expensive vacation, but what we *really* need is the peace of mind that comes when we are engaged in a program that will improve our long-term financial security.

I don't spend a lot of time reviewing my clients' income and expense statements, which they prepare at my request. It doesn't take long to find expenditures that made their way into the "necessities" column that rightly belong in the "luxuries" column. Addiction to tobacco is a tough habit to kick, but everyone knows that they will be much better off if they quit. It amazes me that people will throw down $4.00 and more at Starbucks for a cup of coffee, often more than once a day, and think nothing of it. We all have our "toys"—boats, planes, sports cars, hobbies, and such—and our SUVs, home theaters, high-speed Internet connections, resort vacations, skiing trips, and much more. We splurge on these things because "we deserve it." Many of us go into debt to obtain these things. For the first time in history our national savings rate has turned negative because we have confused "wants" and "needs."

Many of us know the psychological toll that comes from worrying about debt. It is a wonderful thing to replace that worry with a growing feeling of financial security.

We *can* reduce our cost of living. It may take some work, but it is worth the effort. It is also possible to spend less on almost everything we buy. More important, we can save money by not spending it or by "postponing gratification." Americans have an addiction to eating out that has greatly rewarded the restaurant industry for decades. If we eat well-prepared meals at home, we will save a significant amount of money and spend more time together as a family doing the things that can bring families together. Saving just $1.00 per person per day in a four-person household by preparing and meals at home adds up to $41,073.28 over an eighteen-year period, if compounded at 5 percent per year.

"Postponing gratification" can mean waiting until you can pay cash for something before you buy it. If you don't think you will ever have enough cash saved up to make that purchase, maybe you should reconsider whether you can afford it. Just because you can make payments over time with interest does not make an item less expensive.

Many Americans fail to take advantage of one of the easiest ways of improving their financial circumstances. Many of my clients work for employers who offer company-sponsored retirement plans. If your employer offers a 401(k) and you do not participate, you are passing up an opportunity to have Uncle Sam pay a portion of your contributions. If your employer offers a matching program, you are passing up free money.

Eliminating habits and addictions—tobacco, alcohol, and Starbucks come to mind—can contribute significantly to our financial health and perhaps to our physical health as well. For example:

- 1 pack of cigarettes per week = $182.00 or more per year. Invested at 5 percent, that's at least $8,686.33 after twenty-five years.

- 3 beers per week = $129.87 or more per year. Invested at 5 percent, that's $6,198.32 after twenty-five years.

- 3 purchases from Starbucks per week = $416.00 or more per year. Invested at 5 percent, that's at least $19,854.47 after twenty-five years.

These numbers may not look all that impressive, but they ignore several points:

- Prices are for low-priced items on special at the supermarket.

- Your consumption may be greater than indicated.

- You might receive a better return than 5 percent on your money.

- You might have continued your habit for more than twenty-five years.

- The health and social costs of regular consumption of these products (with the possible exception of caffeine) are incalculable.

There are other ways to maintain our standard of living while spending less money. (See chapter eight.) I do not intend to make people "savings poor," whereby they are setting aside so much money that they have nothing left to live on. However, most of my clients will not be able to retire comfortably at the age of sixty-five. Most of us 1) do not save enough, 2) will live longer than our parents, and 3) will live longer in retirement than our parents or previous generations. It's one thing to be "savings poor," but it is quite another to run out of money when you're too old to go back to work.

Some of my most enjoyable and gratifying appointments over the years have been those with people who thought they could not afford to invest. I would show them how, if they could free up some disposable income to invest, I could apply my methods and research to obtain an above-average return. Then I would show them how they could free up some income so that they could invest. It's almost like creating something from nothing.

• • •

Inflation

"In a social democracy with a fiat currency, all roads lead to inflation."

John Templeton

"The CPI as calculated may not be a conspiracy, but it's definitely a con job foisted on an unwitting public by government officials who choose to look the other way."

Bill Gross

Most of us think we understand inflation, but we really don't. We read reports of changes in the consumer price index and think that an increase in the index is inflation. On those rare occasions when the index declines, we think we have deflation. Neither is correct.

Inflation is "falling money," or money that is losing its value. Inflation is brought about by the creation of money that has no backing. It can also come about when prices rise due to increased demand or scarcity. The laws of supply and demand have little to do with real inflation except insofar as the money supply is concerned. Rising prices are merely a symptom of inflation. Since so much of what we see and hear in the media is concerned with "price inflation," it is often difficult to keep the correct definition in mind.

We have seen the effects of inflation for almost a century. The decline in the value of the Federal Reserve note is only the latest in a series of declines in the value of various American currencies. The first inflation took place in the late 1700s when our currency was called the Continental. Too many of them were printed so that the government could meet its obligations. Their value fell to almost zero, thus giving rise to the expression "not worth a Continental." History repeated itself during the Civil War with the rise and fall of the "greenback." (Take a look at Images 1 and 2 on page 262 and 263 for examples of these.)

Take a dollar bill out and look at it. Note that is says "Federal Reserve Note" across the top. Note that it also says it is legal tender for all debts, public and private. Technically, the dollar is not issued by the United States Government; it is issued by the Federal Reserve. The dollar is not backed by the full faith and credit of the government; in fact, it has no backing at all except whatever amount of gold may remain in the vaults of the Federal Reserve. This is "fiat money," "money whose usefulness results not from any intrinsic value or guarantee that it can be converted into gold or another currency, but instead from a government's order that it must be accepted as a means of payment."[2]

Through its actions the Federal Reserve has created far too much money. Each new dollar debases the value of every dollar already in circulation.

In fact, the Federal Reserve was created in 1913 for the specific purpose of protecting the value of the United States dollar. Since its creation the Federal Reserve has managed to decrease the value of the dollar by more than 95 percent.

Much more recently, after World War I Germany was faced with huge claims for war reparations. Unable to pay and facing economic disaster, the decision was made to simply print more money. None of this money was backed by gold. The result shows how quickly money can lose its value.

In February 1923 an attractive multicolor twenty-thousand-Reichsmark note was printed. By that date 20,000 Reichsmarks was just about enough money to buy a loaf of bread. In June of that same year the one-million-mark note was printed. By that time it took a million marks to buy a loaf of bread. In October of 1923 the one-billion-mark note ("*Eine Milliarde*") was printed in two colors on a small piece of plain off-white paper. By the time it was printed, it took about one billion marks to purchase a loaf of bread. (Images 3, 4, and 5 in the center section show these bills.)

You may have seen some of the pictures of people taking wheelbarrows full of paper money to the store. Employees were paid twice a day, and they had to spend their earnings immediately before prices were raised again.

In the summer of 2006, Zimbabwe became the latest in a long line of countries to devalue their currency, in this case cutting *twelve* zeros off of their paper money. Mexico had done the same thing a few years earlier. The history of the world is littered with worthless paper currencies. The United States dollar is following a similar course. We are already at the point where we should cut one or two zeros off of our currency.

Inflation, then, is "falling money." Deflation is its opposite, "rising money." When deflation occurs the currency *increases* in value.

Throughout most of the history of the United States our Federal government felt it important to pay off the national debt. Debt was usually incurred during wartime and was repaid during peacetime. This policy ended after World War I when the United States government decided we should come out of isolation. The Great Depression gave our government another excuse not to pay off the existing debt and to incur a much larger national debt. That debt expanded during World War II and rose tremendously throughout the Cold War. It continues to rise today to the highest levels in history.

Today it would appear from the actions of our Congress and our presidents that deficits and debt no longer matter. Both the executive and legislative branches and members of both parties have become profligate spenders. In a few short decades, the United States has moved from the world's wealthiest nation to the greatest debtor nation in history. The once-mighty United States dollar, like every other debased currency, will become worthless. That's a sobering thought, and the primary reason why I spend so much of my time looking at alternatives to the dollar.

● ● ●

Investment Risk

Most Americans are quite naïve about risk. We'll spend quite a bit of time talking about risk because it is of vital importance and because we need to understand it better. I don't know how many times a client or prospective client told me that they're not afraid to take risks as long as they don't lose any money. It's that type of thinking that makes us vulnerable to financial professionals. We tend to focus our attention on the sales pitch, and we minimize the risk.

In general terms, investment risk has everything to do with the possibility that we will not get back all that we put into a particular investment. It's the old discussion of "the return *of* your investment versus the return *on* your investment." Prior to making each investment, we must determine whether we would be comfortable with the losses we might suffer as a result of owning it. Would we be more comfortable with a 25 percent chance of a 50 percent decline, or a 50 percent chance of a 25 percent decline? Most of us don't even think that way. This is one reason why so many financial professionals talk so much about diversification, as if that were a general panacea to eliminate or at least offset risk.

The theory is that if you divide your money among several different investments you will reduce your level of risk. That wasn't the case in 2008.

In fact, *investment risk* is only one of several risks that we need to consider when we evaluate a particular savings or investment program. Though it is seldom discussed, (perhaps because few people can discuss it knowledgeably) *dollar risk* or *currency risk* is just as important as investment risk. Let's say that you pick a good investment and purchase it with a full understanding of its investment risk. The investment then increases in value by 20 percent, and you take your profits. You then have the privilege of paying capital gains taxes.

What if, during the time you held that investment, the value of the dollar fell by 20 percent? You would have lost money. Even if the 20 percent gain in the stock fully offset the 20 percent decline in the purchasing power of those dollars, taxes would have taken away some of your gains.

Example:

$10,000 invested

+   *$ 2,000* gain (20%)

$12,000 new value of investment

($2,400) Currency declines by 20%

$ 9,600 purchasing power ($12,000 adjusted for decline in the value of the currency.)

In other words, the entire value of your investment declined *in terms of what it will buy.*

There are other ramifications to a declining dollar, which we will discuss later on.

Throughout my career I have struggled with the problem of risk. Only recently have I begun to feel comfortable in being able to manage risk. That comfort level rose as the quality of my analytical tools increased.

Millions of Americans own stock mutual funds. You only have to glance through a prospectus to understand that a stock mutual fund carries a significant amount of risk. Don't be swayed by the notion that the fund's diversified portfolio reduces or eliminates risk; it doesn't. Some of the world's best stock fund managers saw their funds fall by 50%-70% and more in 2008 despite good diversification.

Most people prefer to buy a bank certificate of deposit or insurance company annuity contract because they have a guarantee of principal and interest. In other words, there is no investment risk. However, if your certificate of deposit is paying 5 percent and inflation is running at 7 percent, you are losing 2 percent per year even before you pay taxes on your interest income. That makes certificates of deposit and fixed annuities guaranteed losers during inflationary times.

The methods most financial professionals use to mitigate risk can be ineffective. Diversification and dollar cost averaging are among the most popular, and neither is particularly useful. People in my business use those methods because it protects *them.*

Financial professionals are heavily regulated and are placed under strict requirements of fair dealing with their clients and customers. A stock broker or financial professional is usually quite accustomed to seeing his clients lose money on some of the investments they purchased from him or her. Preaching the "gospel" of diversification helps to take the investment professional "off the hook" by reducing his responsibility and his liability when he puts a client into an investment that turns out badly.

Let's take the example of a "family" of mutual funds, which is simply a group of mutual funds of different types all managed by the same management company. The financial professionals tell you that you'll be saving money by putting all of your money into a particular family of mutual funds rather than spreading it out across several families.

Since we all want to save money, this sounds very appealing. In most cases, however, the investment professional will suggest four or five funds within the fund family almost at random. Everyone wants a "growth" fund, and if you buy one you need to offset the risk of that fund with a lower risk fund such as a "total return" fund or an "equity income" fund. There should also be a "bond" fund in the mix, because bonds are usually less risky than stocks. However, most financial professionals are convinced that the stock market is the best place to be, and they slant their recommendations toward stocks.

There was a short-lived advertising campaign by a mutual fund company on the theme: "There's never a *bad* time to buy a *good* investment." That statement is generally false: it can only be correct if market timing is impossible. I will never forget a conversation with a financial professional who told me confidently that "if the client wants to make more than 6 percent per year I just put him into a growth stock fund." This approach completely ignores the greater risk of stock mutual funds—and making it should cost him his license.

If you accept your broker's recommendations, you might have a "growth" fund, a "total return" fund, a "value" fund, a "bond" fund and a money market fund. If you diversify in this manner–and most people do - it is most likely that in any market two of your five funds will be going up, two will be going down, and one will be "dead in the water."

Millions of Americans have access to a 401(k) at work. Most 401(k) plans have been established by the employer to limit the number of investment choices available to each employee. They don't want to put anything "risky" or "exotic" on the list because that could lead to a lawsuit down the road. They also want their employees to focus on their jobs rather than their retirement plans. For these reasons most 401(k)s are pretty useless in today's volatile markets.

Here's what the choices in a typical 401(k) plan look like:

Choice No.	Name	Type	Objective	Risk
1	Growth	Stock	Higher potential returns from rapidly growing companies	High
2	International Growth	Stock	Higher potential returns from newer, smaller overseas companies	High
3	Emerging Markets	Stock	Higher potential returns from companies outside the industrialized world	High
4	Small Cap	Stock	Higher potential returns from newer, smaller companies	High
5	Value	Stock	Higher potential returns from "undervalued" companies	High
6	Small Cap Value	Stock	Higher potential returns from smaller, unseasoned "undervalued" companies	High
7	Growth and Income (Stocks)	Stock	Higher potential returns from rapidly growing companies plus dividend income from older, more established companies	Moderate to High
8	Total Return	Stock and Bond	Diversification within the fund itself, along with a return superior to that available from income investing or CD rates alone.	Moderate to High
9	Global Growth	Stock	Higher potential returns from companies located all over the world	High
10	International Value	Stock	Higher potential returns from "undervalued" companies outside the U.S.	High
11	Capital Appreciation	Stock	Higher potential returns from domestic "special situations" or "pure-growth plays"	High
12	Growth and Income (Bonds)	Bonds	Above-average return from a combination of fixed-income securities (bonds) and dividend-paying stocks	Moderate
13	Balanced	Stock and Bond	Diversification within the fund itself to provide a high yield along with some capital gains.	Moderate to High
14	Money Market	Short-term Fixed Income	Stability of principal and a fluctuating interest rate	Very Low
15	Stable Value	Guaranteed Income Contract (GIC)	Stability of principal and a fixed interest rate generally higher than that offered by money-market funds	Very Low

Do you see how imbalanced this assortment of funds is? Let's break down the list.

- Ten of the fifteen choices are nothing but stock funds. Most of them are high-risk funds by definition. The only thing mitigating their risk is the inherent diversification of a mutual fund.

- Twelve of the fifteen choices are stock funds or stock and bond funds. All twelve, therefore, carry the higher risk and greater volatility associated with stocks.

- There is only one bond fund available, and that fund is described as a growth and income fund. That means that the manager most likely will take additional risk to increase the fund's overall return by purchasing lower quality, higher-yielding bonds.

- Neither the money market fund nor the stable value fund is deemed to have any risk of principal. Since they have no risk of principal, they likewise offer no opportunity for growth. In the right economic environment, a well-managed bond fund will provide capital gains as well as interest. At least one of the four basic categories of bond funds should be represented on the list. That would be a government-securities fund, a high-yield bond fund, a high-grade corporate-bond fund, or a worldwide-bond fund.

- The most glaring omission is the sector funds. International investing is not a sector; energy or banking or precious metals are. In our day of inflation and a declining dollar at least *one* fund should be available that can beat inflation.

- Nevertheless, this list is very typical of those used by corporations today. Americans deserve better, but we also need to be better educated about our choices.

- In hundreds of interviews with financial professionals, I was amazed at how often I saw this approach used. I decided that there had to be a better way to invest. The idea of diversification, if properly applied, is a good one. Wouldn't it be better, however, to identify five categories of investment that are going up and divide your money among them?

- If you believe that "you can't time the market," you would think that you simply cannot find five investments that are all going up. Much of my work over the past dozen years has been an effort to refute that notion. What I have found is that market timing is no more an exact science than fundamental or technical analysis. That does not excuse a financial professional from making an attempt.

- When I was still in the securities business, the broker-dealer firm I was with prohibited its representatives from also being investment advisers. In other words, we could either make our living selling investments, or by managing them; but we could not do both. Since most financial professionals have to be better at selling than they are at research and analysis, they are forced by experience and temperament to stick to selling. The research and analysis, the prognostication of the future must be left to others.

- The year 2005 provided a classic example. The overall stock market performed poorly during that year. The top-performing market sectors in the United States in 2005 were real estate, oil and gas, precious metals, and energy services. The top-performing bond or fixed-income sector was high-yield bonds. None of those choices appear among the available choices of most 401(k) plans. Most financial professionals, because of their liability, did not use some or all of those sectors. In fact, most of them allocated most of their clients' money among the standard choices, including index funds.

- In 2005 I placed as much of my clients' money as I could in places where they had access to what I believed would be the best-performing sectors in the market. As a result, my clients had their money in energy, precious metals, real estate, and high-yield bond funds. We were diversified, but our diversification was among those sectors of the market most likely to perform well. 2005 was a good year for my clients.

Now that we have identified the five *I*s, we can address and overcome each with knowledge, motivation, and diligent application. Let's start by looking at one of the biggest obstacles people face when they want to become successful investors; the "financial professional."

Part II

The Basics

Chapter Four

What is a "financial professional"?

No more than one man in ten, at least in the United States, is really a master of the trade he practices. The rest take money for doing what they are quite incompetent to do, and thus live by false pretenses.

H.L. Mencken, from Minority Report, 1956

Most Americans are misinformed about the financial services industry. Unlike medicine and other professional fields, you will encounter many unskilled, unprofessional, and even dishonest people. Many of them want to make *your* money *theirs*. Please pay close attention as I review what you can and cannot expect when you work with my peers.

In hundreds of interviews over the past twenty-five years, I have put together a "man on the street" definition of a financial professional. This incorrect definition is based upon the perceptions of those who *utilize* financial services. It lumps together those who call themselves financial planners, financial advisors, stockbrokers, insurance salesmen, accountants, estate planners, and investment advisors. Here are some common characteristics, the things most people expect in a financial professional:

- He (or she) will charge a fee just to visit with him, just as an attorney or CPA would.

- He is knowledgeable about his specific field, a generalist in all areas of personal finance and a specialist in his specific area.

- He has significant experience in personal finance.

- He has specialized education and training in personal finance.

- He has specific skills that the layman does not possess.

- He works for his clients.

- He holds to high standards of ethical conduct and integrity as dictated by his professional standards.

- He is capable of helping me do better financially.

- You have to have a lot of money to invest just to be allowed to talk to him.

I have told thousands of people that the above statements are generally untrue, and the universal response has been one of disbelief. Even if they have never worked with one, most people expect a financial professional to be just that - professional. They expect him to have the same training and skills for his field as their doctor does in the medical field or as their lawyer does in the legal field. Very often this is not the case.

I do not imply that employment in the financial-services industry is not a valid profession. It is—but it is a *sales* profession. You need to understand that due to the complex and sophisticated nature of personal financial management, most people, if they obtain financial skills of any sort, tend to specialize on one area and spend most of their time working in that area. Also, the entry level in the financial services industry is very low. To become a stockbroker, you pay some fees, get fingerprinted, and pass a test. In many cases, the rest of your training is on-the-job training. Much of that training involves making cold calls.

In the early 1980s, I worked for a major brokerage firm in one of their Dallas offices. Every Monday morning everyone in the branch was called into the conference room for a meeting. The branch manager would stand up in front of the group and tell us that we needed to sell $15 million worth of this and $10 million worth of that, and as soon as we had done that we could sell our customers whatever we wanted to for the rest of the week.

One of the biggest Wall Street firms required newly licensed brokers to dial the telephone at least three hundred times every working day. These brokers would utilize a typical telemarketing script to introduce themselves and the company and to try to sell something almost blindly. If they could get someone to open an account and deposit money into it, they got to keep their jobs.

I remember my branch manager giving me his office, the largest in the branch, and moving his desk into the corridor. I had become the top producer in the office, and I cannot recall that he ever asked me what it was that I was selling. He was only concerned that I was bringing in enough commissions to justify *his* existence.

A licensed representative in the financial services industry is a *salesman*, first, foremost and, in some cases, always. Whether or not he becomes a *professional* is up to him. His employer will specify the activities in which he may engage. If he (or she) is licensed for the sale of securities, every word he speaks or writes is (or is supposed to be) regulated. If he wants to offer a client a particular investment product that is not on his employer's approved list, he may not do so even if he feels that that product is superior to anything his employer has to offer. If his employer does not offer a full spectrum of insurance and investment products, that representative must either function without a full menu or risk losing the client to someone who can provide the products he cannot.

Because of the great complexity and sophistication of the financial markets, most investment professionals focus on one specific area and devote their full time to it. For example, there are thousands of people who spend their days on high school and college campuses selling retirement programs to faculty. This business is popular with the representatives because once it is established it provides a regular income almost indefinitely. In some instances the representative does nothing but promote those specific retirement plans; others try to generate additional business from those same clients by selling life insurance, CDs, and other non-retirement investments.

On a given college campus, an employee may be contacted regarding his retirement plan by anyone from a single-product "captive" agent to a "jack-of-all-trades" insurance agent whose primary business is property/casualty insurance. The employee is left to decide whether he should work with a representative who only has one product to sell or someone for whom his retirement plan will be just a side business. It's a difficult decision because the single-product salesman must promote the virtues of his product to the exclusion of all others, whereas the "jack-of-all-trades" spends most of his time working at his insurance business.

Many years ago I hired a young man who represented one of the best-known insurance companies offering products to the educational community. He was referred to me by one of his clients, and he was drawn to me because I was not captive to any company or product. He also appreciated the fact that I took responsibility for my clients' money, something he was forbidden to do. Most important, however, was that his company had instructed him not to talk about their mutual funds because of their poor performance. People with integrity often have difficulty selling inferior products.

There are people in the financial services business who are very successful and who have developed a formula for their success. One in particular claims to spend no more than forty-five minutes with any prospect, after which the prospect—who has now become a client—is ushered out of the room and into a different office where he or she will complete the paperwork and write the checks. I call this the "assembly line" approach to financial services. To me it is cold and impersonal, and is designed to generate commissions for the representative rather than to create wealth for the client. Why is this individual so successful? Part of it may be due to the attractiveness and celebrity of success itself.

Let's review the nine points I brought up at the beginning of this chapter.

He or she will charge a fee just to visit with him, just as an attorney or CPA would.

This is true only of certain individuals, those known as "fee-only" planners. Most financial professionals, particularly securities and insurance sales people, are compensated primarily by commissions. They may also receive trailing commissions, service fees, management fees, and other income and from financial products they have sold to you.

He is knowledgeable about his specific field, a generalist in all areas of personal finance and a specialist in his specific area.

This is generally untrue. Those who are relatively new to the business, in particular, are likely to have very little training or experience in any field of personal finance. If they have been around for a few years and have focused on an area of specialization, they may not be knowledgeable or perhaps not licensed to work in other areas of personal finance.

He has significant experience in personal finance.

This is often untrue except perhaps among those who have many years in the business. "To the person who is good with a hammer, everything looks like a nail." Those who survive in the financial-services business usually do so because they have gotten good at one thing. When their clients need other products and services, they are often referred to friends and associates who specialize in those areas. For middle-class Americans, this makes it difficult to do any "one-stop shopping." We usually have to deal with several different people, and often those people have differing and even conflicting ideas about how we should handle our personal finances.

He has specialized education and training in personal finance.

To the credit of the industry, many financial professionals have been encouraged to seek out further education in their field. To retain and renew most securities and insurance licenses, representatives must receive continuing education on a regular basis. Many professional certifications and designations have been developed during the past twenty-five years, some of which helped increase the professionalism of the industry. Most of them are not mandatory. Most of them have a rather narrow focus.

The certified-financial-planner designation, for example, is rather broad in its scope and provides an excellent overview of investments, insurance, and estate planning. Unfortunately, however, it is only available today to those persons who charge a fee to create a financial plan. I had to drop my certified financial planner designation because my typical client neither needs nor can afford a full, written financial plan.

He has specific skills that the layman does not possess.

Any licensed financial professional possesses *knowledge* which the layman does not, simply because the representative had to pass an often rigorous examination. The *skills,* however, come with training and experience. Even the best educated and most experienced professionals will come up against questions they simply cannot answer. With a federal income tax code that runs into tens of thousands of pages, none of us has all the answers.

He works for his clients.

When you talk to any financial professional, you have to ask yourself who he is working for. If you are buying homeowner's insurance, an independent agent might be the best choice. If he knows his business, he can put you into the most appropriate policy with the best company. He's not restricted to a handful of products from the company to which he is a captive agent, and because he must be knowledgeable in a wider variety of products he might just be more professional.

On the other hand, when you get that dreaded phone call during dinner time from some stockbroker who just wants to get you to open an account, you know he's not working for you.

The real test, however, comes when you are sitting down across the table or across the desk from someone you've never met before and who was referred to you by a friend. At that moment you need to be able to determine whether he is actually interested in you or whether he views you as just another commission. Does he give intelligent answers to your questions? Does he seem knowledgeable about those areas of concern to you? Do you think he is deserving of your trust?

It's always awkward, especially during a first meeting, for you to ask pointed questions about things the representative is suggesting or recommending to you. You could learn a lot about him (or her) by examining the commissions associated with his favorite investment products. Here are some examples:

A. Limited partnerships carry some of the highest commissions available in the securities industry today. Limited partnerships have a very specific purpose and are useful to only a certain relatively small segment of the population.

B. There are several "classes" of mutual funds available today. Class A carries the maximum allowable "front-end" commission; these days, representatives who use class-A funds are often more interested in the commission than in their relationship with you. With Class-B funds you are not charged a front-end commission. However, the representative receives a front-end commission and a small trailing commission. Class-C funds may have a small front-end commission, but most have a larger trailing commission. A representative has to keep you as a client to continue to earn commissions from Class-C funds.

No-load funds charge no commissions; representatives who use them will probably charge you a management fee. They too will need to keep you as a client if they want to keep getting paid, and that means that your account has to do well enough to justify their fee.

C. When you look at life insurance, the agent who offers nothing but whole life may be trying to earn the highest commissions available. In certain instances, however, there are good reasons why whole life is superior to other forms of life insurance.

Commissions are by no means a perfect determinant of the financial professional's motivations; they can, however, provide valuable insights into what he thinks of you.

He holds to high standards of ethical conduct and integrity as dictated by his professional standards.

It has been my privilege to know some honest, competent individuals in my industry. These people are genuinely interested in their clients and want to do what is best for them. In many cases, however, their ability to serve their clients is limited by many of the factors listed above. Some have an area of specialization outside of which they lack expertise. Others work for firms that significantly restrict their activities and the products they may offer.

Then there are those persons—and there are all too many—who are "in it for the money." They don't spend their time trying to find better ways to help you meet your financial needs; they spend their time looking for ways to get their hands on more of your money. Some of these people are misguided, some of them are inexperienced, some are unethical, and some are downright dishonest.

If an investment idea sounds too good to be true, it probably is. You may have to use that adage along with your gut feeling about the person when you're deciding whether you want to work with him or her.

I could devote an entire chapter to people I have met who were only interested in themselves and who were in the financial services field because it was a way for them to make a lot of money. Though there are many regulations in place, it is still up to you to make good decisions. Recouping losses from bad investments or being victimized by unethical sales practices is painful and difficult.

He is capable of helping me do better financially.

This is not necessarily true. You will need to ask lots of questions and make your own judgments. If this professional has used the same products and strategies with every client for several years, you should look elsewhere because he (or she) is probably out of date.

Personal money management is dynamic and ever changing because the world in which we live is dynamic and ever changing. Something that was an outstanding investment for over twenty-five years may no longer be something you should consider. If the management has changed, the laws governing the investment have changed, the fees have increased, the performance has plateaued, or if the investment has gotten too big to be manageable, you need to find something better and more current.

You have to have a lot of money to invest just to be able to talk to him.

This seems to be a reasonably valid notion based upon the familiar, stereotypical Wall Street professional. Often it is true. There are, however, individuals who are willing to work with the middle class. I prefer to work with the American middle class; they need the assistance of a highly skilled financial professional just as much as the wealthy. Besides, their situations tend to be relatively straightforward.

Most middle-class Americans don't need to concern themselves with dual passports, complex estate planning, trust relationships, offshore banking, and some of the more sophisticated techniques and vehicles available only to those who have good lawyers. Instead, they need a knowledgeable, experienced coach who will encourage them to set more money aside and do the best job possible in protecting what they have and making it grow.

• • •

Financial Services Job Descriptions

When you choose a financial professional, you ought to know what to look for. Here are some of the common titles found in the financial services industry today.

Stockbroker. This term has almost gone out of use, as has *bond broker* in the past quarter century. One of the reasons for this is a growing public awareness that stockbrokers do just that—they sell stocks and other investments for a commission - and little else. Twenty years ago some of the larger Wall Street firms wanted to call their stockbrokers something else, such as "financial advisors" or "financial consultants," but because of the regulatory environment and the potential liability associated with such designations, they did not. Today, the term *financial consultant* has gained wider usage, particularly at the larger Wall Street firms. In many cases it still applies to a stockbroker, a person whose primary focus is on common stocks.

As the environment has changed, the job of a stockbroker likewise has changed. Today's stockbroker usually deals with stocks, bonds, mutual funds, limited partnerships, and possibly the sale of insurance products. Certain products like variable annuities require both a securities license and an insurance license. The designation "stockbroker" or "financial consultant" does not necessarily indicate professional qualifications. The requirement to become a stockbroker remains the same; you have to pass a test.

Why would you go to a stockbroker or "financial consultant" you knew had no additional qualifications? Usually they would contact you through telemarketing, or you would go to them because you have been referred to them by a friend who had received a "hot" tip from them. Remember, regardless of what you call them, stockbrokers or financial consultants usually charge the maximum commissions available and as much in additional fees as they can for any other services they provide. If you have access to the Internet, you can do just about everything that a stockbroker could do for you, and pay less in commissions and fees.

Insurance agent. Just as there are many different types of insurance, there are many different types of insurance salesman. You may expect any insurance salesman to have a fair amount of training, though if he or she is new to the industry most of that training may have been sales-oriented. Unless he is selling life insurance through a multi-level marketing organization, the salesman should have some degree of professionalism and some expertise in the products he or she is offering you.

There are several categories of insurance salesmen. They include:

- Property/casualty. These are the folks who sell you your homeowner's, auto, and personal-property insurance. These are areas of specialization requiring ongoing training and continuing education.

- Life and health. As the name indicates, these people focus on life insurance, health insurance, disability-income insurance, long-term-care insurance, and related types of insurance. I have great respect for professional, experienced life insurance salespeople who can put together complex insurance programs either in connection with estate plans or business plans.

- Specialty insurance. These people focus on those types of insurance you often don't hear about, those which often are sponsored and made available by employers. This would include cancer insurance and other specialty medical insurance, which should be purchased by persons who have a family history of that particular illness. Specialty insurance has become much more popular in the last few years because of a very well-known duck.

- Annuities. Many people obtain an insurance license solely for the purpose of selling annuities. As was mentioned above, the sale of variable annuities requires both a securities license and insurance license. Standard, traditional fixed annuities require only an insurance license. Both products have been immensely popular, as are the latest entries to the annuity field, the Total Return Fixed Annuity (TRFA) and the Equity Index Annuity (EIA).

Insurance, like everything else in the financial services industry, is dynamic. Products, laws and regulations, life expectancies, and people's needs change. There are people who focus solely on exclusive lines of insurance. More often, they have an area of specialization, but they use another to attract new business. For example, there are many insurance agents working in the area of retirement called 403(b). 403(b) is their base income and their source of new clients, but they specialize in life insurance, health insurance, financial planning, or something else.

Insurance agents tend to stay away from products that do not compensate them well. Many agents don't like to sell term life, because the commissions are quite low relative to the amount of work required to get the policy underwritten. Some insurance companies actually sell directly to the public over the Internet; other insurance companies use an agency. Since the agency does not have commissioned agents, the compensation paid to the agency is less than what an ordinary agent would receive.

All of this only complicates the process of finding the right products and the right professional. Not only are many insurance products difficult to understand, but buying them requires a series of very subjective decisions. Just as a Cadillac salesman wants to sell you a Cadillac, so any insurance salesman wants to make sure that you can fit into the products that he has to offer.

Knowing what you need and what's available to you is part of what this book is about. We will discuss insurance needs in chapter twenty-one.

Financial planners. These are individuals who in some cases have specific training in the various aspects of personal financial planning, which includes investments, taxation, insurance, and estate planning. Unfortunately, the designation "financial planner" is not restricted, and it can be taken on by just about anyone. Only the designation "certified financial planner" (CFP) is restricted to those who have actually earned it and who charge a fee to produce a written financial plan.

When you get into a discussion with someone about your personal finances who claims to be a financial planner, you need to check his credentials. He doesn't need to be a CFP to charge you a fee to write a financial plan; if he is a CFP and produces a written plan for you, he will charge you a fee. The amount that you pay for a written financial plan may or may not have any relationship to the value of that plan.

Most financial planners, regardless of their professional designation, if any, do not survive in business solely by charging a fee to write a financial plan. There are "fee-only" financial planners, but the fee they charge for a financial plan is only one of the fees they will charge you. Ordinarily, they will put you into "no-load" investments including variable annuities, mutual funds, certain hedge funds, and others. Though you do not pay an upfront commission to purchase these investments, you'll pay the financial planner an annual management fee ranging somewhere between one-fourth of 1 percent and 3 to 5 percent. Management fees are assessed based upon the amount of money under management, and the rate charged decreases as the amount invested increases.

Registered Investment Adviser (RIA). These people manage money—any kind of money—and charge a fee for doing so. They make no guarantees regarding the return you will receive on your money. Their fee is based on a percentage of the assets under management and is usually assessed at least twice a year.

Registered Investment Advisers can do several different things, such as:

- Actively manage a portfolio of stocks or bonds.

- Actively manage a mutual fund account by dynamically allocating your money among a combination of funds within the family of funds.

- Seek out, evaluate, and place your money with one or more third-party advisers. These third-party advisers offer one or more strategies, each of which is designed to help enhance the performance of a particular investment.

- Create a "fund of funds" within your portfolio, which means taking the money you placed with them and allocating it among some dynamic combination of strategies, investments, third-party advisors, and so on.

Registered investment advisers may be compensated by management fees, commissions, or a combination of both. They are not necessarily required to obtain any particular credentials other than their investment adviser license, which they must hold in each state where they do business.

Some registered investment advisers are licensed for the sale of securities and/or insurance, meaning that they will probably be compensated at least in part from the sale of securities and/or insurance in addition to their fees.

Commodity Trading Advisor (CTA). Like RIAs, CTAs manage money and charge a fee for doing so. They make no guarantees or representations regarding potential investment returns. They may be compensated through management fees, incentive fees, commissions, or some combination of them. CTAs, as their designation implies, focus on commodities rather than "traditional" investments.

Incentive fees mean that a CTA may be compensated fully or in part from a percentage of trading profits. That ability has both positive and negative connotations for their clients. They might be inclined to take on too much risk by swinging for the fences in the hopes of increasing their income; it also means that they are more powerfully motivated to achieve significant returns for their clients.

"Alphabet soup." This group includes people who have been granted designations such as Certified Public Accountant (CPA), Chartered Life Underwriter (CLU), Chartered Financial Consultant (ChFC), and Chartered Financial Analyst (CFA). It also includes the Registered Health Underwriter (RHU), Registered Employee Benefits Consultant (REBC), and Chartered Leadership Fellow (CLF) designations.

- A *CPA* is an individual who is certified to practice accounting in a particular state. A CFA is an individual who has passed examinations in accounting, economics, security analysis, and money management.

- The *ChFC* designation is a financial planning designation for individuals in the insurance industry.

- A *CLU* is an insurance professional who has passed examinations for insurance, investments, taxation, estate planning, employee benefits, and more.

- An *RHU* has passed an examination about medical insurance, disability income insurance, long-term care insurance, and managed care.

- An *REBC* has passed an examination in the areas of pensions and retirement planning, group medical plans, long-term care, executive compensation, and personnel management.

- A *CLF* has taken courses to help him serve in a leadership position in the financial-services field, such as general agents, regional marketing managers, and district managers.

New designations are being created all the time, in part because for many people they are simply a marketing tool. In general terms, licenses are more important than certifications and tend to be more heavily regulated. The CPA and CFP designations, however, are quite difficult to obtain, and a person who possesses one or the other should have the tools and training to be a professional. Don't expect your CPA to give good investment advice; accountants look at the past, not at the future. With all professionals you need to consider their point of view, which is reflected in the training, the licenses, and the certifications they hold. Most important, you must know what they are compensated to do.

• • •

Choosing a Financial Professional

The first and most important step in choosing a financial professional is determining what you need. Most of the people I work with have a basic idea of what they need, but their overall knowledge of financial vehicles and planning techniques is limited.

You can do some research on your own, but you will probably waste some time because you don't know exactly what to look for. It will probably be best for you to visit with several financial professionals and find out what each of them does. They will all recommend ways they can help you.

If you're going to work with a professional, you don't want to eliminate his income, but you do want to make sure that you are getting value for the fees and commissions you are paying.

What you really want is someone who is sitting on the same side of the table as you are, someone who is not in an adversarial relationship. He or she should have significant education, training, and experience, and should be genuinely interested in helping you meet your needs in his capacity as a professional. Finding such people is never easy, but they do exist. What is so important about personal finance is that every penny you pay in fees and commissions is directly subtracted from your investment returns.

The final investment decision should always be left up to you. The only time the final decision is not yours to make is when you have hired someone to actually manage an account for you and you leave it up to them to make the day-to-day decisions. This is the case when you buy a mutual fund, a closed-end fund, or a hedge fund, and when you hire a money manager. You make the decision as to whether to buy a particular fund or service, but everything after that is in the hands of the manager.

The more you know the better off you willl be when you work with financial professionals. I encourage you to take the time to get a broad overview by visiting financial websites, perusing *The Wall Street Journal* once or twice, watching CNBC or Bloomberg on occasion, and taking notes about what you see and hear.

I recommend that my clients work with at least two other people besides myself: a lawyer who specializes in estate planning and an insurance agent who specializes in property/casualty insurance. If they own their own business, they may also need a CPA or accountant to take care of their books. I usually try to do the rest, including finding and managing their investments, serving as an independent agent to find the best and most appropriate life, health, disability, and long-term-care insurance policies, and preparing their tax returns. Since my focus is on the day-to-day management of investments and because life, health, disability, and long-term care insurance are constantly becoming more sophisticated and complex, it is difficult for me to remain fully qualified in every aspect of my business.

That means that your "team" will consist of three financial professionals. You pretty much know what to expect from your lawyer and your property/casualty agent; it's the investment adviser or financial consultant that you need to be most concerned about.

• • •

What kinds of people work in
the financial services industry?

About ten years ago, when I was still licensed for the sale of securities, I attended a leadership conference sponsored by the broker/dealer firm with which I was registered. It was both their first conference and mine, and it was a real eye-opener for me. We spent an entire day being instructed by a psychologist who, among other things, helped identify people who have the potential for success in the sales business. The first thing he did was to have us complete a fairly lengthy survey. This was one of those surveys where you define your own personality traits by choosing from two characteristics the one that most accurately described you. Most of these pairs represented things that were almost opposites, which made it fairly easy to complete the survey.

When each of us had completed our surveys, we graded them and arrived at a numerical score, which placed our personalities into one of four quadrants: controllers, promoters, analysts, and sensitives. These were very descriptive labels.

The controllers were those people who had to dominate every situation in which they found themselves, which made them ideal to serve as high-pressure salesman.

The promoters were those with the big egos, people who were constantly promoting themselves with little or no regard to those around them. The promoters would make great used-car salesmen.

The analysts were those who approached life analytically, looking for the why and how in situations.

The sensitives were those who were concerned about their feelings and the feelings of those they served.

I was in a group of almost one hundred experienced, top-producing securities representatives. Of that group, more than ninety were either controllers or promoters. There were four sensitives in the group, and I was the only analyst.

Think about that for a moment. Each of these people had served for a number of years in a profession that demands careful, thoughtful, analytical research in identifying and implementing the best possible strategy to enable their clients to achieve financial success, and yet more than 90 percent of them were disinclined by nature to do that type of work.

This was demonstrated very effectively later in the day as each of us participated in a carefully designed game. The game had obvious appeal to controllers and promoters because its purpose was to win as much money or points as you possibly could, completely disregarding everything else. As each group was sent to different rooms and left to their own devices, those who were psychologically preconditioned to take charge did so and immediately began to tell us what we ought to do. Since I was the only analyst in the room and since it was second nature to me in any event, I decided to take a closer look at the game and how it was structured. It took me all of two minutes to realize that this game was designed to teach cooperation, something for which most of the people in the room had no use and little experience. In fact, if the groups in the different rooms did not cooperate one with another, *none* of them would ever win any points.

I went to the front of the room and asked if I could announce my findings to my group. The instructor had come into our room and was sitting quietly at the back. He was, by his own admission, astonished as I laid out how the game worked, for as he later told us, no one had ever figured the game out in less than four minutes. Needless to say, our group won the game, because we understood how it worked right from the beginning.

I learned a lot about my profession that particular day. I came away much better prepared for leadership in the securities industry, because now I knew what types of people I ought to be hiring. I also realized that if that was the way the securities industry really worked - and it was - I was in the wrong profession. Within three years I had left the securities industry forever.

Please keep this example in mind as you search for a financial professional. I firmly believe that this group of a hundred was typical of the entire industry, and that you may have to look at a hundred people before you find one analyst. Unless you're the type of person who simply needs to be told what to do, you will be much better off working with a real analyst. Even when you find one, however, he or she may not be able to do that good a job for you. Personal financial management is difficult for *anyone* to do regardless of their qualifications and psychological orientation.

I share the following example with you reluctantly because it casts an even more negative light upon my industry. I wish I could say that it reflects the conduct of just a few, but it does not. You will find similar approaches employed by people in this business with any combination of letters after their name. Sometimes, some of the largest firms on Wall Street engage in promotions based upon a simple deception like this.

Recently a client called me to ask my opinion about some advice she had been given by one of my peers. She had attended a seminar that he gave, and even though she told him that she was already working with someone he asked if he could make an appointment with her. She agreed and when he arrived, she again informed him that she was working with someone and had no intention of doing business with him. He was persistent, and he tried to sell her things for over two hours.

There's nothing wrong with persistence; it was what he told her that bothered me. He was a "one-product wonder;" he had been given a track to run on, and that was about all he knew about anything. His track that particular day was some changes to the laws governing IRAs. He had attended some presentation about how people could stretch their IRA distributions to avoid taxation to their immediate heirs and possibly pass on IRA assets to their grandchildren.

This "stretch IRA" concept is a valid estate-planning concept for those people who have significant assets and whose IRAs are big enough that, even though they take the Required Minimum Distributions, there will still be enough left upon their death to merit advance planning. This was *not* the case with my client. I work primarily with the American middle class, and most of them are going to have little or nothing to pass on to their children, much less their grandchildren. In fact, most of them are going to be dependent upon Social Security throughout their retirement. This meant that this young man was wasting his time and my client's.

What was more important was this young man's "solution" to my client's nonexistent "problem." He inquired about her retirement accounts and was given an accurate list—the report I regularly prepare for my clients. From that list, he should have instantly discerned that most of my client's money was not subject to any surrender charges. Less than a third of her money was in a four-year annuity contract with less than two years to go. A small amount of her retirement money was in an annuity product that did have surrender charges. In each case, the account had been opened to serve a specific purpose, and each was functioning well.

The young man then proposed something that was not only preposterous but laughable. Unfortunately, such an approach is highly successful when used on those who really don't know any better. This licensed financial professional proposed that my client move all of her retirement money to one annuity product. Here was his reasoning:

1. My client was wasting time and money by having her money divided up into several different accounts.

2. The annuity product he was offering was superior to any product she currently owned. (The only particular advantage his product had, as far as I can tell, was that it had a relatively short surrender charge period.)

3. By implication, the new product would provide better returns than any or all of her existing accounts. Of course, he knew nothing about the performance of her accounts.

4. At this point, the young man made a very common mistake, one for which he should forfeit his license. He told my client that this product that he was recommending had been enjoying a return of 7–8 percent per year. He implied that it would continue to do so, even though the product offered no such guarantees.

The most extraordinary aspect of this proposal was that this young man wanted my client to save money on surrender charges by having her immediately pay unnecessary surrender charges. She would have had to do so to implement his recommendation, and he knew it. He was simply out to make a sale and a good commission. He said nothing about the service he would provide in the future, or whether he would offer advice to my client. He said nothing about what he was going to do to earn the commissions she was going to pay.

Finally, had my client implemented this proposal, all of her retirement money—reduced by the surrender charges she would have had to pay—would have become subject to a new surrender charge.

You may not know what constitutes permissible conduct in the financial services industry. This young man was violating several rules and certainly should be prohibited from serving in this industry ever again. Nevertheless, these are common industry practices. It is for this reason that the state of California recently passed some new legislation requiring people like this young man, had he made this presentation in the Golden State, to disclose significant amounts of additional information to prospective clients. Many state legislatures are trying to protect their seniors from fraudulent and unethical practices like these because they are rampant.

Here is my response to this young man's proposal.

The accounts my client currently possesses have been carefully designed to maximize her return and minimize her costs of ownership. Those requiring active management have been managed at little or no cost to the client.

There are several reasons for having a number of accounts. The four-year annuity, for example, was purchased with a windfall profit from another annuity. One of my strategies had worked exceptionally well, to the extent that the client was able to close out an existing annuity contract and pay the surrender charge and still take away more profit than she would ever have received had we not utilized the strategy.

Another one of the client's accounts utilized a no-load family of mutual funds. This family of funds has been carefully selected and was chosen because it offers funds in numerous sectors, any one of which can outperform the overall stock market in a given year. In this case, we have had much success in utilizing energy, natural resources, and precious metals funds, and each had produced returns significantly greater than the maximum available from this young man's product.

One of the client's accounts was in place when I first met her. Since it utilized a family of mutual funds for which the client had paid a commission up front, I kept the account open so that she can get more value out of the commission she paid. I would not have done so if this family of funds had not offered the funds my client needed.

I had done an outstanding job for this client. Her investment program was state-of-the-art and was producing strong returns. My client was significantly better off financially than she would be if she implemented this young man's proposal.

What did my client do? She accepted the young man's recommendations, threw away a great deal of money, and is no longer my client. This has happened hundreds of times in my twenty-nine years in the business.

One final example should suffice. A few years ago I had more than one hundred clients in one small West Texas community. I had been working there for several years, slowly and carefully building up my practice and my reputation. One day I learned that another securities representative was working among my clients and having significant success with them. I found out that he and I were licensed through the same broker/dealer firm; I also found out that he was promising 40 percent annual returns. Have you ever calculated what happens if you make 40 percent per year? At 40 percent annually, $10,000 becomes $289,000 in just ten years. Forty percent is a very attractive number; unfortunately, no one has ever attained it consistently.

I lost a lot of clients to this individual, all of them people who should have known better. Each client who went away had been earning an average of 10 percent per year on the accounts under my management. We had earned that return without exposing most of their money to the risks of the stock market. Nevertheless, the clients went away. This other securities representative was nothing more than a thief. When he was found out he fled the country and had to be extradited back to the United States. Much of my clients' money was gone, never to return. Not one of those clients ever came back to me.

Key Questions

If all you need is someone to supply you with stock tips, find a broker with a proven track record and make an agreement with him to discount your commissions. If you need a true professional to help you assemble your own financial plan, try to find one of the analysts I mentioned above. They do exist, though they are rare.

When you meet with a prospective financial advisor, make sure you ask him certain important questions about the services he provides. Here are some important questions you should ask:

- Are you trained and experienced in creating written financial plans for your clients?

- Do you focus on the financial plan itself, on investment strategy, unspecified investments, or do you have a different focus?

- How are you compensated?

- What products and services that we might need are you *unable* to provide for us?

- What financial products and services do you offer, and how did you select them?

- What is your basic philosophy of financial planning?

- How often do you communicate with your clients? What is the nature of your regular communications?

- Do you or does your firm produce comprehensive statements? Do these reports include complete investment summaries, realized gains and losses, unrealized gains and losses, income and expense reports, and others?

- Do you work alone or with a team? If you work with others, who are they and what additional services do they provide?

- Whose advice do you follow when you make investment recommendations?

- Do you perform fundamental or technical analysis on the investments you recommend?

- Is the bulk of your time spent serving your existing clients or looking for new clients? (Most people will feel pretty uncomfortable asking that question, but it is important that you know.)

Above all, you really do not want to work with the one-size-fits-all person who is going to make his product fit your needs, no matter what. Even if everyone had the same basic financial situation, we still would have different ideas and opinions. A true professional will carefully weigh your needs, desires, and risk tolerance and evaluate your current situation. He will talk to you about what you would like to accomplish.

The professional who accurately determines what you need in the way of financial management is rare, for his work involves numerous skills and significant experience with people and with his industry. He or she must know how to discern your needs based upon what you say; they must have experience with appropriate solutions to each aspect of those needs; and they need the skill and patience to teach you why your needs differ from what you thought you wanted. Those rare individuals are the "keepers."

If you are like the vast majority of the American middle class, your single greatest need is to keep more of the money you earn and make it work for you to improve your financial situation.

• • •

How I Serve My Clients

As a financial professional I take responsibility for my client's money. That does not mean that I will reimburse them when they lose money on something I recommend. That is both illegal and unprofessional. Instead, I make sure that I have done my homework in seeking out and identifying trends in the markets that will affect their money. I spend much of my time performing research in many parts of the world as I try to find products and services suitable for my clients. In most cases, I invest my own funds into a new product first and introduce my clients to it only when I am satisfied it will do what they need. Over the years this has meant that my clients have avoided numerous losses.

For example, when a new family of mutual funds is introduced, I like to examine it for at least two years before I recommend it to my clients. I'm not concerned necessarily with an investment's "track record"; a mutual fund's performance history is worthless once the market changes or the manager moves on. Likewise, performance history can be meaningless for limited partnerships and insurance products. For companies like banks that offer FDIC-insured instruments less research is required.

I rely on my own method of technical and fundamental analysis. What I want to find out is the investment's underlying soundness or the lack thereof.

I not only carefully screen the products and services I offer to my clients. I also keep constant watch over their money. When something is underperforming, I try to find a way to improve its performance.

In addition to my research into investments and investment vehicles, I must also keep tabs on the Congress, the IRS, the Federal Reserve, the White House, the Supreme Court, the European Union, Japan, OPEC, Hong Kong, China, India, and a few other political and economic entities scattered throughout the world. No one can closely monitor everything that is going on; my job is to sift through massive amounts of information and find what my clients need. This research affects every recommendation I make to my clients.

Financial products change every day, and keeping up with them is more than a full-time job. I need to solicit the opinions and recommendations of people I trust who focus on areas for which I have no time. This helps me narrow the scope of my research and focus on those products and services most likely to be of benefit to my clients.

Despite the quantity and quality of my research, I am not always right. Losses are part of the game, but if we manage risk properly we can minimize them. You can expect unpleasant surprises in investing from time to time.

I choose to work with clients who have, by comparison with the wealthy, rather limited options. Unless they get involved in a side business, are self-employed, or build a multi-level marketing organization, their investment opportunities follow a common thread, and much of my research applies to this common thread. These clients' goals are much the same; it's usually just a matter of how much they will need and how soon they will need it. My primary responsibilities are 1) to make sure that the client is motivated to set aside as much of his disposable income as he can and 2) to do everything I can to increase his "bottom line" through an appropriate combination of investments and strategies.

Now let's look at the *next* major obstacle to your financial success: Wall Street.

Chapter Five

Guaranteed to Win: How Wall Street Takes More People for More Money Than Las Vegas Ever Will

Many Americans seem to believe that Wall Street has the noble purpose of funding worthwhile enterprises. These enterprises, they believe, make us wealthy and enable us to be the masters of our domain. Wall Street, as the conventional wisdom goes, provides the financing that allows us to span the seas, harvest the farmlands, build the cities, transport our goods and ourselves, and build this great economic powerhouse into the envy of the world. People believe this mostly because that's what they have been told. If only it were true.

Wall Street is like a vulture, but it doesn't live on carrion. Wall Street feeds on only the best. For example, it takes its cut right off the top when your savings are put to work in an "investment." It then takes annual fees, commissions for each transaction, management fees, and more. It makes money from the use of money in ways that bankers cannot.

The average American who invests in Wall Street's offerings either loses money or makes only a small return. Not only do most of us have bad timing, but the game is clearly rigged in favor of the "house." Wall Street is the biggest house there is. A former branch manager of a securities firm I worked for once told me, "Our job is to take the customer's money and turn it into commissions." I thought he was joking; it took me a while to realize he was serious.

The primary job of Wall Street is to separate you from your money, and for many people that is exactly what happens. It's kind of like welfare in reverse; money is transferred from the many to the few.

Because there is so much money on Wall Street, the big financial firms can hire expensive lobbyists to promote their interests before Congress and other legislative and regulatory bodies. These firms' influence is enormous and growing every day, all at the expense of those who are not the firms' primary beneficiaries. When even the janitors receive an annual $500,000 bonus (or more), you know something is out of whack. When a major Wall Street firm can lose 60 percent of its customers' money in a hedge fund and in the same year pay billions of dollars in bonuses to its employees, you begin to suspect that something is just not right.

The issue is not just one of unrestrained greed and complete disregard for both customers and shareholders; what we see today is a huge manipulation of the rules to benefit those at the top of the heap. America was once the industrial capital of the world, and huge fortunes were made by providing products to the people; today that industrial base has largely moved offshore, and the resulting vacuum has been filled by financial firms. Not too many years ago financial firms represented about 5–6 percent of our economy; in 2007 the figure was 21 percent.

I spent twenty years in the securities business. When I was new in the business I became familiar with corporate underwriting, the process by which companies "take themselves public" or issue additional shares of stock. It didn't take long to realize that the "investment bankers" made immense and, in my opinion, obscene profits on underwriting. They were working with other people's money and therefore had little or none of their own at risk. They charged tremendous fees to create a stock or bond or preferred stock, but assumed no responsibility for the product's performance. In other words, it was no concern of theirs whether the investment failed or became the next Google. However, if it looked like it would work out well, they made sure that they and their buddies got the lion's share.

I observed these investment bankers acquiring brokerage firms, and it was easy to see why they would. Once they created a corporate underwriting, someone else was paid to actually sell the stock to customers. Here was an entire profit center they had been missing. Now they became "soup to nuts" firms, though they still bore very little risk. I have seen many, many deals come out that seem to have been deliberately underpriced by the investment banker. Why would they do that? Because they were reserving stock for themselves and their friends in anticipation of making a killing on this "hot" new IPO (Initial Public Offering).

I worked at a couple of different brokerage firms during those years. I became a top producer, and I wondered why I was never able to obtain shares of these "hot issues" for my clients. After some research I learned the answer. Deals that had the potential to take off like a rocket were reserved for the investment banker and his buddies, the big institutional investors (banks, insurance companies, and pension plans). I was able to get stock for my clients only in secondary offerings and in IPOs that were expected to fizzle.

The securities industry today—the investment bankers and the brokerage firms they own—are second in line only to the Federal Reserve in their ability to "print money." Their best and brightest are working the trading desks, taking positions opposite yours and those of every other American who is trying to make a little money by investing. You don't stand a chance against them; that's why more than 90 percent of day traders lose money and are eventually wiped out. Your chances are better in Las Vegas *unless* you have a plan, know what you are doing, and stick to your plan with all the intelligence and discipline you can muster. Even then, your profits will literally be the crumbs that fall from Wall Street's table. A "good" trader, for example, makes a profit on 51 percent of his trades. If that is his percentage, he had better make sure that he makes at least as much on each profitable transaction as he loses on the others.

• • •

Private Equity–A New Name for Theft

There are other ways Wall Street "prints money." Here is an example borrowed from the S&A Digest (Stansbury & Associates) that typifies how Wall Street firms operate today.

The S&A Digest

by Porter Stansberry

October 31, 2006

Baltimore, Maryland

In January, three private-equity firms bought Hertz from Ford, paying $2.3 billion. They're already selling, dumping 28 percent of the company on the public. But . . . before they let the public in on the deal, they will have taken $1.43 billion out of the company, roughly 60 percent of what they paid for it, less than a year ago. Have you ever seen a large public company pay a 60 percent annual dividend? Neither have I. These private-equity deals are all the same. They load the firms with debt and operate them on a shoestring budget, essentially living off the capital investments of the former owners. By the time the companies are completely sold to the public, they're ruined.

Guess who's selling this deal to the public? Merrill Lynch. Guess who was one of the three private-equity investors? Merrill Lynch. Guess who arranged the first billion-dollar loan? Merrill Lynch. It's amazing what you can get away with if you have a tall building, a huge advertising budget, and the right lawyers.

If you understand what Porter is describing in the preceding paragraphs, you get a small inkling of why it is so difficult to make money as an investor. Merrill Lynch probably didn't do anything illegal in the Hertz deal, but anyone who bought Hertz in the public offering was buying a crippled company. This sounds similar to the "junk bond" deals of the 1980s put together by Michael Milken at Drexel Burnham. Initially, those deals were also legal.

• • •

Selling Something You Don't Own

In recent months a major Wall Street firm was convicted of selling a commodity (in this instance, silver) that they didn't own. Customers, thousands of them, bought silver from this company and were told their silver was being held in a vault somewhere for safekeeping. The customers had only a piece of paper, and it did not reference specific bars or bar numbers. The silver simply didn't exist.

In its own defense this company pleaded that they were engaging in a widespread industry practice. That was true; many Wall Street firms do exactly the same thing. Of course it's illegal, but on Wall Street if you have enough clout or powerful friends you can often get your way. In this case the judge must have been convinced that this scam was of no significance. Even though the company was found guilty, their punishment was merely being required to evaluate their accounting standards. If you or I were caught engaging in the same "widespread industry practice," we would soon find ourselves in prison for a long, long time.

● ● ●

Don't Follow the Crowd; Do Your Own Thinking

Every day my mail and my e-mail are crammed full of solicitations from people who have a get-rich-quick scheme. It never ceases to amaze me how these people, whom no one has ever heard of before, have been spectacularly successful in trading obscure stocks and who, for the price of a subscription, are willing to share their secrets with you so that you may go into direct competition with them. It reminds me of those campaigning for public office who boast that they are not politicians. Anyone who seeks elective office had better be an excellent politician, or his political career will be stillborn. Anyone who has stumbled upon the key to Wall Street's back door had better keep that secret to himself lest he risk being labeled a scam artist.

Several years ago I read the results of a scientific study of investor performance. In this study real data was used. One particular mutual fund was selected, and customer returns were compared with fund performance. The results were shocking. During the five-year period under examination, the fund produced about a 60 percent return, or about 9.9 percent annualized. The average investor in that fund *lost* money, and I believe the average loss was about 14 percent over the same five-year period.

You ask yourself how that could happen, and the answer is not intuitive. Timing was the downfall of the fund's investors, for they had gotten in and out of the fund at the wrong times. Human nature works against us when it comes to investing our money; fear and greed tend to override our analytical processes, with the result that we buy when we should sell and sell when we should buy. Such behavior has been labeled "herd mentality" by some, but most people are sufficiently unwise all by themselves to make a mess of their investments.

Being an analyst by nature, I always try to find a rational basis for things, a fundamental premise that drives something. I decided long ago that I wanted to buy things that were cheap, not things that were expensive. That kind of attitude gives you a significant advantage over most investors and traders today. Cheap stocks can become cheaper, but expensive stocks almost certainly will.

What's the difference between a trader and an investor? When a stock a trader has bought falls, if he holds onto it thinking it will come back he has just become an investor—and a poor one at that. His failure to exercise discipline and cut his losses opens the door to additional losses.

In addition to our own natures and our desire to seek pleasure and avoid pain, we can add peer pressure to the list of things that can tempt us to make poor decisions. You have probably heard the adage "rags to riches." You may not be familiar with its follow-on, which is "rags to riches to rags in three generations." If creating wealth is a skill, spending and depleting it is not. Many fortunes have slipped through the fingers of the generation that only inherited it. When we talk about money around the water cooler or at a party, we seldom bring up our losses, but we are more than happy to brag about our gains. One of the biggest mistakes people make is to jump into an investment that has just soared in value. When an investment has made a strong move in one direction, the odds are high that its next direction will be either the opposite direction or sideways. When you buy at the top, you are giving someone else the profit he deserves. After all, he got in when you should have.

This is why I never followed the "momentum" school of stock trading and why I seldom concern myself with trendlines, moving averages, and support and resistance. A trend remains in motion until it is complete. Once it is complete, it ends, and a new trend or the lack thereof begins.

My best trading—my lowest-risk, most profitable trading—has always been suggested by seeking out good companies that are currently undervalued or, in the case of commodities, seeking out things that are selling below their cost of production and that have not recently been rendered obsolete. Yes, there are reasons why a stock falls, just as there are reasons why a stock rises, but reasons change over time. The critical decision with stocks is, will this company be forced to file for bankruptcy? With commodities it's, has this commodity been replaced, or have vast new supplies of it become available at lower prices?

This, by the way, is another great reason to like commodities right now. Never in its history has the world been faced with the likelihood of running out of key commodities, but that is the situation in which we find ourselves today. Oil and natural gas are just two; silver is another. We will never run out of gold because gold is seldom consumed beyond recovery, but its price can still rise when demand exceeds supply.

· · ·

Stocks and Bonds Are Paper Assets

That is another key to why so many people lose when they compete with Wall Street. Wall Street never runs out of stocks to sell. If they have a shortage, they just print up more shares. You can't do that with aluminum, platinum, uranium, or silver. If these elements are irreplaceable in a particular application, we will be forced to pay any price to find and extract them from the earth until the remainder is unrecoverable at any price.

That's what happens to oil, you know. Petroleum engineers determine through exacting procedures both the amount of oil in the ground and what percentage of it is expected to be economically recoverable.

Through a century of experience, they have also learned that when you open the spigot too wide you decrease the amount of oil that is recoverable. We may soon enter a period in which there will be a trillion barrels of oil in the ground throughout the world and not one drop will be recoverable at any price.

We see, then, that Wall Street is an enormous "self-regulating" casino that stacks the odds heavily in its favor. A quick study both of the history of the stock market in the U.S. and the Federal Reserve should convince even the most skeptical that the game is unfair and the playing field not level.

Why would anyone play a game so vitally important to his or her success in life and yet one we are so likely to lose? The answer is simple; most of us have no choice.

● ● ●

What can you invest in?

Think about the things you can use to make your money grow:

- Stocks

- Bonds

- Mutual funds and ETFs

- Savings accounts

- Certificates of Deposit

- Annuities

- Rare stamps and coins

- Precious metals

- Commodities

- Real estate

- Chinese porcelain

- Art

- Rare books

- Other collectibles

Making money in each of these requires knowledge and experience, some more than others. Some have *perceived* risk; others do not. Anything that does not guarantee your principal and interest has perceived risk.

All of them have *real* risk, whether the risk is expected return relative to inflation and taxes or an application of the greater fool theory[3].

• • •

History

All of these categories have a *history*. Sometimes, to make the story more impressive, the history cited is measured in decades. Since you probably won't own any investment for decades, you will need to take a closer look at its more recent history and its future potential. Most of us take the easy way out and assume that the future trend will be the same as the current direction, which is why we get it wrong two out of three times. In fact, one of the most frequent errors made by those who make predictions is expecting current trends to continue indefinitely.

• • •

Liquidity and Marketability

All of these categories have varying degrees of *liquidity* and *marketability*. Liquidity is your ability to get all of your money back at any moment; marketability means that an investment trades on an exchange with at least a minimal volume. All of them have a *spread,* which is the difference between the amount you would pay to buy them today and the amount you would receive if you sold them today. Despite what I have said about how the odds are stacked against you on Wall Street, if you invest carefully, your costs can be the lowest in any time in history. There are discount brokers and deep-discount brokers; most of the stock markets now use decimal pricing[4] instead of the old fractional pricing. There are many no-load mutual funds available, and there are other ways to reduce or eliminate your costs of investing. In fact, some of the best mutual funds are *only* available without a commission. When you invest in securities, you never need to find a buyer when you want to sell.

• • •

Dealers

All of these categories have *dealers.* The dealer's job is to maximize the seller's profit and his cut. The dealer justifies maintaining a spread between what he will sell you something for and what he will pay to buy it from you by talking about the risk he assumes. In low-margin businesses, such as gold and silver bullion, there is a significant risk. The dealer may sell you something and then have to go find it somewhere so that he can deliver it to you. Or, if you sell something to him, he has to find someone willing to buy it from him at a higher price. If he trades in something with volatile pricing, like gold or silver, he does incur substantial risk. That's why you never buy gold or silver bullion on Friday, Saturday, Sunday, or Monday. Over the weekend, including Friday, the dealer doesn't know how the markets will open next Monday; on Monday he is still trying to balance his accounts from the past three days' activity.

The stock market historically has produced an average performance of 7 percent per year. When the stock market went exponential a few years ago that performance rose to about 11 percent even including the year 2000 collapse. Under ordinary circumstances, if you can achieve a "market return," you can keep up with inflation and taxes. If you carefully and correctly "time" the market and avoid downturns, you can do even better.

Finding the right dealer is one of the ways in which you will reduce your cost of investing. If you can reduce your investment costs from 2% per year to 1% per year, you will improve your overall investment return by about 20 percent. Here is the math:

Example 1. $10,000 investment

$ 700 7% annual return

($ 200) investment costs

$ 500   Net annual return, or 5%

Example 2. $10,000 investment

$ 700 7% annual return

($ 100) investment costs

$ 600 Net annual return, or 6%.6% is 20% more than 5%.

Finding the right financial advisor can help as well.

Your net return (after commissions) on your investments is not the final real return. There are additional and often indirect costs associated with investing. They may include a safety deposit box or other storage facility as well as insurance for your hard assets, the costs of preparing your tax return, hidden fees, and the value of the personal time you spend in managing your investment portfolio. Of course, all of your investment returns must be diminished by the taxes you pay on your gains and the effects of inflation, but that is the subject of another chapter.

• • •

The "Talking Heads"

Before I leave this chapter I have to advise caution in one important area. There are a great many people in the financial media who are free to share their ideas and opinions, to debate issues, and to provide a running commentary on the markets. I have listened to many and met many over the years. Most of them are just doing a job. Many of them are slaves to a methodology, and their opinions and public statements come directly from what their computers tell them. Others, those who are called economists, have their own computer models that they use to try to micromanage the economy. Finally, there are traders who always promote ideas that will be out of date by the time the interview is finished.

My warning is this: you cannot rely on what others say unless you are completely familiar and comfortable with their sources, believe that their analysis and/or recommendations are correct, and are positioned to act instantly on their statements. In other words, most of what you hear and see on the Internet, on TV, and on the radio is not going to do you much good because you don't know where the information is coming from and you are not qualified to determine its objectivity and authenticity.

I'm not saying that people in the media speak anything less than the truth. What I am saying is that each of them has their own bias and approach.

If I am going to be critical of the media, I also must point out those whose opinions I find to be reliable. It's a very short list. One of the few is Rick Santelli on CNBC, who reports from the former Chicago Board of Trade (CBOT) on interest rates and bonds. I am sure that many people who watch CNBC don't fully understand everything Rick says. However, he has the experience in the trading pits to know what he is talking about, and his commentary is timely, to the point, and accurate because he is reporting on market activity as of that moment. He has given me some valuable insights that have helped me to make some critical decisions.

If you utilize the electronic media to get trading ideas, you really ought to turn the sound down so that it is no more than background noise. Most of what you hear will only confuse you or get you into something too late to profit. The media won't notice a trend until it is well developed, and at that point the trend is more likely to change than it is to continue. This is especially true in these times of day trading and microscopically short holding periods.

Even if those in the media and their guests were providing timely and accurate information, you must be concerned about who writes their paychecks. There are at least two sides to every story. Just because someone says he has an existing position in something doesn't mean you ought to run out and buy some for your portfolio. That person may have been holding the stock for years and have a huge gain; he may be looking to get out at a certain price level that might be very close. In fact, you might just be the one to help give him the profit he has waited for—and make yourself the "greater fool" in the process.

• • •

Summary

The financial markets, known to us collectively as Wall Street, offer you the opportunity to invest your hard-earned money in good faith and in the hope that you will receive an honest return for your money. However, Wall Street has its own set of rules. Wall Street's rules—some of them unwritten—include these:

1. Wall Street is in business to make money for Wall Street.

2. The playing field is slanted in Wall Street's favor.

3. Wall Street takes at least one piece of the action in every transaction.

4. Wall Street lobbies aggresively for the promulgation of rules that enable the Street to do pretty much whatever it wants.

5. When Wall Street can't get the rules rewritten the way it wants, it often ignores the rules. Here is what *USA Today* had to say:

    "New York Attorney General Eliot Spitzer charged that major mutual fund firms pump up profits using illegal trading schemes that cost small investors "billions of dollars" annually.

    "'The full extent of this complicated fraud is not yet known,' Spitzer said. 'But one thing is clear: The mutual fund industry operates on a double standard. Certain companies and individuals have been given the opportunity to manipulate the system.'

    Spitzer says Canary gave four mutual fund companies banking business in exchange for the ability to engage in illegal after-hours trading and market exploitation.

    "This is another example of the little guy being told to play by the rules, while the big player gets the breaks,' says Jim Cramer."[5]

Elliot Spitzer continued his investigations for two years, and in the process reached a settlement with a number of securities firms in which they would pay millions of dollars in restitution to their customers. Did this end all the illegal activity in mutual funds? Of course not.

6. Wall Street *creates* a stock IPO (Initial Public Offering) and makes a percentage. Wall Street *sells* the stock created in the IPO and makes another percentage. Wall Street *trades* the stock as a broker and makes commissions. Wall Street *trades* the stock as an institutional investor and makes profits in competition with you, the disadvantaged personal investor. Wall Street creates mutual funds

and ETFs that buy and sell the stock; Wall Street makes trading commissions, management fees, and origination fees for the fund or ETF. Wall Street charges margin interest for margin accounts, maintenance and other fees for accounts that do not meet certain arbitrary rules, and "wrap account" fees just for the privilege of placing your money with their firm. Many of Wall Street's mutual funds even charge you a fee (called a 12-b-1 fee) to advertise their fund to new customers.

7. If all of that was not enough, Wall Street also keeps the spread between the "bid" and "ask" prices. The spread is much narrower for listed stocks these days now that we trade in pennies, but in options and many other securities, the spread can be very large indeed. I have seen commodity options with an ask price as much as three times the bid price. You buy at the ask and sell at the bid; with a bid of $10.00 and an ask of $10.20, if you buy and sell immediately afterward you have just thrown away $.20 (the spread) plus the commissions in both directions. In an investigative article, *Business Week* said this:

"Amex (American Stock Exchange) options specialists and traders are said to regularly engage in price-fixing. The aim is to keep as wide as possible the 'spread' between the bid—what the public can get to sell an option—and the ask, which is what the public must pay to buy an option. Because the prices are allegedly skewed to favor the denizens of the Amex floor, the public is hurt each year, BUSINESS WEEK estimates, to the tune of $150 million."[6]

1. Wall Street provides, for a fee, numerous streams of information about its various offerings, the markets, and the economy. Much of this information is created to motivate you to buy something and pay them a commission. Some of it is incorrect, some of it is outdated, and some is deliberately misleading. Much of it is not actionable and can be hazardous to your wealth.

When you invest you compete against an army of highly trained, experienced professional traders who take the opposite side of many trades. They have highly sophisticated computer tools at their disposal. Some of them are paid millions of dollars each year in bonuses based upon how much of your money they can take away from you.

The vast majority of investment vehicles will not, from year to year, provide a return that will keep you ahead of inflation, taxes, and the declining dollar. In other words, most investments are useless for you most of the time.

You can learn how to compete and earn a good return even with the odds stacked so heavily against you. In the next chapter we will talk about how you can get your hands on useful information.

Chapter Six

What You Don't Know—How to Get The Right Amount of the Information You Need

When I was in graduate school, the personal computer had not yet been invented. There was no cable TV or Internet, and certainly nothing like CNBC or any program that had a running stock-market ticker at the bottom of the screen. Print media were still very popular as a means of conveying significant amounts of information efficiently and accurately. Investors read the *Wall Street Journal* every day, along with *Fortune* or *Barron's* or some other financial magazines. There was a significant delay in getting good information to investors, and that delay gave Wall Street firms and traders on the exchanges a significant advantage. In those days the only "day-traders" were those who worked at the exchanges or those who maintained direct telephone contact with the trading floor during the trading day.

Back then you depended heavily on the print media and on the research offered by your brokerage firm. Your brokerage firm was a full-commission firm. You didn't have a "wrap account." You simply paid a commission for each purchase and sale you made in your account. Those commissions heavily favored the larger investors. If you were only buying one hundred shares of General Motors, you were still going to pay at least a $40.00 commission. A single-options contract might also cost you a $40.00 commission.

The personal computer and the Internet helped to change all of that. We have gone from a relative dearth of information to "information overload." Now there is so much information about companies, industries, stocks, the economy, Congress, the world situation, and so much more, it is difficult and time-consuming to sift through what's available and figure out what has any value to you.

The first thing you must do with financial information is separate fact from opinion. You can work solely from factual information; I will show you how. Most of what is available is opinionated and editorialized, and it is tempting to accept someone else's ideas as a substitute for our own analysis. Most of us tend to be a bit lazy. We have other things to do with our time. If someone tells us he's never bought a losing investment in his entire life and goes on to list twenty or thirty winning stock picks he made over the past six months, we are inclined to believe him (or her).

If you are going to be a successful investor, you have to learn how to separate the useful analysis from the fluff and the deliberate deceptions. The financial industry is a sales profession; everyone wants to sell you something. They are not concerned what happens to you after you have made your purchase. Once you have identified useful data and analysis, you still need to weed out what is irrelevant. With the small amount of remaining data, you are ready to perform your own analysis.

• • •

How to Become the World's Greatest Investment "Expert"

I read a story several years ago that was supposed to be hypothetical. It was about a person who wrote a quarterly financial newsletter. Actually, he wrote two. In the first he described a particular stock in glowing terms, recommending that his readers buy the stock immediately. In the second, he recommended that his readers sell short the same stock immediately, describing it in terms that made you think the stock was about to fall off a cliff. Initially, each letter was sent to one hundred thousand people.

You can see where this is going. When it came time to send out the next issue of the newsletter, this writer had one hundred thousand very happy readers and one hundred thousand "unhappy" readers. Only if the stock price had gone nowhere would this scheme fail. In the new issue the writer recommended that his readers sell the first stock and buy a second stock. He only needed to send out fifty thousand copies, and those went to half of the people for whom his initial recommendation had been accurate. The other half of that group received a newsletter recommending that they sell short the second stock. The one hundred thousand unhappy readers received nothing—except possibly a refund on their subscription, if one had been promised.

Now this writer has a group of fifty thousand readers for whom he has been right on the money twice in a row. If he repeats this process twice more, he will have the most loyal group of 12,500 readers you've ever seen. These folks will think he just about walks on water, and he could be wrong for years before they would ever think of canceling their subscriptions.

This is only a hypothetical example—or is it? It's obviously a strategy that could work very well for the newsletter writer, but is it legal? The answer is yes. Most newsletter writers are not required to be registered as investment advisers, and newsletters are protected by the Constitutional guarantees of free speech. The fact that the writer is expressing two very countrary opinions does not, as I understand it, violate any law.

• • •

Get to the Motive

When you read something about investments and have decided whether the information was fact or opinion, you then have to figure out what the writer's motivation is. How is he or she compensated? Who pays their salary? Are there visible conflicts of interest? Does the information contain any disclaimers that might detail conflicts of interest?

What would happen to the writer if here she were proven wrong or, to put it more politely, if history went against her? Does the writer bear any responsibility for the consequences of having made a bad recommendation? Does the writer have any of his or her own personal funds invested in this recommendation? It's been interesting to watch interviews on CNBC in the last couple of years since new disclosure rules have been put into effect. Fund managers talk about how wonderful a particular stock or industry is and then say they don't own any of it, either personally or in the fund they manage.

And what about those pesky economists, the people who tend to predict twenty-two of the last seven recessions? Is there any point in listening to them? For that matter, is there any point in listening to what Congress has to say or what the EU is doing or whether Iran is building nuclear weapons?

The answer is yes in every case. You don't invest in a vacuum. There are different types of risk, and you need to have at least a nodding awareness of them. Each in its own way can have a positive or negative impact on your investments. You don't necessarily need to be an intelligence expert qualified for the diplomatic service, but *you need to establish a context in which your investments can work*. You cannot afford to be blindsided when history goes in a different direction than you thought it would.

• • •

What is the trend?

I'm also not saying that you have to predict the future in anything other than your investments. Just a general knowledge of the current trends can be very helpful. For instance, knowing that the Federal Reserve is systematically raising interest rates has an impact on your decisions about investing in bonds. When China is building a new city of twenty-five million inhabitants every six months, your investments in commodities and infrastructure will be affected accordingly as building materials become more expensive. When Congress is talking about reducing or eliminating capital gains taxes, you might want to do some repositioning in your portfolio to increase your capital gains potential.

As you create and build your investment portfolio, you'll also build a list of sources you feel you can rely upon. At any hour of any day, you can find opinions across the entire range of the spectrum. You can even find analysts discussing a single company whose opinions at any moment in time range across the entire spectrum.

In my work I follow the opinions of many people, and before I take a specific idea too seriously, I perform my own analysis on the recommended investment. In this way I can eliminate more than 90 percent of what is recommended for one reason or another. Even though I do this full time, I simply cannot look at all the investment opportunities available to me, and neither can you. How often have I read that the Turkish stock market, for example, was the best performing stock market in the world for the previous year, rising some 55 percent, and I didn't know anything about it? That will happen most of the time. You have to devote your efforts to those areas of investment that you believe are the most valuable to you.

• • •

Create a List

You should create a list of things—stocks, bonds, mutual funds, ETFs—that you will follow, and from time to time you'll either add to that list or subtract from it. I used to watch coffee very carefully, but found that I was trading it very infrequently. I switched to cocoa instead and found it to be closer to the type of investment I was interested in because of its price action.

• • •

Information Is Worth What You Pay for It—Sometimes

Should you pay for investment information? Yes, but you should only pay people who have a demonstrated and proven track record of good, solid recommendations. With over sixteen thousand financial newsletters to choose from, that can take a lot of research. Fortunately, there are newsletters like the Hulbert Financial Digest (go to www.marketwatch.com). The Hulbert people track the performance of a large number of financial newsletters and rank them in accordance with the return generated by the recommendations. This is ideal for a stock trader, because they have done a lot of the research for you. Still, all they have done is to identify historical events that may or may not be repeated; their rankings are based upon past performance.

In other words, you are paying for advice that was good yesterday. If you receive your information by e-mail, it may be a little more timely. However, if the information is based upon past performance, such as information already made public by a particular company, the fundamental analysis performed either by the newsletter writer or by yourself may have little or no value at this point. If the newsletter writer is providing you technical analysis, it may be out of date, or it may not utilize methods that have a valid premise. There are a lot of newsletter writers who actually have a pretty decent track record but whose record will someday fall flat on its face because their luck is going to run out.

• • •

Chasing the Money, or Don't Follow the Crowd

One more point: "chasing the money" can be hazardous to your financial health. Many people look for people with a track record. I recently met a retired doctor at a financial conference. He told me that he opened an account with a "famous" broker who had made vast sums of money for himself and his clients. I knew the broker; he had been recommended by numerous newsletter editors whose work I have read over the years. The doctor told me that he had called to open the account but had never actually spoken to the broker. He was immediately referred to one of his associates. Undeterred, the doctor transferred an account in which he had accumulated a $500,000 gain. Three years later, that $500,000 gain had become a $300,000 loss. The doctor was quite disturbed that none of the standard risk management techniques had been applied in the management of his money.

The doctor had made a common mistake. In fact, he had made several mistakes. His biggest mistake was to think that someone who had a word-of-mouth reputation of long standing would devote personal time and attention to his account. That's not what a broker does.

The name of the game on Wall Street is *accumulating assets*. That's every broker's job, as it is for every financial advisor, financial planner, and investment advisor. Assets are accumulated in three ways: prospecting, referrals, and "bluebirds" (people who walk in when you happen to be "broker of the day"). Prospecting for new customers is the primary activity of just about every financial professional. When they start bringing in a large income, they can hire people to do their prospecting for them. A broker who is widely recommended often enjoys large numbers of referrals.

There are more than a million licensed persons in the United States who would like to take a commission out of your pocket. Financial professionals have to find a way of differentiating themselves, of making themselves stand out from the crowd, because only those who stand out will be successful at accumulating assets. That's why brokers get themselves onto radio talk shows or have a weekly column in the local paper or give dinner seminars or send out mass mailings to keep their name in front of people.

In a more perfect world, financial professionals would be compensated for their honesty, diligence, and knowledge. In this world, however, they are compensated for perceived performance. I have personally interviewed more than eight hundred individuals and couples about their personal finances, and each of them has developed a working relationship with me. Of those eight hundred, well over half went away because someone promised them better performance than I had delivered. In most of those instances, of course, the person to whom my client went had no idea of what my actual performance had been. Likewise, in most of those instances the likelihood of that other person outperforming me was remote, even if he were to take on far more risk for that client.

The average person who works with a financial professional has no idea what their actual annual investment returns are. We don't know because we don't care; we tend to choose financial professionals the way we tend to choose new cars. We want the "sizzle" far more than we want the steady, conservative pace of the true professional.

I'm not going to change human nature; I would be foolish to try. I just want you to be aware that what is "hot" today will probably be "cold" tomorrow, and what is appropriate for a friend may not be appropriate for you.

The methods I will teach you in this book will enable you to perform your own analysis and come up with useful answers. It won't matter who came up with the recommendation; you will be able to put it quickly through several screens and decide whether it is worth any more of your time. Once you start rejecting 95 percent to 99 percent of the recommendations and "hot tips" you receive, you will be a more effective investor. You will be able to rely upon your own decisions.

Will you get blindsided from time to time? Of course you will. We all do. If you write your own set of rules and follow them, you will be more successful than most people. You will have the confidence that your analysis has removed much of the uncertainty from your investment decisions.

Chapter Seven

"Do It Yourself"

We Americans are proud, independent, and entrepreneurial. We have a "can do" attitude, which sometimes gets us into trouble. We tend to act on insufficient information, vacillate in our ideas and opinions, and substitute common knowledge for common sense.

In today's highly complex world, there are many things that require the services of specialists. We need competent accountants, doctors, and engineers. In those instances where lawyers are necessary, we need competent lawyers as well. Professionals study for years and often serve in apprenticeships or internships to hone their skills before being released onto the market.

Investing and personal financial management are skills that require significant training and experience to master. Few professionals ever obtain the necessary skills, and very few among the general public do. If you have a lot of money, you can hire advisors and pray that they will be honest and keep you out of trouble. (How many lottery winners will die broke and divorced? More than you think.)

If you are like most people, you are on your own. You have an insurance agent you seldom hear from except when he wants to sell you something. You pay someone to prepare your tax return each year. If you own a business, you probably have an accountant who keeps your books and prepares your financial statements. The faces at your bank change constantly, and they only call you when they want to move your CD into an annuity.

· · ·

What You *Should* Have Learned in School

Public schools are notorious for their failure to prepare teenagers for financial responsibilities. You didn't get it in high school, and it is unlikely you will receive any useful financial education in college. There are few places we can go to learn about money and investing except, of course, for the very expensive school of hard knocks.

Instead, much of our financial education comes from what we hear at parties or around the water cooler. Sometimes a broker will manage to get our attention and spin a tale about a hot stock he is touting. Maybe a next-door neighbor or a fishing buddy or someone who also attends PTA meetings suggests to us that a new product or service could be beneficial to us. Worse, we may get our investment ideas from the shopping channel or some late-night infomercial—or CNBC.

There is no systematic financial education available today that would enable Americans to handle their finances intelligently. We are not taught how to produce a meaningful income, minimize our taxes, obtain consistent returns on our savings and investments, or plan for our children's education or our retirement. Likewise, we are not educated about how to protect and preserve what we have.

• • •

Rationalizations

Most of us cloak ourselves with numerous rationalizations, which, we hope, will adequately defend us from our own failure to plan and prepare. For instance, we love the notion of safety in numbers; we want to believe that the government will somehow "fix" Social Security simply because most of the people we know will be dependent upon it. We are in the same boat as our entire circle of friends in saving for the future; we can't put money aside because our spending on necessities takes all our available income. We use our homes like ATMs and borrow to the hilt just to maintain the lifestyle that "everyone says" we deserve.

Another rationalization is the one about long-term performance. We buy stocks and mutual funds with little regard to the timing of our purchases because we have been told that over time "the stock market always goes up." All we have to do is make the minimum payments each year into our 401(k) or IRA, and the law of averages virtually guarantees us a million dollars by age sixty-five.

One of the most common and dangerous rationalizations is the one that says we don't need to save for a rainy day because the government will be there for us. We want to think we don't need disability insurance, we don't need our own health insurance, we don't need insurance that will pay our nursing-home expenses, and we certainly don't need that cancer insurance (even though one or more members of our family has died from cancer). Couple this rationalization with the common belief that we are already "stretched to the limit" financially, and you end up with a nation of dependents. The fact that such behavior is encouraged by all levels of government is, of course, purely incidental. Governments thrive on creating and maintaining dependencies, even though hard evidence demonstrates time after time that the social programs they invent are almost always disastrous failures.

• • •

Procrastination

When it comes to planning, the most dangerous mistake may be procrastination. Do you have a will? A durable power of attorney for health care? A trust to minimize taxation and probate costs? Most people do not have these things because creating them takes conscious thought, time, and money. Besides, they frequently become obsolete because the laws change all the time. Even if the laws didn't change, our relationships with our beneficiaries do. Liberal divorce laws have only added to the problem of keeping an estate plan current.

• • •

Control What You Can Control

What can you do to become successful in managing your personal finances? You can begin by making a commitment in your own mind as to the importance of taking personal responsibility for your own future. Some things are out of your hands, and it is all too easy to be blindsided by unanticipated events. However, there are things we can control. We can control our thoughts, and we can educate ourselves. We can have discipline and we can implement a well-thought-out plan. We can set and achieve meaningful goals.

Keep in mind that we don't have to fund it all ourselves. If we expect your children to go to college, there are thousands of sources of scholarship and fellowship funds available. There are even a few programs for home schooling. We don't have to bear the full burden ourselves, nor should our children expect us to. (Have them talk to their grandparents.) If we have a family medical history of certain illnesses, we can insure against them by supplementing our regular health insurance. And if it looks as though we will live longer than our parents, we can insure against the possibility of higher expenses incurred in the preservation of life. Of course, most Americans hope and pray that Social Security will still be there when they retire to supplement or even provide the majority of their retirement income. For most Americans, retirement will be the most expensive thing they ever do.

• • •

Establishing a Plan

You've got to have a dream. If you don't have a dream, how you gonna have a dream come true?

from *South Pacific*

First and foremost, you've got to have a plan. The plan identifies your goals and objectives, and it gives you a document you can refer to occasionally to make sure you're still on track. The plan is not cast in concrete; it is a dynamic, living thing, subject to frequent revision. You can even change your goals and objectives because the whole purpose of the plan is to enable you to fund the things you want to do in life, not to dictate what you will do.

How do you develop a plan? Before you even consider talking to a financial professional, I think you need to make some basic decisions. Decide what it is you're trying to accomplish in terms of specific targets. These targets will include retirement, children's education, and all planned major expenses. In considering these expenses, understand that you don't need to plan to pay cash for everything; the responsible and careful management of debt can be a powerful financial tool.

On the next several pages, you'll find some worksheets you can use in establishing your own financial plan, preceded by a description of each page. In these pages we focus on three specific areas:

- who and where you are today

- where you want to go

- the means available to you for getting there.

Once you have completed and reviewed these pages, you will be ready to make some decisions and create a plan.

• • •

Financial Worksheet Page 1

Page 1 contains objective information with which you are most likely quite familiar. It is important to fill this page out because you just might take these pages to a financial professional at some future date. Having this entire survey, along with your income statement and balance sheet, might save you some money in fees later on.

Please pay special attention to the last section on page 1, where you will provide information about special needs and dependencies. The success or failure of any financial plan often hinges on such potential situations.

• • •

Financial Worksheet Page 2

Most of the information on page two is self-explanatory; please use an additional page or more if your situation warrants it. *Sources of income* refers to your employer or your self-employment; the annual amount is either the current salary or the average anticipated net income from the business.

Note the four categories of ownership in the next section: joint account, yourself, spouse, and children. Again, you may need additional pages for this section. The distinctions about ownership are important when it comes to drafting your will and trust documents. The institution called for here is the bank, investment company, insurance company, or other financial institution that holds the accounts you are listing.

The *other* section can include things like collections, rare coins, antiques, jewelry, and other valuable items that can be readily converted to cash.

The *marketable securities* section is for stocks and bonds, mutual funds, ETFs, and the like. If you trade options, it is unnecessary to list them here.

• • •

Financial Worksheet Page 3

The objective information continues on this page. Fixed annuities include traditional annuities as well as multi-year guarantee (MYG) annuities, total-return fixed annuities (TRFAs), and equity-index annuities (EIAs). Be sure to indicate ownership and whether they are non-qualified (NQ) or inside retirement programs such as an IRA.

In the section on *limited partnerships,* the last question about how much you have received to date refers to *distributions,* not tax deductions or credits.

The *real-estate* section should include your own home(s) and all other real estate in your possession, including raw land.

The last section, on *consumer debt,* is one of the most important in the survey. Most people have difficulty answering the questions. Quite a few of my clients have been shocked to discover the actual interest rate on their credit cards and even on their mortgage, if they have an adjustable-rate mortgage.

The question that is not asked in the debt section is the direction your indebtedness is moving. Is your debt increasing or decreasing? Do you make only the minimum required payments on your credit cards, or do you pay the balance in full every month? Are you accelerating your mortgage(s) or just making the regular payments?

• • •

Financial Worksheet Page 4

Now we get to the subjective information. Many people are unsure about whether their income exceeds their expenses. Far too many people have no emergency fund at all. The section on goals could take a fair amount of your time if you have not previously considered these types of goals.

The final questions have to do with risk. Please fill out everything on this page carefully and thoughtfully. This exercise can have tremendous value to you as you think about what the future may hold. With this information you'll be able to construct your own balance sheet and income statements, which I will describe shortly. Once you understand what is on those documents, you are ready to confront your situation as it is today.

CONFIDENTIAL FINANCIAL PLANNING SURVEY			
Family Data: Information about You		Information about your Spouse	
Full Name		Full Name	
Date of Birth		Date of Birth	
Birthplace		Birthplace	
Soc. Security No.		Soc. Security No.	
Citizen of	U.S. Other	Citizen of	U.S. Other
Occupation		Occupation	
Self-employed?	Yes No	Self-employed?	Yes No
Employer		Employer	
Work Phone		Work Phone	
Years of service		Years of service	
Medical Problems (list)		Medical Problems (list)	
Home Address		City, State ZIP	
Home Phone		Fax #	
Cell Phone		Cell Phone	
E-mail address		E-mail address	

Your Children	Name and other information	Birthdate
Child #1		
Child #2		
Child #3		
Child #4		

Previous Marriages	
Financial obligations to spouse or children of previous marriage	
Special Needs (describe briefly)	
Physical limitations of family members, if any	
Will anyone become dependent upon you in the near future?	

All Current Sources of Income: You		Your Spouse	
Source 2		Source 2	
Annual Amount	$	Annual Amount	$
Source 3		Source 3	
Annual Amount	$	Annual Amount	$
Source 4		Source 4	

Checking, Savings, Certificate of Deposit, Credit Union, Money Market, IRA and Retirement Accounts					
Account	**Institution / Interest Rate**	**Joint Account**	**Yourself**	**Spouse**	**Child(ren)**
Checking #1		$	$	$	$
Checking #2		$	$	$	$
Savings / CU		$	$	$	$
Cert. of Deposit		$	$	$	$
Cert. of Deposit		$	$	$	$
Money Market Fund		$	$	$	$
401(k)		$	$	$	$
IRA, SEP, KEOGH		$	$	$	$
Profit-sharing plan		$	$	$	$
Other (describe)		$	$	$	$

Marketable Securities - Stocks, bonds, mutual funds, options, etc. (Amounts are approximate)					
No. shares	**Description**	**Jointly held**	**Yourself**	**Spouse**	**Child(ren)**
		$	$	$	$
		$	$	$	$
		$	$	$	$
		$	$	$	$
		$	$	$	$
		$	$	$	$
		$	$	$	$

Fixed Annuities and Limited Partnerships				
Limited Partnerships: Company / Type		Amount Invested	Date of Purchase	How much have you received to date?
		$		$
		$		$

Real Estate You Own or are Buying					
Real Estate	Address	Purchase Year	Price Paid	Owned by	Current Mkt Value (est.)
Your Home			$		$
Other (describe)			$		$
			$		$
			$		$

Mortgages and Other Debts (list balances for credit cards only if they are not paid off each month)						
Mortgages	Location	Amount Borrowed	Interest Rate	No. Payments Remaining	Is the Loan Insured? (Y/N)	Unpaid Balance (est.)
Home Mortgage		$	%			$
Other Mortgage		$	%			$
Other Mortgage		$	%			$
Other Loans	Company / Description	Interest Rate	Monthly Payment	Credit Insurance?	Unpaid Balance (est.)	
Credit Card 1		%	$		$	
Credit Card 2		%	$		$	
Auto Loan		%	$		$	
Line of Credit		%	$		$	
Other (describe)		%	$		$	

Other information and details

_____

_____

Which statement is correct?

☐ I spend <u>more</u> than I earn each month.

☐ I spend <u>less</u> than I earn each month.

☐ I am uncertain as to whether I spend more than I earn each month.

How much money do you feel you should have available for an emergency? $

(Some people like to keep 3 months' income under the mattress for a rainy day; some rely on their unused credit card balances.)

Briefly describe your personal and family goals and your financial needs:

Children' Education _____

_____

_____

Self-employment – current or planned _____

_____

_____

Travel / Vacations _____

_____

_____

Retirement _____

_____

_____

_____

At what age do you wish to retire? Husband _____   Wife

Desired monthly retirement income in today's dollars $ _____ (total from all sources)

How much risk are you willing to accept overall in your **savings?** (Each spouse gives a response).

1 2 3 4 5 6 7 8 9 10   (1 is low risk, 10 is high risk)

1 2 3 4 5 6 7 8 9 10

How much risk are you willing to accept overall in your **investments?** (Each spouse gives a response).

1 2 3 4 5 6 7 8 9 10   (1 is low risk, 10 is high risk)

1 2 3 4 5 6 7 8 9 10

It's all right to feel a little uncomfortable as you go through this exercise. I would rather that people were uncomfortable having confronted their situation than allow themselves to be lulled into a false sense of security. Besides, I'm going to show you how you can improve your situation every day of your life.

• • •

Evaluating Your Input: Debt

Once you have completed the survey, you're ready to begin evaluating the data. When I review a survey like this, after I familiarize myself with the personal details, the first thing I look at is debt. That small section tells me more about the person or couple than almost anything else. For example, it tells me whether these people are good savers or good spenders, whether they are getting ahead or falling behind, and whether I can help them if they become clients.

There are some people I cannot help because they lack the discipline to do what they need to do. I have had a few clients like that over the years, and despite my best efforts they simply could not keep up. You've probably seen the surveys that find that money or the lack of thereof is the leading cause of divorce. That's probably true. The way people manage their money weighs heavily on their ability to succeed as spouses and parents.

When I see a survey that shows high debt levels, I ask my clients about their experience with debt and how well they think they're doing. I get the full range of responses; some people whose debt appears completely out of control are quite complacent and feel they're doing fine. Others recognize that even though their situation is not particularly bad it can easily become worse, and they have a desire to fix things. It is said that the person standing at the top of the stairs and looking down is in a far worse position than the person at the bottom who is looking up. If we want to improve our circumstances, we can.

What does unmanageable debt look like? It can take the form of a large adjustable-rate mortgage, plus, in some cases, a second mortgage. It also includes at least one car loan, and it almost always includes significant amounts of credit-card debt. Many people think that their home equity will continue to grow and will therefore bail them out of their situation. I try to show them why that may not be a real solution after all. If they have recently refinanced their home and taken out some of the equity, I ask them where the money went. Did they take out equity to pay off credit-card debt? If so, what is the current balance on their credit cards? If it has gone back up again, these folks are probably in trouble. It's very simple; their spending exceeds their income. Until they can bring their spending under control, they have little hope for improving their circumstances in the future.

Some of my interviews end at this point with some council from me regarding getting out of debt. I'm not a credit counselor or a psychologist, and there is little else I can do for these people. We are both wasting our time if I proceed to talk about setting up an investment program as long as they have no disposable income to invest.

My counsel to all of us is the same: avoid debt as if it were a plague. The only appropriate debts are your home mortgage, which should be a fixed rate loan of twenty-five years' duration or less, and student loans, which should be avoided whenever possible. If you cannot handle the payments on a twenty-five-year mortgage, you are probably buying more house than you can afford.

I know that most people cannot pay cash for a car. I always recommend that you own the car longer than you make payments on it. If your vehicle is properly maintained, it should continue to give you several years of faithful service after it is paid off. I don't believe that leasing is a good idea for most people.

Credit-card debt is the worst. Far too many people have told me about how they keep rolling their debt from one credit card to the next so that they can take advantage of the introductory rate until it runs out. Many people who do this are living literally on the edge; their spending is out of control, and when the credit card solicitations stop coming in the mail, they will find that their expenses have increased even more due to the high interest rates they will be forced to pay. One of the credit cards I carry has a current interest rate of 32 percent. No one who is struggling to make ends meet can afford a rate like that.

I use credit cards very differently than most people do. I keep only two or three active credit-card accounts, each of which offers some incentive. One gives me frequent-flyer miles with my favorite airline; another gives me cash back on every purchase. Each charges a low fee or no annual fee at all. Since I pay them off in full every month, I never pay interest or finance charges. Over the years this has produced more than forty free flights and thousands of dollars in cash back, and I haven't paid a penny in interest.

When you complete your income statement, you will discover how much of your income is being eaten up by debt service. If the total (principal and interest) that you are paying on your debt is in excess of 50 percent of your income, you have a problem that needs to be addressed immediately. Refinancing your home is an option but not necessarily a good one because it doesn't require you to change your spending habits.

If you do decide to refinance your home, please avoid "negative amortization" loans and interest-only loans. You should also avoid adjustable-rate loans. All three can be very hazardous to your financial health. The number of foreclosures in this country is increasing dramatically every month, usually because the homeowner did not read the fine print in his mortgage contract or he bought more house than he could afford.

Negative amortization loans are not promoted as such by mortgage brokers. Most people may not understand that term, but it certainly has a bad connotation. Such loans are advertised as "1 percent" or "reduce your interest rate" loans. They do just that; they reduce your interest rate because you pay only a portion of the interest that is due on your loan. The rest continues to build as part of your mortgage balance, and as a result your mortgage balance increases every time you make a payment. Does this give you some idea of how dangerous these things can be?

• • •

Evaluating Your Input: Assets

The next thing we look at is, of course, your assets. For many people their biggest single asset is their home, and the second is their 401(k). (If you rent and do not own any real estate, you may skip the following section.)

Try to find out what your real estate is really worth today, even though you have no intention of selling it. If you talk to a couple of realtors, you can get a pretty good feel for the way your local real-estate market is going. Now ask yourself some questions. You might want to take some notes on your answers.

• How much could your house sell for today?

• How much did you pay for it?

• How much do you *owe* on it?

• How much longer do you plan to live there?

Here's a question it will take some work to answer: how much does it cost you to live in your house each month? That answer may surprise you.

Could you and your family live as comfortably less expensively somewhere else?

What I am trying to do here is to help you decide whether your house is really an asset or liability. Let's take the analysis a little further:

What do you expect housing prices to do over the next year? Two years? Five years?

If you believe that the value of your house will continue to rise, will its value increase faster than the rate at which you are putting money into it?

If you believe that the value of your house will fall or stay the same, is there enough added value to owning that house to make it worthwhile when renting or owning a less expensive house might be a viable financial option for you?

I don't want you to run out and sell your house. I just want you to make an objective decision about it. Since it is the most valuable single asset most people possess, it is certainly worth your while to make it work as hard for you as it can. If it is a "money pit," you might do well to sell and look elsewhere.

Now that you have answered these questions, is your house an asset or a liability? If its net cost of ownership[7] is more than its future increase in value, it's a liability. Will it "sustain itself" if prices level off or even move down? Probably not.

Now let's move on to your other assets. For many of us, our 401(k) is our next largest asset, often because there's no easy way to get to it. I once heard of a young man who quit his job so that he could draw from his 401(k), pay the taxes and penalties, and net out enough to purchase that pickup truck he really wanted. Two weeks later he applied for and was given his old job, but he had wiped out his 401(k) and his eligibility to participate. That's throwing away free money.

How is your 401(k) doing? Are you actively managing it? Are you actively contributing to it? Does your employer provide a matching contribution?

What is the current value of your 401(k) account? Is it fully vested to you? If not, how much longer do you need to work for that employer for your plan to become fully vested? People sometimes quit or get themselves fired just prior to an important vesting anniversary. It's generally a good idea to stay with the company long enough to receive your full vesting and to take necessary steps to protect your account. Under some new legislation, it may even be possible for you to remove all or a portion of your 401(k) balances, particularly your vested balances, and transfer them to a regular or Roth IRA. The nice thing about IRAs is that they are always 100 percent vested to you and solely under your control. What you might be giving up, however, is the loan provision that some 401(k) plans offer.

How is your 401(k) invested? Are you using an aggressive strategy or something more conservative? Are you taking any risk at all?

What do you expect your 401(k) to do for you? Assuming that Social Security will still exist when you retire, and if you add your anticipated Social Security income to withdrawals from your 401(k), will that provide you enough to live on? Since it is virtually impossible to answer that last question, we will relegate it to the "hypothetical" basket for now, but we will return to it. We will also discuss how much you can reasonably afford to withdraw from your 401(k) each year in order to avoid running out of money.

Some of your remaining "assets" are probably liabilities, because if and when you ever sell them you will take a loss on them. I'm thinking of your collections, your hobbies, your boat, private airplane, RV, jet ski, and all the things you enjoy in life. Let's leave them alone for now and move on to any remaining investments you may have.

Savings accounts, certificates of deposit, stocks, bonds, and mutual funds may all be listed at their current net asset value, whether that is a paper gain or a paper loss for you. The same is true for annuity contracts but not for limited partnerships. It's very difficult to put a price or a value on limited partnerships at any time. A good rule of thumb would be to list them at 30 to 50 percent of what you paid for them, less any distributions you have already received.

• • •

Creating a Balance Sheet

Once you have completed the survey, you are ready to prepare a personal balance sheet. A balance sheet is a snapshot of your financial situation at a particular moment. It derived its name from the fact that it usually has two columns of information and the numbers must agree for the report to be "in balance."

On the left side of the balance sheet, you list all of your assets, whether you own them outright or owe money on them. All are organized logically, which in this instance might mean starting with the most liquid (cash) and proceeding to the least liquid (hobbies and personal effects.) Your list might look something like this:

Assets

<u>Liquid assets</u>	
Cash on hand	$300
Checking account	$1,650
Savings account	$2,200
Money market fund	*$1,200*
Total, liquid assets	**$5,350**
<u>Time deposits</u>	
Certificate of deposit	$5,000
Savings bonds	$975
T-bills	$50,000
Fixed Annuity	*$30,000*
Total, medium-term liquid assets	**$85,975**
<u>Marketable assets / long-term assets</u>	
Discount brokerage account	$12,250
IRA account	$27,500
401(k) account	$68,300
Cash value life-insurance policy	*$3,750*
Total, long-term and marketable assets	**$111,800**
<u>Illiquid assets</u> (stated at fair market value)	
Home	$374,900
Home furnishings	$12,300
Car	$14,100
SUV	$16,700
Precious metals	$3,750
Other household items	$3,000
Other personal items including clothing	*$2,600*
Total, personal assets	**$427,350**
Total, all assets	*$630,475*

That's a pretty impressive number when you add it all up. However, most people owe money against some of their assets, and that debt directly subtracts from your assets when you calculate your net worth.

Liabilities

Short-term debt (to be paid off in five years or less)	
Credit card 1	$6,500
Credit card 2	$2,200
Medical bills	$3,750
Long-term debt (to be paid off in five years or more)	
Auto loan-SUV (6.0 percent, sixty months)	$12,350
Mortgage (thirty year, 6.25 percent fixed)	$235,000
Total liabilities	**$259,800**
Net Worth (Assets - liabilities)	**$370,675**

The idea of a balance sheet is to balance your assets against your liabilities. Any excess of assets over liabilities constitutes your net worth. Let's look at these numbers a little more closely.

First, this family is actually better off than many "middle-class" families in America today. Their net worth is actually positive; for far too many people, it is negative, and as the value of our homes declines most of us are seeing our net worth shrink. Add to that rising inflation in terms of the prices we pay for everything and the possibility that the stock market over the long term is heading down, and an awful lot of people could see their net worth cut significantly.

If you have a positive net worth, what does it really mean? In this case, this family has $260,000 of indebtedness that needs to be paid off. They do have $630,000 in assets; however, only about $203,000 of their assets are available to pay off that debt. If this family had no income, their short-term and medium-term liquid assets would need to be sold to pay off their debts. The remaining assets, including all their personal assets, are the things that they nominally need to live and therefore would not be candidates for sale. Besides, if any of them *were* to be sold, they would probably fetch a price well below the price originally paid for them. That, by the way, is why I mentioned that personal assets need to be stated at fair market value.

Can this family, with $427,000 in personal assets including their home, live for any significant period of time without an income? The answer is no. What about the possibility of retiring? How much benefit will their 401(k) and their IRA provide as supplements to Social Security, assuming that this couple has already reached the age at which Social Security benefits are available? If these two retirement accounts, with a total current value of about $96,000, were to yield the very generous rate of 10 percent per year, they would only add $9,600 to the couple's annual income, or $800 a month.

Two important points need to be made here. First, a net worth of over $370,000 is almost certainly not enough to enable a person or couple to retire. For most people, such an amount is usually tied up in personal assets that provide no income. Second, this couple, like most American couples, needs to bring in a steady income in order to "service"[8] their debt and meet the expenses of daily living.

Now let's continue our financial analysis by assembling an income statement.

•••

Creating an Income Statement

This step is often easier than creating a balance sheet. All you have to do is list all your sources of income and all your regular and irregular expenses.

Income includes your salary or hourly wage and overtime, retirement income, self-employment income, Social Security, disability income, interest, dividends, capital gains, rents from properties you own, royalties, awards, and a few others. Income earned in an annuity or retirement account, because it remains in the account and is not sent to you for you to spend, doesn't count because it is not currently taxable; it will count as income in the year you *withdraw* it from the account to spend it.

Expenses include regular expenses like food, clothing, and shelter, education, medical costs, insurance, transportation, personal items, vacations, raising children, and so on. If you own rental property, you include the expenses you incur in maintaining and managing that property. Don't forget to include income, sales, property, and other taxes. Don't include investments you are making except for salary reduction contributions to a 401(k) or 403(b) plan at work. Those are "mandatory" in that you contractually agree to them and will make them automatically; any and all other contributions you make to savings and investment accounts are voluntary and can be changed at will.

•••

A Sample Income Statement

Here is a hypothetical income statement for a salaried employee whose spouse also works outside the home. All figures are annualized, though it is often easier to calculate an income statement on a monthly basis.

Income

Salary	$47,000
Salary (spouse)	$38,000
Rental income	$9,000
Interest (checking account)	$116
Interest (certificate of deposit)	$1,250
Interest (savings accounts)	$424
Interest (credit union)	$225
Mutual fund interest	*$160*
Total annual income	$96,175

Expenses

Federal income taxes	$18,000
State income taxes	$1,000
FICA (Social Security) taxes	$5,475
Medicare taxes	$2,465
Property taxes, personal residence	$5,400
Food	$6,000
Clothing	$1,800
Mortgage	$9,600
Utilities	$210
Other housing-related expenses	$120
Transportation	$375
Unreimbursed medical expenses	$1,200
Charitable contributions	$2,700
Travel	$4,800
Loan payments	$9,420
Other household and personal expenses	$1,000
Insurance: life, health, auto, homeowners	$4,400
Investments *	$3,000
401(k) Retirement-plan contributions *	*$14,500*
Total expenses	$91,465

* Note that contributions to investments or retirement accounts are not considered current spending. However, they must be subtracted from your disposable income and for that reason are included here.

What's the first thing you do when you have created an income statement? You subtract total expenses from total income. In the example above, there is a surplus of $4,710 per year; most of the people I meet with show a deficit. The obvious question you should ask yourself if you arrive at a deficit when completing your own income statement is this: *how can I spend less than I earn?* There are few easy answers. Many Americans borrow on their home equity and spend it, and many pay only the minimum on their credit cards each month. They are literally living on "borrowed time." When the payment comes due, they stand to lose their home, their credit rating, and even some of their possessions.

Even if you come up with a surplus, you must ask yourself a tough question: where is the surplus going? Many people find they have understated their actual expenses.

How do you know when you have arrived at an accurate number? The best way is to track your expenses for at least three and perhaps as many as twelve months. If you use Quicken or Microsoft Money, you may already be doing that. In fact, this entire process can be greatly simplified by using either of those software packages. Both of them automatically generate your balance sheet and income statements. The key is to track, literally, every penny both in and out the door. If you don't have any training in accounting, you may find yourself inventing all sorts of "creative financing" methods, but if they work for you that's fine. The exercise itself can be very worthwhile, if for no other reason than when done properly the time it takes to complete your tax return is greatly shortened. Besides, you will have a much better idea of where the money goes.

Even if you track your expenses for three months with pencil and paper, you will still learn things about your spending habits that may surprise you. It's similar to the experience of doing your own tax return; many people have absolutely no idea how much they are actually paying in taxes. They think that if they're getting a refund they're either paying very little or even nothing at all. Tracking your expenses will enable you to visualize how much you are spending in each of the various categories. It can also help you to better distinguish between "luxuries" and "necessities." Finding that you are running a deficit each month can be very motivating in shifting items from the necessity category to the luxury category.

Once you have reviewed your balance sheet and your income statement, think about what you are looking at, where you are today and what you have accomplished throughout your life. These numbers give you strong hints into your ability to deal with money and even with your personality. This is especially true if you get on the Internet and find some comparisons between your situation and that of your peers.

Some people are surprised to find that their spending habits are extravagant or that their savings habits are not up to par. There are, for example, many Americans who think nothing of patronizing nice restaurants several nights a week. That can be just as dangerous a habit as smoking, both in terms of money and health. For most people, your own kitchen is a much better place to control diet and nutrition, and it should be a much better place to control the food budget.

Are you making as much as your peers? Are you progressing, in terms of building your resources and setting money aside for the future? Do you have good money habits? If not, what can you do now to improve? Married couples ought to discuss these things together and make decisions about them together. Since money is the cause of so much marital strife and divorce, you would hope that trying to decide together to resolve money problems should strengthen your relationship with your spouse.

Now consider the future. If you take your current situation and extend your income and spending and investing trends along their current path, where would you be five years from now? Ten years? At retirement? Are you setting enough money aside for major planned expenses, such as college tuition for your children? Note that we're not talking about the return you are making on the money you have set aside; at this point were only concerned with your diligence in setting money aside in the first place.

$$\bullet \ \bullet \ \bullet$$

Your Financial Plan

Once you have thoughtfully reviewed these numbers and considered the future, you have almost finished your own financial plan. You haven't dealt with risk just yet. You will need to consider what sort of risks you ought to insure against and how you can afford to do so. You will also have to figure out how to achieve a return on your savings and investments that will keep up with inflation and taxes and the declining dollar. You have, however, made some significant discoveries about yourself and your situation. You now have a much better idea of where you are financially and where you are going so that you may get on track to accomplish your financial goals. Of course, if you have realized that it would be very difficult for you to get yourself into a more positive situation because you can find very little disposable income, that too is a significant piece of information. That knowledge can motivate you to improve your employment situation and/or work toward a promotion and still work the same number of hours each week. That is literally free money. That money, after taxes, goes straight to the bottom line of disposable income because it hasn't been spent yet.

Please don't beat yourself up if you can't at present find your way out of a deficit or cannot find a way to increase your disposable income so that you can set more money aside. If you hadn't gone through this exercise, you might not know that you had that type of a problem. You should already rest a little easier because you have taken the first steps in taking responsibility for your own finances. At this point it may be appropriate to talk to a financial professional who is trained, knowledgeable, and experienced in personal financial planning, because such a person may be able to help you to identify ways to do the things that you need to do that you couldn't find on your own.

Should you have a detailed, written financial plan? That's up to you. People like me ordinarily have a written plan. They also have a daily to-do list and lots of other written reminders that keep them going throughout the day. There are many others who prefer the seat-of-the-pants approach, and that can work every bit as well.

For me, being able to check the boxes on the to-do list creates a very simple system of rewards, just like burning the mortgage is a very big reward that comes after a long period of effort. I like to keep a tally of what's going on; I look at my net worth every day, and I am pleased when it has increased from the previous day. If it hasn't, I want to know why. The financial software makes it possible to know these things.

If you are not that detail-oriented, all you need to do is to make a list of the things you want to do that money will help you accomplish and then figure out how you're going to raise the necessary funds. If you have young children at home and plan to put them through college or if retirement is more than twenty years away, I would suggest that trying to hit a specific dollar target in either case is going to be little more than useless because of inflation.

The effects of inflation and the declining dollar are going to become more extreme in the years to come. This makes it more difficult to try to set specific dollar goals, especially because right now we don't even know if the dollar will still exist twenty years from now.

Fifty to a hundred years ago it was much easier to set specific dollar targets. Inflation was insignificant compared with what we have experienced in the last thirty years, particularly in terms of medical and educational expenses. Retirement was easier to plan for because people didn't live very long in retirement. The world has changed, and we need to adapt to it. In the rest of this book, I will show you how I think you will be able to do so.

Now let's look at ways you might be able to free up money for investment.

Part III

Tools and Techniques

Chapter Eight

Saving More and Spending Less

We have discussed the effects of inadequate income and inflation on our personal finances. It's time to talk about the inadequate income portion in more detail. The American middle class is shrinking rapidly, at least in part because our national net savings rate has fallen to zero and below. A few have migrated to the upper class, but most of us are seeing ourselves slip ever closer to the lower class. If we do not save, we cannot expect to be better off financially than we are today. We cannot depend upon:

- Career advancement with significant raises

- Continued rapid appreciation of our home and other real estate

- Above-average performance of our investment portfolio

- The continued expansion and profitability of our own business

- Winning the lottery

There are just too many uncertainties in today's economy. The population of the United States would be stable or declining if it were not for legal and illegal immigration. We are among the most heavily taxed and over-regulated people in the world. There are significant weaknesses in the American infrastructure. The costs of doing business are constantly increasing, and that cuts into profitability. Our natural resources are rapidly being depleted. Our manufacturing base has been moving offshore for decades.

In other words, if we are to create wealth, we cannot do it by relying on things that seemed to work well in the past. We have witnessed a forty-year bull market in residential real estate, for example, with little volatility along the way. Artificially low interest rates made it possible for real estate to rise even more toward the end of the cycle.

That bull market has ended. We can no longer expect the rising value of our home to bail us out as it has done in the past. It is essential that we regularly devote a portion of our disposable income to savings and investment. It may be difficult to do so at first, but it is by no means impossible.

It used to be that when you retired you had perhaps five to ten years to live. In the first half of the twentieth century, sixty-five was "extreme old age." If our circumstances were meager, we might end up moving in with our children. Our medical needs were cared for largely out of pocket.

Since we are living so much longer and most of us want to retire earlier, we have set up goals that often turn out to be unachievable. If you don't know how long you will live, you dare not eat into your principal. We have to live on the income from our savings and investments. Because of inflation, the need for medical and long-term care insurance, and the high cost of living, our income has to be stretched further than ever.

For example, let's say that you are sixty-two and want to begin retirement today. You are eligible to draw on all of your retirement accounts without penalty because you are past the age of fifty nine and a half. You may receive Social Security through early retirement. You are married, your children are grown up and (hopefully) gone away, and you are receiving $1,200.00 per month from Social Security. You also have saved $1 million in your savings, investment, and retirement accounts. Taking a number out of the air, let's say that you are able to earn 6 percent consistently on your million dollars. Here's how the numbers work out:

• • •

Example 1

Investment yield: 6 percent on $1,000,000 =	$60,000 per year
Social Security income:	$14,400 per year
Gross income:	$74,400 per year

Now, that part sounds pretty good. But before you get too excited, that's take a look at taxes and inflation and how they erode your income.

Taxable income:	$50,000
Taxes:	$ 9,057
Net income after taxes:	$65,342

If inflation is "only" 3 percent per year, you have to reinvest 3 percent of the total value of your investments.

Net income after taxes:	$65,342

Reinvestment to retain purchasing power: (3 percent of $1,000,000) $30,000

Net income after taxes and inflation: *$35,342*

Suddenly you find yourself living on about $3,000.00 a month, and it doesn't look like a lot of fun. If you have a net worth of $1 million, you probably ought to have long-term-care insurance. If you procrastinated buying a long-term-care policy because you couldn't afford it, as most people do, that insurance alone is now going to cost you at least $3,000 to $5,000 per year out of pocket. It will cost your spouse about the same amount.

The somewhat demoralizing point of this example is that a million dollars doesn't buy what it used to. I think it's safe to assume that $3,000.00 a month will not be adequate to meet your financial needs during retirement. But remember, in this example we are preserving your principal indefinitely because we have no idea how long you will live and need income.

Now let's summarize the flaws in this example, any of which may render it worthless.

1. Your real rate of return will vary. It may not keep up with inflation. It may even be negative if you purchase an investment that is not guaranteed as to principal and interest.

2. The rate of inflation will vary. When inflation is higher, you must reinvest a larger chunk of your income to maintain your purchasing power.

3. Your tax rate will vary.

4. The government could fail to honor its Social Security obligations. This may not seem possible, but the corollary certainly is: the government could raise Social Security and Medicare taxes drastically to be able to pay benefits to recipients. Taxes paid by retirees could also increase. Your Medicare co-pay can increase, and the cost of your Medicare Supplement insurance can rise as well.

● ● ●

Example 2

Let's look at the same example, but this time we will allow you to erode the principal and not reinvest to keep up with inflation. This is a more practical example for most people, but it is not necessarily a valid one. In this example you look at the mortality tables and your family's medical history as well as your own personal medical history. You make a subjective determination as to how long you may reasonably expect to live, including whether you expect to end up in a nursing home or will need long-term care of any sort for any significant length of time. Long-term care today can easily cost $300.00 per person per day, unreimbursed by medical insurance, and those costs are only increasing.

Let's say you have determined that your reasonable life expectancy is to age eighty-eight. Your spouse will outlive you by three years. It would be nice to have a financial legacy to pass on to your heirs, but in this example you will have nothing left. You can only hope you won't leave any bills behind. If you do, you should try to cover them with life insurance, but life insurance begun above age fifty can be *very* expensive.

Here's how the numbers work out. We assume that your million dollars will continue to generate 6 percent per year. Now, however, you will be drawing down those million dollars over your combined life expectancy which is 29 years (88 + 3 = 91; 91 - current age of 62 = 29). Based on these numbers, we would receive an income of $72,840.00 per year.

Drawdown of investments:	$72,840 per year
Social Security income:	$14,400 per year
Gross income:	$87,240 per year
Taxable income:	$55,000 *
Taxes:	$10,307
Net income after taxes:	$76,933 per year

* Note that the amount of taxable income will never actually be $55,000.00. It will be more in the early years and less in the later years, when more of the money you receive is principal. If you are withdrawing funds from a traditional IRA or 401(k), all of the withdrawals are fully taxable; if you withdraw from a Roth IRA or Roth 401(k), none of what you receive is taxable.

In this example the only component of your income that will keep up with inflation is Social Security; the rest of your income will be in the drawdown of your investments, and you will take the same amount from them each year.

The difference between Example 1 and Example 2 is your staying power. Example 1 gives you a fighting chance of being able to afford a very long retirement, while in Example 2 you will run out of money (except for Social Security benefits) at a certain age.

In Example 2, as long as we have inflation, your purchasing power in real dollars will decline year after year for the rest of your life. Unfortunately, that makes this example much less attractive as long as the Federal Reserve continues to destroy the dollar.

Here is how the million dollars are depleted over twenty-nine years:

Year	Month	Balance	Average Monthly Interest Earned	Amount Paid Interest + balance	Monthly to Investor	New balance
1	1	$1,000,000.00	$5,000.00	$1,005,000.00	$6,070.00	$998,930.00
	2	998,930.00	4,994.65	1,003,924.65	6,070.00	997,854.65

	3	997,854.65	4,989.27	1,002,843.92	6,070.00	996,773.92
	4	996,773.92	4,983.87	1,001,757.79	6,070.00	995,687.79
	5	995,687.79	4,978.44	1,000,666.23	6,070.00	994,596.23
	6	994,596.23	4,972.98	999,569.21	6,070.00	993,499.21
	7	993,499.21	4,967.50	998,466.71	6,070.00	992,396.71
	8	992,396.71	4,961.98	997,358.69	6,070.00	991,288.69
	9	991,288.69	4,956.44	996,245.14	6,070.00	990,175.14
	10	990,175.14	4,950.88	995,126.01	6,070.00	989,056.01
	11	989,056.01	4,945.28	994,001.29	6,070.00	987,931.29
	12	987,931.29	4,939.66	992,870.95	6,070.00	986,800.95
2	24	973,987.87	4,869.94	978,857.81	6,070.00	972,787.81
3	36	959,184.45	4,795.92	963,980.37	6,070.00	957,910.37
4	48	943,467.98	4,717.34	948,185.32	6,070.00	942,115.32
5	60	926,782.16	4,633.91	931,416.07	6,070.00	925,346.07
6	72	909,067.19	4,545.34	913,612.52	6,070.00	907,542.52
7	84	890,259.60	4,451.30	894,710.90	6,070.00	888,640.90
8	96	870,292.00	4,351.46	874,643.46	6,070.00	868,573.46
9	108	849,092.84	4,245.46	853,338.31	6,070.00	847,268.31
10	120	826,586.17	4,132.93	830,719.10	6,070.00	824,649.10
11	132	802,691.33	4,013.46	806,704.79	6,070.00	800,634.79
12	144	777,322.71	3,886.61	781,209.33	6,070.00	775,139.33
13	156	750,389.41	3,751.95	754,141.36	6,070.00	748,071.36
14	168	721,794.93	3,608.97	725,403.90	6,070.00	719,333.90
15	180	691,436.79	3,457.18	694,893.98	6,070.00	688,823.98
16	192	659,206.24	3,296.03	662,502.27	6,070.00	656,432.27
17	204	624,987.77	3,124.94	628,112.71	6,070.00	622,042.71
18	216	588,658.79	2,943.29	591,602.08	6,070.00	585,532.08
19	228	550,089.11	2,750.45	552,839.56	6,070.00	546,769.56
20	240	509,140.54	2,545.70	511,686.24	6,070.00	505,616.24
21	252	465,666.35	2,328.33	467,994.68	6,070.00	461,924.68
22	264	419,510.77	2,097.55	421,608.32	6,070.00	415,538.32
23	276	370,508.41	1,852.54	372,360.95	6,070.00	366,290.95
24	288	318,483.70	1,592.42	320,076.11	6,070.00	314,006.11
25	300	263,250.21	1,316.25	264,566.46	6,070.00	258,496.46
26	312	204,610.04	1,023.05	205,633.09	6,070.00	199,563.09
27	324	142,353.08	711.77	143,064.84	6,070.00	136,994.84
28	336	76,256.24	381.28	76,637.52	6,070.00	70,567.52
29	348	$6,082.70	$30.41	$6,113.11	$6,070.00	$43.11

Note that after the first twelve months only one payment per year is illustrated. In total you would have received $2,112,360.00 over the period of twenty-nine years and would have only $43.11 left.

Now let's summarize the flaws in this example, any of which may render it worthless.

1. Your real rate of return will vary. It may not keep up with your withdrawals, which would deplete your funds even more quickly.

2. The rate of inflation will vary. If inflation continues, your purchasing power will decline year after year.

3. Your tax rate will vary.

4. The government could fail to honor its Social Security obligations.

5. You could outlive your income.

Assuming that you are on track to have $1 million when you reach retirement age, I hope you don't get particularly excited about either of these examples. No prudent man[9] would recommend that you systematically eat your "seed corn." Running out of money, already a serious problem in the United States, will become a much more significant problem as the baby boomers retire.

The solution should now be obvious. If you start today and reevaluate your situation and if you make and hold to a commitment to reduce your spending and increase your saving, you'll have a far better chance of enjoying your retirement and being able to accomplish some of the other things you want to do. There is a double benefit to embarking upon a disciplined program of saving and investment; your net worth increases, and you begin to be savvier about your personal finances. As you learn more, you should be able to earn more by making your money work harder for you.

• • •

Spending less

Controlling our discretionary spending is a lot like dieting; both require us to rein in our passions, and both leave us feeling somewhat deprived. I want to help you get to the point where you get excited about the way in which your personal net worth is increasing. It's a game with a very serious purpose, and like any game, it's more fun when you're good at it. Here are some suggestions for regaining control over your spending, in the order of their impact.

• • •

Housing

Historically, housing has taken up as much as 40 percent of our income; today, for some people, the percentage is even higher. Loose lending standards have enabled us to borrow far more on our homes than we should, with the result that many people are far deeper in debt than they ought to be.

How can you reduce the cost of housing? That depends upon how flexible you are and whether you can separate wants and needs. A house or a condominium is usually viewed as an appreciating asset, but in reality both are depreciating liabilities. If you understand that, you are one step closer to getting a handle on your housing expenses. You never really *own* real estate; you just use it for a while. Someone else will own it after you are gone.

I believe in owning a home of the appropriate size in an appropriate neighborhood. I'm a firm believer in regular maintenance, and it is always best to have a yard that is not too big to be manageable. Depending upon where you live, what is appropriate can vary significantly. For example, in Southern California, building lots are measured in terms of square feet; in many towns in New Hampshire, the minimum lot size for a house is three acres. That house in New Hampshire on three acres will cost significantly less than the house on fifty thousand square feet of land in Southern California. A house on forty acres outside of Omaha will cost less than either one.

If you have or plan to have a growing family, you probably ought to buy more house rather than less. Moving can be very expensive, especially if you include real-estate commissions, closing costs, and taxes. If you own a house you like, bought at a good price, and have a fixed rate mortgage, you are better off than many people.

There are several things you can do to reduce the cost of living in your house. You can:

- Make it more energy efficient.

- Negotiate a reduction in your property taxes.

- Accelerate your mortgage and pay it off early, saving yourself thousands of dollars in interest.

- Perform regular maintenance in order to avoid some major repairs.

- Shop around for a better mortgage than you have now, especially when interest rates fall.

There are also some things you can do to reduce your homeowner's insurance premiums; talk to your agent about them.

If your "depreciating liability" is in a market that has experienced rapid and significant price appreciation, as is the case on both coasts, you might want to consider selling and taking a profit. That always raises the thorny question of where you would live once you sell, because everything else in your area is just as expensive. That's where some knowledge about real-estate markets can come in handy. Although the housing market collapse I predicted for several years is under way, there are still people who could sell at a profit—if only there were any motivated buyers.

There are times to own, and there are times to rent. This is one of the better times to rent, if you can find a place that you like. We have seen decades of price appreciation in many markets, and now most of these markets have seen prices fall. It's taking longer to sell a house, and many deals are falling through for one reason or another. We are beginning to see a significant change in the way people buy residential real estate.

You can "take your money and run" now, live in a place you rent for two to five years, and in a few years buy a home just as nice as the one you sold for significantly less than you sold it for. If housing prices resume their ascent, following this strategy will put you at a disadvantage. I strongly recommend that you talk to a few real-estate agents candidly about what they are seeing in your area in terms of price stability, length of time on the market, availability of financing, and so on. You could also go down to your county courthouse on a regular basis and take a look at the houses being sold due to foreclosure.

If you live in California and have been enjoying the false savings created by Proposition 13, this strategy might not work at all. Even if you bought a house for half as much as what you sold yours for, the increase in property taxes could offset any savings on the price you paid.

If you are at the age when you are looking at buying your first home, I would suggest that you shop very carefully. We're getting close to the time when you can make ridiculously low offers on properties and they will be accepted. I don't think you should plan on seeing the value of your home increase significantly after you buy it.

I would not recommend purchasing a condominium, now or ever. Condominiums are even more subject to the whims of the market than single-family dwellings. Besides, after thirty years, when the property is ready to be torn down, you own nothing. As far as I can tell, buying a condominium is very much like paying too much rent for an apartment. I am sure that there are people "out there" who have actually made money when they sold their condominiums; I haven't met any of them.

When you own your home please be careful to maintain it well but don't go overboard in lavish decoration and additions. Making your home more energy efficient can pay off for many years to come. If you check with your local electric utility, you might find that they offer a free energy audit. In New Hampshire a professional inspector walks through your entire house and drafts a list of recommended changes. He then schedules a contractor who will come in and do up to $4,000.00 worth of those changes. The total cost to you is $100.00.

Sometimes self-sufficiency can pay dividends. There are numerous ways to heat and cool your house, and most often the house was designed around those fuels and sources that are currently the most cost-efficient. I have discovered that propane, though it offers fewer BTUs per unit than oil or natural gas, can be significantly less expensive. Its price is not as subject to the extreme fluctuations we have seen in the oil and natural gas markets in the last several years.

If you live in an area where firewood is readily available you could supplement your heating system with a wood stove which utilizes firewood more efficiently than a fireplace. There are attractive, efficient wood stoves today that can easily heat an entire house. By placing an open container of water on top of the wood stove, you can keep enough humidity in the air.

As a backup source of electricity, I usually put a propane-fired generator in the backyard, away from the living quarters and close to the garage. That may not pay for itself in the usual sense, but if you live in an area that is subject to severe weather, thunderstorms, and power outages you will quickly come to appreciate a backup generator.

Though it is not yet cost effective, a solar array could be a good way to help preserve the environment and provide a steady, reliable source of electricity. With the combination of solar cells mounted on the roof, a propane-fired generator, an inverter and a battery bank in the basement, you should never be without power for more than one-one hundredth of a second. Keep in mind that if you sell a house equipped in this manner, you may not recover all of your additional investment in technology.

While we are on the subject of housing, let's talk realistically about building equity in your owner-occupied dwelling. You can think of home equity as "dead money" because it isn't paying any interest or dividends. Your home equity is saving you mortgage interest, but for most people that interest is an important deduction. We have come a long way from the days when a home was a sanctuary, something sought after and faithfully cared for through an entire generation or more. Today many people don't keep their homes up but rather let them run down. We think of them as investments; we speculate on them, and we're willing to borrow the maximum we can against them. There is a difference between a house and a home, but that's not what I'm getting at. I'm thinking instead of those who have put themselves at risk because they have dealt imprudently with that most important asset.

You have to decide for yourself whether you are speculating on your house or plan to use it as your home for an extended period of time. If you intend to be there for a long time, the only decision you have to make regarding whether to build equity or to "invest the difference" is the guaranteed rate of return you can receive on the money. If your fixed mortgage is at 6 percent and you have a safe, secure investment paying 7 percent, you may be better off paying less on the house and more into the investment. That is a purely subjective decision, however, and not something I recommend on one way or the other.

• • •

Transportation

Some people buy new cars; other people buy used cars. For some people a car is a status symbol; for others it is just transportation. I prefer to buy new, pay off the loan as quickly as possible, and keep the car long after the payments end. Yes, there are bargains to be had when you buy a used vehicle, and these days you can check the car's history on the Internet. The thing you *can't* check is the way the car was driven.

There are significant resources available on the Internet today to help you identify and get the best price on the car that you want. In today's soft economy, deals and rebates abound; you need to know the difference between the invoice price and the retail price, and the blue-book value for your trade-in. You probably already know that the options you want are not cheap; in fact, in many cases most of the dealer's profit comes from the options.

Even more important is the expected after-purchase cost of the vehicle. There are Web sites which detail the average expenses for maintenance for most cars available today. Warranties do not cover standard maintenance items, but they can be helpful when you have unexpected problems. Extended warranties are also very high profit margins for dealers, as are the "paint and fabric" treatment they try to sell to you. If you live in an area with cold winters, the undercoat and clear-coat treatments can be worth the money.

You can shop around for car insurance and talk to the agent about the coverage you must have and the coverage you don't really need. Make sure that you don't get yourself into a financial bind because of the car payments. Know what you can afford before you start going to the dealers. These days some people actually refinance their car loans so that they can save money on interest.

If the lease payments they offer you sound better than the loan payments remember that in almost every case leasing is more expensive than buying. At the end of the lease, you own nothing, but if you have driven the leased vehicle too many miles you may have to pay an additional fee.

• • •

Food And Household expenses

We've already discussed home-cooked meals as opposed to dining out. The savings can be very significant, especially over a long period of time. You can spend too much on groceries just the same as you can spend too much on restaurants, however. If you avoid the more expensive packaged meals, you can save quite a bit of money while adding just a little time for meal preparation. It doesn't take much time to look through a store circular, and it's always a good idea to "shop the specials" when the things that you eat regularly are on special.

Keeping a supply of food in the house, especially food that has been purchased "on special," can be a very good idea. Many grocery items have a useful life of a year or so before they began losing nutritional value, color, and flavor. Leave the children at home if you can when you go to the supermarket and avoid impulse buying. (The counsel about impulse buying applies to homes and cars as well.)

Household items—those things that fill hundreds of thousands of storage units all over the country—can be more judiciously purchased as well. Don't go to the mall unless you need to buy something there. Decide what you need before you go to the store or get on the Internet to make a purchase. Take some time to look for bargains but make sure you get quality sufficient for the life expectancy of the item you're buying. A $20.00 pair of shoes can be uncomfortable and be worn out after one season, but a well-made, attractive, all-leather pair of shoes for $250.00 can look good for years.

• • •

Big-ticket Items

College education is expensive. College tuitions and other costs have risen much faster than the general rate of inflation for decades, and there is no leveling off in sight. The obvious choice if you can't afford an Ivy League school is a state school or lots of scholarship and grant money. More private and public funding for college education is available than ever before, and some of it goes begging because no one knows it's available.

When you are buying other big-ticket items, from vacations to cars to major appliances to "toys" (boats, SUVs, RVs, and such), there are ways to save money by shopping around and finding the best deal. The greatest money-saving technique is to separate needs and wants and place expenditures in the appropriate category. Just because there are vast quantities of consumer goods available for a price doesn't mean you have to partake of a fair share of them.

• • •

Retirement

Don't envision retirement as that opportunity to do all the things you couldn't afford when the kids were growing up. It doesn't happen that way any more, at least not for the vast majority of Americans. I recommend downsizing your home as appropriate (which could make it more difficult for your kids to move back home again) and saving money that way by living in a cozier, more intimate environment. (That sounds a lot better than "scrimping and saving.")

I suggest that you plan to do more things at home. Yes, clients of mine have purchased that RV and put tens of thousands of miles on it, and they have a great time; but they are now facing more expensive gasoline or diesel, and it's beginning to pinch a little. Most of my retired clients are busier in retirement than they were while they were employed; if you're not, I strongly recommend getting involved in local organizations where you can serve. Being involved and needed can be much more rewarding than being pampered, and it usually costs much less.

These are just a few ideas to get you thinking about how you can live less expensively. You will certainly come up with your own, and I encourage you to make this a part of your regular thought processes. Money not spent can be invested and if invested wisely can provide a greater feeling of security as you look to the future.

Chapter Nine

Making It Grow: Stocks, Bonds, Mutual Funds, and ETFs

It's time to make what may be the most important point in this book:

> Opinions, no matter whose they are, are worthless. Uninformed opinions, those formulated in the absence of facts, can be downright dangerous.

Each of us views the world through his or her own set of lenses. Those lenses are formed through our entire life of observation. The way we observe things is a function of our personality, our upbringing, our education, and the fundamental set of values to which we hold. The way we feel about things is shaped by our previous experience.

We live in a world that claims to celebrate diversity, but in reality it rewards conformity. Our friends tend to be people whose incomes are within 10 percent of ours on either side. We join organizations but tend to be very casual about our participation. Most of us function within a belief system that promotes our self-interest. We prefer to do the things we see those around us doing. Even when we become politically active, we align ourselves with one or another prominent ideology or party to free us from having to think about what's really important. We like to let others do our thinking for us, and we want to be left alone to do pretty much what we please. As a result, most of the time we end up getting what we *deserve* instead of what we *want*.

Opinions are not "right" or "wrong"; they simple exist and are always subject to modification. Many of us hold opinions about things that, if analyzed, conflict with other opinions that we hold. The psychologists call that cognitive dissonance. It's one thing to have an opinion about who will win the World Series; it's entirely another to have an opinion about the solution to global warming. Most of us have better informed opinions about the former than about the latter. If a million of us gather to voice the same opinion, we are nothing more than a faceless mob.

Everyone has opinions about money and investments. These tend to be based upon what we have personally experienced, what we have heard from our friends, or what we hear and see in the media. Our opinions tend to be poorly researched, based on material inaccuracies, and may be dangerous to our financial well-being.

The markets illustrate this point perfectly. When you buy an investment, you think it's going to go up. The person who sold it to you (not the broker, but the person on the other side of the transaction) thinks it's going to go down or at least stay flat for some period of time. The two of you have opposite or contrary opinions, and that's what makes the markets work. Which of the two of you is right will only be determined over time.

I have been reading market research for thirty years. Much of it is produced by highly paid analysts who specialize in their field of research. Most of what they produce is worthless, in part because they are required to slant their research in the direction their employer tells them to. Even those who are more ethical and honest are often wrong.

I include myself in that group whose opinions may be of no value. It's fine to listen to the opinions of others, but you must make your own decisions. You have to do your homework. I evaluate thousands of opinions, sifting through them and performing additional analysis on those that look attractive. The few that survive my scrutiny are watched carefully until it is time to add them to my portfolio and my clients' portfolios.

You have probably received solicitations in the mail in which a particular investment is described in glowing terms. You have no way of knowing whether the information is correct. All that you know is that someone has sent you a marketing piece to try to get you excited about something. Whether they're trying to promote a specific investment or selling a newsletter, the intent is to get you to take action without thinking about it any further. This is usually dangerous.

In chapter four, "What Is a Financial Professional?" we looked at what motivates those in the financial services industry. Understandably, their personal income always tops the list. If something you read, hear, or see arouses your interest, the first thing you have to do is to identify the motive of the writer. Sometimes this is quite simple.

Almost every day I receive a newsletter or tabloid-style publication in which some unknown author raves about a particular stock. In each case I do exactly the same thing. I look for the box at the bottom of one of the pages that says "This is a paid advertisement" or language to that effect. When I find it, the material goes into the wastebasket. There is no point wasting your time on advertising any more than there is in looking at the past history of a particular investment.

When you find something pertaining to an investment that is not labeled as an advertisement and that might actually be research material, as you read through the material you will usually find that the author recommends that you buy the stock. Most of the time no mention is made of an appropriate *price* or *timeframe* in which the investment should be purchased. The appeal is to your greed, and the whole idea is to get you to hustle into that investment immediately.

To my knowledge there were no more than two people in my industry who accurately predicted the year 2000 stock-market crash. Some had been predicting a crash, but had begun doing so as much as seven years earlier. Their adherents had missed out on some of the most spectacular gains ever seen in the stock market. The majority of writers constantly recommended increasing your exposure to the stock market, and many were 100 percent invested in stocks at the peak. It has been interesting to me over the past several years to read articles written by many who now claim to have predicted the year 2000 peak. They did not.

The most egregious example of such "hindsight forecasting" I have seen came in the form of a newsletter-style solicitation. This author, someone I had never heard off, talked about how if you had followed her recommendations during the previous twelve months you would have taken $200.00 and turned it into several million dollars. There followed a trading history of more than a dozen stocks, each of which had risen in value as much as fifty times (5,000 percent) during those twelve months.

Amazingly, the author of this solicitation claimed to have recommended buying and selling each of these stocks one after another and at exactly the right moments. It was only when you read the fine print that you realized the truth: this person had *not* been in business last year, had *never* actually made these recommendations, and had *no reasonable expectation* of ever being able to generate such an astonishing market performance. What this person *had* done was to find stocks that had enjoyed a spectacular run in the previous year and placed them in sequence for maximum gains. In any year you will find stocks that make significant moves up or down; the trick is always to get into and out of them at the right moment.

• • •

Be Your Own "Expert"

If you are going to make your money grow, you are going to have to become your own "expert." After all, you are responsible for the results. There are no guarantees in investing; that's the nature of risk. You have to limit your risk by doing your homework and having a very good idea of what to expect from each investment you make. If you fail to keep ahead of inflation, taxes, *and* the declining dollar, your purchasing power will shrink. If you rely on uninformed or biased opinions, you are probably heading into trouble.

The markets humble the best of us. There are some people in this business whose advice is so poor that you should do exactly the opposite of what they recommend. There are some who have lost their clients' entire investment. Most of them just start a new company and look for new customers.

That's why I try to provide my clients with a framework, a structure that can help them to make the right decisions. I attempt to educate my audience. This approach tends to make me long-winded considering the average person's attention span, but it gives my clients enough information to make their own decisions.

You need to know the reasons why an investment might not work. You need to know what the alternatives are. Sometimes there are no good alternatives; sometimes you just need to "park" your money in a money-market fund until conditions improve. The analogy of a boat seeking a safe harbor to ride out a storm is a good one. You should invest when it is appropriate to do so and only then.

Investment involves risk. When you take a risk, you can lose. If you choose the route of safety, you may earn some interest, but you will never experience growth of your principal.

The number of dollars you own may *increase* if you place them in an account where they will earn interest; however, adjusted for inflation and taxes, the purchasing power of your money will usually be *less*. Making your money *grow* means taking appropriate and necessary risks in the hope that the *value* of your principal will increase over time. That's my definition of the objective of investing; *your purchasing power must increase year after year.*

● ● ●

Let's look briefly at some of the best-know forms of investment.

● ● ●

Stocks

Own a piece of any publicly traded company and have voting rights

These days millions of Americans have money in the stock market, but some of them don't realize it. On numerous occasions a prospective client has told me "Oh, I don't own any stocks; I buy mutual funds."

In the United States millions of people make their living directly or indirectly from the stock markets. Thousands of people who have been laid off from their full-time employment turn to "day trading" in stocks to try to replace their income. Most of them fail at it. There are many good books about stocks available today. What follows is just a brief description.

The two basic types of stocks are common stocks and preferred stocks; I work with both, as appropriate. *Common stocks* have voting rights. *Preferred stocks* have no voting rights, but they tend to pay higher dividends. In the event of a bankruptcy, those holding preferred stocks will get paid off before those holding common stocks. In fact, in a bankruptcy the common stockholders are the last to be paid off; those at the top of the list are those who own the company's "senior debt," the highest-rated of the company's bonds.

When you buy a stock, you are buying a piece of a company. Shareholders participate in the company's profits, if any, as well as its losses, without having to lift a finger. Your vote is even solicited for the company's annual meeting, to which you are invited. Commissions on stocks are very low compared to what they were back in the eighties. If you hold your stock(s) for a year or longer, you receive preferential long-term capital gains tax treatment.

Many of my peers will tell you that the stock market produces average returns in excess of 7 percent per year. Therefore, they say, all you have to do is to put some or all of your money into an index fund and sit back and watch your money grow. An index fund attempts to "mirror" a market index such as the Standard & Poor's 500 (S&P 500) or the Dow Jones Industrial Average; normally it does so by buying and holding a proportionate amount of each stock in the index.

What most of my peers *don't* tell you is that the stock market today has significant risks. In fact, the

U.S. stock market has probably never posed a greater risk than when it double-topped in 2007. Charts 1 and 2 show what's called an "exponential" rise (some people call it a "parabolic" rise, but they're not married to a mathematician). You don't need to be a chart expert to identify these trends. When anything rises exponentially, it is time to be very careful.

Turn to the section of color charts and photos. As you can see on Chart 1, the first chart, the exponential rise of the Dow Jones Industrial Average has been broken. Note that the DJIA hit a new all-time high in 2000, then bottomed in 2002 and 2003, after which it hit an all-time high in 2007. The risk at today's levels is very high compared with the risk from 1928 through 1983. You get a sense of that just by looking at the chart, because a trend that was virtually *horizontal* for decades suddenly became almost *vertical.*

The second chart (Chart 2) is another good example of a exponential rise. BHP Billiton, headquartered in Australia, is one of the world's largest natural resources companies. This chart looks quite similar to the DJIA chart, but note that the BHP chart starts in 1999. Note also that BHP has fallen more in percentage terms than the DJIA has. The entire natural resources sector fell sharply in 2008 when it appeared that a global slowdown was coming.

The problem with these charts is that this index and this stock (the DJIA and BHP), after chugging along for years with relatively minor gains and losses, suddenly began to move up faster than in previous years. There are many reasons why this can happen, but they all point to one thing: *there was a fundamental change in the way that investors looked at these things.* To take advantage of this change, you should have gotten in when the trend was relatively flat—and you should have gotten out by now. There are many ways to get out of a stock; we will discuss them later in the book.

What rate of return is "appropriate" for the DJIA? Let's look at a table showing the average returns for different periods:

Dow Jones Industrial Average Historic Returns			
			Annualized
	DJIA,	DJIA,	Percent
Time Period	January 1	December 31	Gain / Loss
1900-2007 107 years	66.61	13450.65	5.04%
1928-2007	203.35	13450.65	5.38%
1933-2007	59.29	13450.65	7.50%
1945-2007	152.58	13450.65	7.37%
1973-2007	1031.68	13450.65	7.61%
1988-2007	2015.25	13450.65	9.96%
1992-2007	3172.42	13450.65	9.45%
2003-2007	8607.52	13450.65	9.34%
1900-1950	66.61	235.41	2.51%
1950-2007	200.13	13450.65	7.52%
1900-1972	66.61	1020.02	3.81%
1972-2007	889.3	13450.65	7.84%
		Total change	
Best five years	1924-1928	214.07%	
Worst five years	1928-1932	-70.39%	
Best ten years	1989-1998	323.39%	
Worst ten years	1929-1938	-48.41%	

These numbers speak volumes, though we won't go into much detail here. Note that for the first half of the twentieth century, from 1900 through 1950, the DJIA averaged a gain of just over 2.5 percent per year. Over the next fifty-seven years through December 2007, that annual rate tripled to just over 7.5 percent per year. That's the fundamental change I mentioned earlier.

Note also that from 1988 through 2007, despite the fact that the DJIA fell almost 39 percent between March 2001 and October 2002, the average annual return rose to just under 10 percent. But that's enough of a difference to make 1988 the year of another fundamental change in thinking about the stock market.

In fact, the DJIA returned just over 6 percent per year on average between 1950 and 1988. That gives us three distinct return periods for the Dow:

- 1900–1950 2.5 percent per year average return

- 1950–1988 6.0 percent per year

- 1989–2007 10.1 percent per year

As we will discuss later on, the way in which investors look at the fundamental data pertaining to a stock, an industry, or an index like the DJIA changes from time to time. Most investors take the wrong approach to the fundamentals. When the market has fallen for a long time, people tend to think it's going to continue to fall and vice versa. Most of us have a "herd mentality" and find it very difficult to be contrarians, or to go against the crowd.

Peter Lynch, who became famous for managing the Fidelity Magellan Fund, remarked that even though his fund had seen extraordinary gains for several years, the average investor in the fund was only averaging about 3.5 percent per year. This was due to the fact that most investors do a poor job of timing the market.

Let's make a couple more points about these numbers. First, we speak only of average *gains*. We can safely do so because the DJIA has risen over most periods of time greater than one year since 1900. We can also do so because the DJIA cannot go negative; the most it can fall over any period of time is 100 percent. Therefore, since the likelihood of the thirty stocks in the DJIA going to zero is very small, we have learned to expect gains.

Second, let's not forget those years of losses. The Great Depression was only one of several periods in which the market took away most investors' money very quickly.

Do I believe that the stock market has more risk solely because it has moved to a period of "exponential" gains? No. There are many factors involved. Some of them are subjective and based upon opinions and attitudes; others are objective and based upon hard data. Still others are based upon inaccurate or even fictitious data. Some of those factors contributed to the exponential rise, and some made it possible.

The U.S. stock market has entered a new phase in which *volatility* will be a key consideration. A volatile market moves more quickly in *both* directions. It is more difficult to make money in a volatile market because the odds of your getting in and out of an investment at good prices are not as good.

The other reason why the stock market has greatly increased risk—and the reason why this book is so important right now—is that the stock market has reached a critical level. The S&P500 has double-topped, first in 2000 and next in 2007. The market has decided its future direction, and it is *down*. At this point, now that the U.S. stock markets have lost more than half their value, strong arguments can be made for movement in either direction. That means that uncertainty about the market is greater than usual. My research indicates that it could be several years before the DJIA gets back up to its 2007 double top.

This is why an appropriate equity-index annuity can be helpful in minimizing risk while offering the potential for significant gains. An Equity Index Annuity, which is a recent innovation in the insurance industry, can give you some of the stock market's gains while preventing you from experiencing losses. As long as you meet all the contract provisions you can expect to get back no less than you have invested regardless of the performance of the stock market.

Many stocks, particular those of older, more mature companies, tend to pay cash dividends. If you own a common stock that has paid a 4 percent dividend each year and is appreciating at an average rate of about 7 percent per year, most of the time you will keep ahead of inflation and taxes. What's not to love about that?

Stocks are marketable; they are bought and sold whenever the markets are open. With overnight and overseas trading, some stocks can literally be traded twenty-four hours a day. You are not obligated to hold onto your stocks for any period of time; you simply have to pay a commission when you buy and when you sell. You don't even need to hold on to the stock certificates. Everything is done electronically, which has been a great benefit to the industry and to most investors.

Stocks are issued by companies in many industries and in many countries. On any trading day, there are tens of thousands of stocks available for purchase or sale. Choosing the one right ones to buy or sell is never easy. You start by deciding the objectives of the particular investment you wish to make ("top-down" management) or you investigate a "hot tip" or other recommendation you received ("bottom-up" management). You might use the first method when you are building a portfolio; you could use the second when you are trying to invest the available cash in the portfolio.

For example, you may be trying to build an *income portfolio*. You might do this because:

- You want the income over the long term and are not particularly concerned about market fluctuations.

- You believe that income-producing investments with an equity component can provide both income and growth.

- You believe that interest rates are steady or about to decline.

- You believe that the stock market is stable or rising.

- You believe that even if the stocks you purchase stay the same or decline slightly in price, the dividends they pay will be greater than the interest you might receive in a certificate of deposit or other fixed-rate investment.

To identify appropriate stocks for this portfolio, you can do your own research or rely on the opinions of brokers or the media. There are many places on the Internet where you can do investment research at low cost or even for free. Sites like moneycentral.msn.com, Bloomberg.com, morningstar.com, biz.yahoo.com, and hundreds of others offer useful information, some of which is accurate. Every online broker also provides research either for free or at a certain price.

Information about almost every publicly traded company is available at the company's Web site. This information will be about the company's *fundamentals;* sales, earnings, financials, and so on. If a stock has good fundamentals you need to find out when to buy it, and that requires *technic*al analysis. That's where charts become important, and we will discuss them later.

• • •

Finding a Broker

How do you buy stocks? The first thing you do is to identify a broker and open an account. If you want to pay high commissions, you can use a full-service broker. The research he or she will provide to you, however, may or may not be any better than what you can obtain for free on the Internet. Most people are better off using an Internet-based discount broker.

Choosing an online broker involves determining how much research and tools you wish to use and doing a comparison among various firms for services, commissions, and fees. Many online brokers today offer different levels of service; the larger your account and/or the more transactions you make each month, the lower your costs per transaction. In many cases you also get monthly fees waived based on the volume of transactions.

The real test comes when you are actually trading. If you place one or two trades per month, you really don't care about trade execution as long as you get the price you want. If you trade several times a day, you should care about execution, and you want to make sure you are with a company that can give you the best service possible. I would make some recommendations, but the features and benefits offered by the many different companies keep changing. There are several print publications that offer an annual review of online brokers. You probably won't know exactly what to look for the first time around, and that's fine; changing from one broker to another is usually free and can take less than ten days.

• • •

Opening an Account

When you open the account online, you should request both a margin account and an options account. You may not need them now, but you probably will later on. You then transfer funds to the account or mail a check and watch your account online to see that it is funded in a timely manner. The margin account allows you to borrow money to purchase securities, which is usually a bad idea. However, certain options strategies require that you have a margin account.

• • •

What Should You Buy?

Once the account is open and funded, you are ready to trade. Then comes the big question: what are you going to buy? The list of available investments in a regular brokerage account is staggering. If someone were to try to publish a list, it would have to be updated literally every second, for companies get into and go out of business constantly.

You begin your selection by reviewing your plan for that particular account and update the research you have performed on stocks you had considered purchasing in it. We will discuss appropriate analytical methods you might want to use in chapter fifteen. When you find one or more stocks that meet your criteria, you place your orders. Those criteria always include making sure that the stock's price is in an acceptable range for you to buy it.

It is said that most of the profits in stocks are made when you *buy* them, not when you sell them. You should always try to pay the lowest possible price for every investment you purchase. That may sound like common sense, but it is actually contrary to the "momentum" method of trading. It is an important part of value investing, however, and if you want to emulate Warren Buffett or Benjamin Graham you buy value. Value investing includes looking for stocks that are "trailing the pack" rather than "leading the pack."

• • •

The world's smartest and best investors usually pursue a "value" strategy. The term means just what it says; you are buying stocks that you believe are worth more than people are paying for them. This is the approach I always use when I work with stocks or commodities. In addition to buying something for less than it is worth, I like to try to buy it as low as it is going to go. That's where technical analysis is very important.

Your strategy can be as simple or as complex as you care to make it. . You can name your strategy whatever you want to call it; the only thing that matters is whether it works. If it doesn't work you need to fix it. I will give you some ideas about how to develop and improve your strategy in chapters fourteen through nineteen.

• • •

Bonds

There are four principal types of bonds: corporate, municipal, government, and convertible. Bonds represent the issuer's debt. When you buy a bond you are lending money to a company or a government entity. Let's say IBM issues $100,000,000 in thirty-year bonds and pays an annual interest rate of 5.875 percent. If you purchase ten of these bonds, you will pay $10,000 and receive $293.75 twice a year. When the bonds mature after thirty years, you will receive your $10,000 back. You may, however, sell those bonds anytime during the thirty-year period; the amount you receive when you sell them prior to maturity is determined by three things: the remaining time to maturity, IBM's current credit rating, and the current level of interest rates.

When cities, counties, states, toll roads, airports, sewer districts, and other government agencies issue bonds, they are usually municipal bonds, which pay tax-free interest. In most other ways, municipal bonds are identical to the corporate bonds described in the IBM example above. The government entity will pay your promised interest regularly for the term of the bond, and then you will receive your principal at maturity.

The U.S. Treasury is one of the biggest issuers of government bonds in the world. Unlike municipal bonds, U.S. government bonds do not pay tax-free interest.

One of the big problems with bonds is that in inflationary times you have no idea what your principal will be worth by the time you get it back. We will discuss this problem a little later.

Convertible bonds are different from regular bonds, which are more suited for capital preservation and income than growth. Convertibles are a hybrid somewhere between common stocks and regular bonds. They usually pay a slightly lower interest rate than regular bonds because they are convertible to the company's stock. The prospectus for the bonds specifically states the provisions for their convertibility. Typicallly, the prospectus might indicate that a single bond with a value at maturity of $1000 can be exchanged for fifty shares of stock of the issuing company. Doing the math, we recognize instantly that there would be no point in converting the bonds to stock if the stock is selling for less than twenty dollars a share. Also, since we will lose the interest the bonds are paying when we make the conversion, we might want to pick some stock price above twenty dollars per share as the level at which we would be interested in making the conversion so that we can offset the interest we will no longer be receiving. If the stock is paying a dividend, we should consider that as well.

Convertible bonds can be a win/win for both the issuing company and the bondholder/shareholder. The issuing company uses your thousand dollars per bond and pays you less than they might otherwise have to. If the price of the stock goes up and you convert your bond, the company will no longer have to pay you interest. They have received for that stock a price that at the time was greater than the amount they would have received when they sold the bond.

You have purchased a bond that will pay you an interest rate that is often better that you can get in a money market fund or a bank CD. You have the right but not the obligation to convert your bond to stock, and if you convert to stock it will be because you will experience a gain.

From this discussion you would think that convertible bonds would be a conservative and fairly profitable investment strategy. In practice, however, these strategies usually disappoint. Back in the 1980s there were a handful of mutual funds that specialized in convertible bonds; most have changed their names and strategies because of their relative underperformance.

• • •

Mutual Funds
A Professionally Managed Pool of Money

Mutual funds were invented back in the 1920s, just before the Great Depression. Because they were designed with very low minimum investments, mutual funds brought millions of new investors into the markets.

A mutual fund is a pool of money with a professional manager who is paid out of that pool. The manager's compensation and the fund's other expenses are stipulated in the prospectus. The prospectus also gives complete information as to the objectives of the fund. The fund's semi-annual and annual reports give a complete description of the fund's holdings as of those dates.

Mutual funds come in several different commission (or "load") varieties; front-end load, back-end load, level load, and no load. You ought to buy nothing but no-load funds, because they charge no commissions. If you choose to work with a full-service broker, however, they will probably try to sell you a fund that has a commission. If you can get a no-load mutual fund with an identical track record to a mutual fund with a full commission, which would you buy? Every penny that you pay in commissions comes out of your pocket in one way or another. Every penny you pay in commissions is subtracted from your overall return. It is difficult enough to keep ahead of inflation and taxes without paying unnecessary commissions and fees.

There are two types of mutual funds, *open-end* and *closed-end*. Both have professional management, charge fees, and buy and sell securities based upon the fund's objectives. The best-known mutual funds are open-end, which means that every time someone invests money into the fund additional shares are created. Open-end funds are usually priced only when the market closes, and they always sell at their Net Asset Value (NAV).

How do you compute the NAV? At the end of each trading day the fund manager totals the value of all the securities in the fund's portfolio, then divides the total by the number of shares the fund has issued.

Closed-end funds trade like stocks. They have a NAV which is calculated every day, but the closed-end fund doesn't always trade at its NAV. I like to buy closed-end funds when they trade at a discount. In some cases closed-end funds have traded for as little as half their NAV.

When you buy or sell a closed-end fund you will pay your broker's regular commission.

Mutual funds also come in different types based upon their objectives. There are growth funds, income and growth funds, government-bond funds, total-return funds, sector funds, junk-bond funds, money-market funds, index funds, and many more. If you are going to buy a mutual fund, you should have an opinion about the market. If you are going to buy a mutual fund that focuses on a particular sector, you ought to have an opinion about that sector.

For over fifteen years, I have used high-yield bond funds, otherwise known as "junk" bond funds, with significant success. I began buying them when they were looked upon with disfavor by almost everyone. Of course, that's the best time to buy, when everyone else is selling. There had been numerous scandals about "junk" bonds, and several people had gone to prison over the way they were created and promoted. By 1990 it seemed as if "junk" bonds were permanently out of favor. For the next five years my clients enjoyed spectacular returns significantly better than the stock market's performance during that period.

I still use junk bonds when the timing is right for them. The returns are significantly less these days because all the very high-yielding bonds of the eighties and nineties are gone. Still, there are opportunities for better-than-average interest and some capital gains. It just takes more careful analysis to determine when to buy and when to sell.

Mutual fund managers break the stock market down into components. Components would include large cap, small cap, "value," international, and the various sectors. Sometimes we can identify a component with potential by looking for the underperformers from the previous year. The strategy has been known to backfire, however, and should be used only with proper technical analysis as well.

There is a problem with mutual funds that stocks do not have. Mutual funds—what we call open-end mutual funds—do not lend themselves to technical analysis. The reason for this is quite simple; unlike stocks, open-end mutual funds do not generate the type of statistics that make technical analysis possible. There are five things you can chart and track for every stock: open, high, low, close, and volume. Those numbers are what drive all of technical analysis. Mutual funds have only one of those five, the close. They are priced only once a day. They have no volume because they are not traded like stocks.

This is not to say that a mutual fund does not exhibit a pattern; it does. You can look at the chart of a mutual fund and think that you can perform technical analysis on it; the fund exhibits cycle highs and lows, trading ranges, and many of the characteristics of regular stocks.

There is another problem with open-end mutual funds. A stock is a stock; what the company does doesn't change (much) from one day to the next. Companies don't change CEOs at the drop of a hat. Unless a company acquires other companies or is itself acquired, its business continues much the same from month to month and from year to year.

Mutual funds are different. Their basic business remains the same, but the portfolio they use to meet the fund's objectives can change daily. Fund managers change too, and with them changes the approach to investing used by the fund. Certain types of mutual funds often see their entire portfolios turn over more than once a year, while some more conservatively managed bond funds may experience very little turnover at all. This is the nature of mutual funds and is neither a positive or a negative for the fund's potential. It is a big negative, however, in your ability to evaluate the fund's future prospects.

If you insist on finding the fund that performed the best over time, you're going to have to get complete details about the fund's history. This includes all the significant management changes that have taken place in the period of time you're looking at, as well as all the significant portfolio changes.

You'll pretty quickly discover that you have no benchmark against which to perform these analyses. Besides, as any stockbroker is required to tell you, past performance is no indication of future return.

Mutual funds are often promoted as a way to avoid making investment decisions. After all, you are paying someone to manage your money for you, and he or she is supposed to be good at it. All you have to do is buy the fund and relax. The truth is that mutual fund managers have good and bad years just like every other investor. In 2008, one of the worst years in market history, the average mutual fund lost over 30%.

One famous mutual fund, the 44 Wall Street fund piled up a tremendous record in the early 1980s, and then went bankrupt within two more years. The fund's managers lost almost all of the fund's money.

There is one other drawback to open-end mutual funds that needs to be understood. Even if you select a no-load family of funds, each fund within the family has management fees and charges. The fund also incurs expenses; as securities are bought and sold, commissions must be paid. The fund has other expenses associated with a financial firm. A mutual fund operates under certain restrictions and regulations that can render it less nimble in dealing with volatile markets. For example, a mutual fund cannot purchase more than 5 percent of the common stock of any company, nor can more than a certain percentage of the fund's assets be invested in any particular company. The fund also describes in its prospectus how much of its assets can be held in cash at any moment. That number is often right around 10 percent. There are times, as in the year 2000, when a lot of people wished that their fund manager could have gone to 100 percent cash.

Mutual funds also operate under certain rules that are designed to protect current investors. For example, the mutual fund may reserve the right to prohibit new money from being invested into the fund. This often happens with precious-metals funds. The total value of all the gold and silver mines on earth is so small that the Fidelity Magellan Fund would require only about a third of its entire portfolio to buy them. If a large number of mutual funds were to simultaneously hit upon the idea of allocating a portion of their assets to the precious metals sector, you can imagine the effect on such a tiny industry. Likewise, if a large number of wealthy individuals decided to dump a large amount of money into a precious metals mutual fund, the dilution effect would hurt all those who had invested previously.

$$\bullet \ \bullet \ \bullet$$

Exchange-traded Funds (ETFs)

Exchange-traded funds are mutual funds that trade on a stock exchange. If you think that makes them very similar to closed-end funds, you are correct. Here is the difference between them.

"An ETF is also a mutual fund with shares that trade on an exchange. The difference is that an ETF allows in-kind redemption by big institutional investors. This prevents the fund's price from deviating much from its NAV . . . No deviations as with [closed-end funds] CEFs."[10]

ETFs are the "new kid on the block." Exchange-traded funds, or ETFs as they are commonly called, were created to compete with and perhaps to replace open-end mutual funds. ETFs are more closely related to index mutual funds and closed-end funds than they are to traditional open-end mutual funds because most of them are passively managed. That has two advantages over open-end mutual funds; first, the costs of operating the ETF can be less than that of a corresponding mutual fund. Second, mutual funds have a nasty habit of declaring capital gains distributions late in the year, usually in December. In fact, they are required to do so. You can buy a mutual fund in early December and by the end of the year have a slight loss in your account, but you still have to pay capital-gains taxes on the gain that was declared by the fund.

The big advantage of ETFs is their marketability. ETFs trade like stocks and can be bought and sold any time the market is open. The big advantage for which they are widely marketed is that many of them mimic specific indexes or sectors. You can pay the price you want to when you buy them, because you can place limit orders on them. Some ETFs offer options that you can trade in conjunction with the ETF or separate from it. ETFs can also be bought on margin, and they can be sold short. ETFs offer a great deal of flexibility not previously available in any investment that represented a "basket" of securities. And, for those who like to do their homework, ETFs are "transparent," meaning that you can find out what the ETF's portfolio holdings are on any given day.

I look at ETFs both from the point of view of a financial adviser and an investor. In both roles I like them because they give me a measure of freedom I have not previously enjoyed. Before ETFs came along, if you wanted to buy the stocks of a particular country or industry or all the stocks represented in a particular index like the S&P 500, you had to go to a mutual fund. You needed to make sure that you purchased a family of funds that offered all the different funds you might want, in addition to the one you wanted to buy right away. That usually limited your choices to one or two families, Fidelity or FranklinTempleton, and at least one of those two was going to charge you a commission. Those commissions can be significantly greater than the brokerage commission you pay to buy or sell an ETF. When you wanted to change investments, it was more convenient and less expensive to keep your money in the same family of funds.

When you move from a family of funds carrying a commission to a different family of funds also carrying a commission, you will pay a new commission (or incur a new deferred sales charge). If you move from a no-load family of funds to another no-load family of funds, you may incur transaction costs. In contrast, you can purchase any ETF, regardless of the firm that sponsors it, and pay the regular commission your broker charges. When you sell it, you pay another brokerage commission, and you can take your money and purchase anything you want to. This can both increase your flexibility and reduce your costs.

Stocks, mutual funds and ETFs are the foundation of many investment portfolios. They represent ownership. Now let's look at some sophisticated ways to employ leverage as an enhancement to or replacement for outright ownership.

Chapter Ten

Making It Grow: Options and Leverage

Too few investors understand options, which can add significant value to an investment portfolio and can help reduce risk and increase income. Options can be part of a very sophisticated strategy. I will describe only the simplest ways of using them.

An option is a contract. It is an agreement between two parties regarding a specific right or obligation that is conveyed from one party to the other. All of the details are set out in advance, including price and expiration date. Specifically, a stock option conveys the right to either buy or sell, depending upon the type of contract, one hundred shares of a specific stock at a certain price by a certain date. Options have two types of value, time value and "in-the-money" value.

Widely traded common stocks have a *spread* of as little as a penny per share, depending upon the price range of the stock. The spread is the difference between the *bid* (the price the highest bidder is willing to pay) and the *ask* (the lowest price a seller is willing to accept). Options, because they are thinly traded by comparison, tend to have much larger spreads. The trading of options, particularly with thinly traded commodity options, literally demands the use of limit orders where you specify the price you are willing to pay (or receive if you are selling).

Options fall into the category of investment we now call *derivatives*. By definition, derivatives are derived from something else; they exist only on paper and don't stand on their own as true investments. For example, options are available on many stocks, stock indexes, and commodities. The price of a stock's options is largely determined by the price of the stock, and not the other way around. Let's see how options work and begin with a discussion of leverage.

• • •

The Principle of Leverage

Here is a simple way to look at leverage.

When you bought your house, you probably borrowed money to make the purchase. For example, if you paid $200,000 for your home and made a $20,000 down payment, you borrowed $180,000 to complete the purchase. Having done so, you are now using *90 percent leverage;* $180,000 divided by $200,000 = .9 or 90 percent.

If you sell your home and receive more than $200,000 for it, you can measure your profit in dollars and in percentage terms. If you sell it for $220,000, your profit is as follows:

Selling price	$220,000
Purchase price	($200,000)

Profit $20,000 or 10% of the purchase price

In *percentage* terms it looks very different:

Profit	$20,000
Your down payment	$20,000

Your gain = 100 percent of the amount you invested

(This assumes that you sell the property before you have paid the mortgage down to any great extent.)

Why do you have a 100 percent gain when the property only increased 10 percent in value? By borrowing money to make the purchase, you used 90 percent leverage. Your investment in the house was only your $20,000 down payment.

Now let's look at what happens if your home *loses* value.

Selling price	$180,000
Purchase price	($200,000)
Loss	($ 20,000)

In percentage terms it looks like this:

Loss	($20,000)
Your down payment	$20,000

Your loss = 100 percent of the amount you invested

Obviously, leverage can work for you or against you. Now let's see how leverage works in the stock market.

• • •

Using Margin

When you buy on *margin* you are borrowing a portion of the purchase price. Whenever you use someone else's money to buy something you are using leverage.

You purchase one hundred shares of General Electric at $50.00 per share.

Your investment is $50.00 x 100 shares = $5,000.

You borrow half the purchase price from your broker, and your investment is $2,500.00.

If General Electric rises in price to $75.00 and you sell your shares:

$75.00 x 100 shares =	$7,500.00
Your cost is	($5,000.00)

Your gain is $2,500.00 or 50 percent of the total purchase price

The gain based upon your $2,500.00 investment is:

Gain	$2,500.00
Your investment	$2,500.00

Your gain =100 percent of the amount you invested

Note that you can borrow as much as 125 percent of a home's value, but in the stock market you can borrow only 50 percent.

If the value of General Electric falls to $25.00 per share:

$25.00 x 100 shares =	$2,500.00
Your cost is	($5,000.00)

Your loss is ($2,500.00) or 50 percent of the total purchase price

The loss based upon your $2,500.00 investment is:

Loss	($2,500.00)
Your investment	$2,500.00

Your loss = 100 percent of the amount you invested

A simple rule of thumb: if you borrow half the purchase price, you effectively double your losses and your gains.

• • •

Using Options for Leverage

Options enable you to utilize leverage to your advantage without risking more than 100 percent of your investment. Options can also hedge against the risk in the underlying investment, or they can even be used as a substitute for buying the stock itself.

An option contract conveys the right but not the obligation to buy or sell something. Once again we can use the analogy of buying a house because options may be used in real estate.

Let's say that you are house hunting and have found a house you like very much. The market is hot, and you don't want to lose this house to another buyer. However, you want to look around for a little longer just in case you find something you like even more. What do you do?

You can approach the seller and offer him a deal something like this:

"I will give you a thousand dollars today if you will promise to sell your house to no one but me for the next thirty days. In addition, if I do purchase your house you will sell it to me at an agreed upon price, and the thousand dollars I pay you now will be applied to the purchase. If I choose not to purchase the house the thousand dollars are yours to keep."

If the seller agrees, you have created a call option contract. You have purchased the right to "call" that house to you at a certain price by a certain date.

• • •

Stock Options: Long Calls

Now let's relate that to the stock market.

General Electric is selling for $50.00 per share. You believe it is going to rise in price. You make the following purchase:

You buy one "GE DEC 55 call" at $2.50 per share. Here's what this means:

"DEC" refers to the month of expiration. A December call expires on either the third Friday in November or December, depending upon the particular stock. Some options actually expire in their contract month, and others expire the month before. It may be bought or sold at any time during market hours prior to expiration.

"55" refers the share price you want to pay. This gives you the right to purchase the stock at $55.00 per share.

Your purchase price for the option is $2.50 per share x 100 shares = $250.00. This is all you can lose, no matter what happens to the price of General Electric stock.

This is what's known as a long call. It gives you some of the benefits of stock ownership without requiring you to pay the full price for the stock. You bought one call option instead of actually buying one hundred shares of stock. One option contract is good for one hundred shares of stock. Commodity options each correspond to one commodities futures contract, and each commodity has its own contract specifications. One contract of wheat, corn, or soybeans is for 5,000 bushels; one contract for gold is for 100 troy ounces.

Let's look at what might happen with your long call:

1. Just prior to the expiration of the contract, General Electric is trading at $60.00 per share.

Your contract is worth roughly $5.00 per share. That's $60.00 (current stock price) minus $55.00 (option strike price) = $5.00. $5.00 times 100 shares per contract = $500.00

You invested $250.00. You have made $250.00, or 100 percent.

2. Just prior to the expiration of the contract, General Electric is trading at $70.00 per share.

Your contract is worth roughly $15.00 per share. That's $70.00 (current stock price) minus $55.00 (option strike price) = $15.00. $15.00 times 100 shares per contract = $1,500.00.

You invested $250.00. You have made 500 percent.

3. Just prior to the expiration of the contract, General Electric is trading at $40.00 per share.

Your contract is worthless.

You invested $250.00. You have lost 100 percent. Had you purchased the stock at $55.00 instead of buying the option, you would have a loss of $15.00 per share ($55.00 minus $40) x 100 shares = $1,500.00. The options contract limited your losses without limiting your profit potential beyond a certain point.

With options you can develop a chart of potential profits and losses because you will know in advance exactly how much you can make or lose at each possible price in the underlying security (in this case, General Electric). Such a chart helps you decide which option to purchase.

This is one of the simplest and most basic types of options strategies. When you buy a call option on a stock instead of buying the stock itself, you are increasing your leverage while reducing your risk.

Understanding Options

An option is a contract. It has specific terms and conditions. The four basic terms are:

- the underlying security or commodity,

- the option's strike price,

- whether the option is a call or a put, and

- the expiration date.

There are two types of options contracts: call options and put options. You can buy them or sell them. They come in different expiration months and strike prices. You can use options with stocks or by themselves.

Options are wasting assets; they will expire on a certain date, and on that date they will have only "in-the-money" value or no value. Most options expire out of the money and worthless.

You can use options when you anticipate something will rise or fall.

A call option conveys the right to buy something at a certain price by a certain date.

A put option conveys the right to sell something at a certain price by a certain date.

There are four basic strategies for single options:

- You can buy a call option instead of buying the stock. This is sometimes referred to as "synthetic stock."

- You can sell a call if you think the stock will fall or stay where it is. If you own the stock and sell a call option against it you are reducing your risk while giving up some of your upside potential.

- You can buy a put if you think the stock will fall.

- You can sell a put if you think the stock will rise or stay the same.

Those are the simple strategies, each involving one option contract or position. Options become very sophisticated when you combine them in some of the various strategies including spreads, calendar spreads, straddles, butterflies, and strangles.

One other thing: options possess time value, and they may possess "in the money" value. If General Electric is selling at $55.00 per share and we buy the $50.00 call, we are buying $5.00 of "in the money" premium. In other words, we have purchased an option with a strike price $5.00 per share below the current market price of the stock. We have to pay for it, and every dollar of "in the money" value increases the option's price by the same amount. The rest of what we pay for an option is its time value. In the example above, the GE $55.00 call had no "in the money" value; we paid $5.00 solely for the option's time value. A $55.00 GE call with a later expiration date will cost more than $5.00 because buying that option gives us more time for General Electric to rise to the strike price of $55.00 per share.

There are sophisticated models available that can help you determine which options are overvalued and which are undervalued. Professional traders have used them for years, and they are now available to regular investors. Before you open a brokerage account, you should ask the firm about the models they make available and what they charge for them.

Now let's look at using call options in the opposite way.

• • •

Covered Calls

You own one hundred shares of eBay, for which you paid $28.00 per share. You think the stock is a long-term hold; you bought it for its appreciation potential. You believe that the stock will be somewhere around $35.00 a share by next April. Since that is your price target, you might not mind obligating yourself to sell the stock at that price, especially if someone pays you for the privilege. That's what a "covered call" strategy is all about; someone pays you for the right to buy your stock from you at a certain price by a certain date. In this case, that someone is willing to pay $1.50 per share for the privilege.

1. You bought one hundred shares of eBay at $28.00
   100 x $28.00 = $2800.00

(Note that we are ignoring commissions and not using margin.)

2. You sold one DEC 2007 $35.00 call at $1.50
   (One options contract is for one hundred shares of stock.)
   1 contract x $1.50 per share = $150.00
   $2,800.00 - $150.00 = $2,650.00 net cost of owning one hundred shares of eBay stock

Selling the call option reduces your net cost of owning the underlying security. You have traded some cash for an obligation. The December 2007 call option expires on the third Friday in November 2007.

If at expiration eBay is at or below $35.00 per share, you get to keep your stock. You always get to keep the option premium, which is the money you received when you sold the call. If eBay is selling for more than $35.00 at expiration, that option is going to be exercised and you'll be required to sell the stock at $35.00. It doesn't matter if eBay is selling for $70.00 at expiration; you still must sell it at $35.00 per share.

This can be a useful strategy, but you have to be careful in how you apply it. I use it primarily with dividend-paying stocks and ETFs to enhance income and reduce risk.

You have to think about the underlying stock. You bought eBay thinking that it was going to go up in price. In the example above, it did, and you took your capital gain from the sale of the stock and kept the option premium. The net effect is that instead of making a 25 percent gain ($35.00 - $28.00 = $7.00; $7.00 ÷ $28.00 = 25 percent) you actually made a gain of 30.4 percent ($35.00 + $1.50 = $36.50; $36.50 ÷ $28.00 = 30.36 percent).

But what's going to happen over the next three to six months? If eBay has met your price target, it may well have met other people's price targets. There may be fewer people expecting eBay to tack on an additional $7.00 per share. If so, that means there will be fewer people willing to pay $1.50 for the privilege of buying eBay from you for $42.00 per share.

It's the nature of the stock market that dooms this strategy. Stocks, like trees, don't "grow to the sky." Stocks go up, stocks go down, and stocks stay flat. They only do one of those things at a time, and when they have finished doing one they're going to do another. You cannot expect to be able to hold onto a stock indefinitely while you sell one call after another against it. If the stock's price remains flat, the next available call option is not going to sell for as much as what you received for the one that just expired. Even if the stock continues to rise in price, there is always a growing awareness that it is getting closer to its peak.

Covered calls, like any other strategy, need to be utilized with proper timing. There are times when the strategy works very well and others when it doesn't work at all. You can use covered calls to increase your income and/or to reduce your cost basis in the stock. (That's cost basis for investment purposes, not tax purposes, by the way.)

● ● ●

Protective Puts

Let's look at one other options strategy. First, we must define the other type of options contract, the put option. Options are very simple instruments; it's the combinations that make them complicated.

A put option is the opposite of a call option. A call option gives the buyer the right to *buy* the stock at a certain price by a certain date. A put option gives the buyer the right to *sell* the stock at a certain price by a certain date. Let's look at a simple put strategy.

In this example let's assume that you have a pretty good idea about where a stock's price is going to go over the next several months. Let's use General Motors as an example. This beleaguered industrial giant has run into tough times over the past few years, and some people are even talking about its potential bankruptcy. (Please take a look at Chart 3 in the center section, the General Motors monthly stock chart.)

You watched the stock fall from its high of almost $95.00 back in the year 2000 to its low in the year 2008 of $8.51 on 29 September, a decline of 91 percent. $8.51 per share can be a lot of money for a company that might be faced with bankruptcy, especially because so much of its future earnings were coming from the financial side (GMAC) rather than from manufacturing. Much of GM's liabilities were tied up in its pension obligations. You would be hesitant to pay $8.51 for General Motors stock even with the analytical techniques we'll discuss later.

In this example let us assume that the time is October 2008, and it seems likely that GM will test its recent low and perhaps fall beneath it. We never know what lies to the right on a chart; all we can do is to weigh the potential for bankruptcy against the increasing possibility that the company has begun its turnaround.

Because of all the uncertainty in the markets, in the economy, and the auto industry, you might want to reduce your risk as much as possible in a stock like General Motors. You could consider buying the stock as a long-term hold if you felt it had value. You might also believe that there could be a short-term "pop" in the stock, as there was in the airline stocks a few months earlier. Either way, options can significantly reduce your risk in this rather risky trade.

GM closed at $9.45 on October 1, 2008. That's a huge discount from its 2000 high, but you should have no expectation that the stock will return to those lofty levels anytime soon. In fact, you can certainly make the case that stock was overpriced at any level above $80 a share. What would a reasonable target be for GM for the next six months?

I would suggest that in six months time the stock could be trading 1) where it is today, 2) much closer to zero if GM does indeed declare bankruptcy, or 3) in the $15 to $20 range. If you just buy the stock, you have about a one in three chance of making money over the next six months. That means you have a two in three chance of either breaking even or losing money, and it's not a good idea to invest with odds like that. Let's look at three other ways to approach this trade using options.

• • •

We have discussed covered call options, where you buy the stock and sell a call option against it. The call option has a higher strike price than the price you paid for the stock. No matter what happens, you get to keep the premium you received when you sold the option. If the stock closes at or above the strike price at expiration, your option will be exercised, and you will be required to sell the stock at a profit.

With GM having fallen 90 percent and with a very real possibility of bankruptcy, a covered-call option simply isn't going to do it—at least, not by itself. When you buy the stock at $9.45 a share, you can also buy "protection" for that investment by buying a put option. Remember, a put option gives you the right to sell a stock at a certain price by a certain date.

This is October 2008, and we want to give this trade six months to produce a profit for us. The March 2009 options expire on 21 March 2009. If we are going to buy a protective put, its strike price must be higher than the price we paid for the stock. Let's take a look at the available options.

The first and most obvious choice for a protective put is the GMOB, the March 10 put. Remember, you buy something at the Ask price and sell it at the Bid price.

GM put options prices, 1 October 2008				
Contract symbol	Contract Expiration	Contract Strike Price	Bid	Ask
GMOB	21 Mar 09	$10	$3.60	None
GMOS	21 Mar 09	$12.50	$5.25	None
GMOO	21 Mar 09	$14	$5.55	None
GMOC	21 Mar 09	$15	$7.00	None

You would pay $3.80 plus the $9.45 per share for a total of $13.25 per share, and your downside–the lowest possible value of your investment at option expiration - is $10 per share. That means the your risk is reduced to $13.25 minus $10 = $3.25 per share. You have just cut your risk by about two-thirds, but you have also cut your potential profitability. Why? Because GM has to be higher than $13.25 per share at the expiration of the option, or you will not make a profit. At $13.25 you will break even. Between $10.00 and $13.25 you will lose money.

Since we believe that GM might be in the $15 to $20 range by March, we might be willing to look at a put option with a higher strike price. The GMOS would protect us to $12.50, and our total cost would be $14.90. The cost of protection in this case is $2.40, a better number than $3.25 in our previous example. Note once again the trade-off in this relationship; the cost of protection is lower, but GM has to trade at a higher price for this trade to be profitable.

The GMOO option looks like the best choice in this instance. It's only $.30 more than the $12.50 put, but it gives us an additional $1.50 of protection. We pay $9.45 for the stock and $5.85 for the option for a total cost of $15.30. The cost of protection is now $1.30, but GM must rise higher than $15.30 for us to make a profit on this trade. This is not a particularly good trade, but we can make it better. That involves Strategy 2.

• • •

Strategy Two: Protective Puts and Covered Calls

GM call options prices, 1 October 2008				
Contract symbol	Contract Expiration	Contract Strike Price	Bid	Ask
GMCR	21 Mar 09	$7.50	$3.60	$3.95
GMCN	21 Mar 09	$9.00	$2.91	$3.30
GMCB	21 Mar 09	$10.00	$2.56	$2.89
GMCS	21 Mar 09	$12.50	$1.78	$2.10
GMCO	21 Mar 09	$14.00	1.43	1.72

Now let's buy the GMOO option and sell a covered call against the position. The GMCD March $20 call is selling for $.76. (See Table 6.) We paid $15.30 for the GM stock and the GMOO put; now we reduce that amount by the $.76 we receive for selling the GMCD call. We are still ignoring commissions, but the math is simple: $15.30 minus $.76 equals $14.54. That is our new net cost for this position in GM stock, and we are profitable at any price over that. Because we sold a covered call, we receive no additional profit if GM is above $20 per share at expiration. If GM is at or above $20 when the options expire, we will be exercised and have to sell the stock. Here's the profit calculation:

$20 minus $14.54 equals $5.46

$5.46 divided by $14.54 equals a 37.5 percent profit in six months.

Our total risk: $14.54 minus $14 equals $.54.

$5.46 divided by $.54 equals 10.11, or a maximum potential profit of over 1000 percent

That's a fairly attractive deal *if* you think the GM is going to rebound sharply in the next six months. Since you own the stock, if GM pays any dividends (which is unlikely), you get to keep them.

Chapter Eleven

Making It Grow: Commodities

We can't live without them.

You have undoubtedly heard horror stories about your uncle Fred who invested in pork bellies and lost his shirt. In every gathering I have addressed, a high percentage of the attendees had heard such stories, and as a result they stayed away from commodities. The public perception is that they are just too risky.

The simple truth is that commodities are, if anything, *less* risky than common stocks. This has been verified by numerous studies, and institutional investors have almost universally come to the conclusion that placing a portion of their fund's assets into commodities is an essential strategy for diversification and risk reduction.

Why are commodities perceived to be so risky? The simple answer is leverage, and a variety of leverage that produces far greater risk than the long options we discussed above. When you purchase a commodity, whether through a cash transaction or a futures purchase, you do not need to put up 100 percent of the money. Your stock brokerage account allows you to borrow 50 percent of the money you use to purchase a stock, but your commodities broker will allow you to borrow 90 percent or even more. You can get yourself into a lot of trouble very quickly with commodities, but you don't have to assume all that risk.

Commodities you can trade on the commodities markets include energy (crude oil, natural gas, unleaded gasoline, and so on), agricultural products (wheat, corn, soybeans, oats, and the like), meats (pork bellies, live cattle, etc.), metals (gold, silver, platinum, aluminum, copper, and more), currencies, stock indexes, softs (cocoa, coffee, sugar, and others), and more. As with stocks and options, there is a definite learning curve with commodities. They trade on several different exchanges, but most exchanges handle only a few commodities. Trading hours vary, contract sizes vary, and the amount of leverage you may utilize varies from broker to broker and even changes with market conditions and volatility.

Because they can utilize significant leverage, commodities are subject to more regulations than stocks. For example, some commodities have contract limits; the price of corn, for example, cannot rise or fall more than $.40 per bushel per trading day. That rule gave rise to the expression "up the limit." When commodity prices fluctuate violently the exchange can change the the daily limits and the brokerage firms can increase the margin requirements.

There are far fewer commodities than there are common stocks, which simplifies the business of trading commodities. Unlike stocks, commodities trade in *contracts*, which are created and expire on a regular basis. Some contracts pertain to the seasons, as with many of the agricultural products; others are created every month of the year, though certain months are much more heavily traded than others. Many contracts are created quarterly; most commodities have options available.

For example, you can trade the commodities contract that represents the Standard & Poor's 500 (S&P 500), one of the best known stock market indexes. The S&P 500 is an index reflecting the stock prices of the five hundred largest companies in the U.S. The S&P 500 index also trades as a commodities future. Options on these futures contracts are available just as options are available on stocks.

Very few traders trade more than just a few commodities. In my work I deal with dozens of stocks, but the commodities I focus on are silver, gold, the S&P500, Euros, Canadian dollars, and just a handful of others.

I am discussing commodities here not because I want you to open a commodities account with some Chicago brokerage firm, but because commodities have significantly better potential than stocks do in our current environment. Let's do a quick comparison. Please take a look at the charts in Charts 4 and 5 on pages 269 and 270.

Let's compare buying one thousand shares of Exxon Mobil with buying one crude oil contract. One thousand shares of Exxon Mobil at $90 per share will cost you $90,000, and your broker will allow you to borrow up to half that amount to make the purchase. One crude oil (CL) contract is for one thousand barrels (42,000 gallons) of oil and with oil at $90 a barrel each contract will cost you $90,000. Your broker will allow you to borrow up to 90 percent of that amount or $81,000.

When you buy a futures contract, if you hold it to expiration, you will receive physical delivery of that particular commodity. Traders never do that; either they close their position outright, or they roll it to a contract that expires later. Each one-dollar-per-barrel change in the price of oil will increase or decrease the value of your contract by $1000. With oil in relatively short supply compared to ever increasing demand and because oil is subject to so many risks, the potential for oil to rise in price is significant—especially after its price plummeted after soaring to an all-time high in 2008.

When you buy one thousand shares of Exxon Mobil, you are buying a proportionate interest in the company rather than any particular amount of oil in itself. Exxon Mobil stock fluctuates in value based upon the amount of money the company is able to make from one quarter to the next on all of its operations. There is no direct correlation between the price of oil and either the profits Exxon Mobil will earn or the value of Exxon Mobil stock. There is, however, a rough correlation between their prices as you can see.

Note that crude oil bottomed in late 2001 at $17.12 per barrel, while XOM bottomed a few months later in 2002 at $29.75 per share. From those respective lows XOM rose 220 percent to its May 2008 high of $96.12, while oil rose 484 percent to its July 2008 high of $147 per barrel. The amount of money you invested was the same, and the risk was roughly the same if you used no leverage or identical leverage in each case. Which would *you* rather have owned?

Before you answer that question let's consider a few more characteristics of these two investments. When you buy a futures contract, you are purchasing all of the gains or losses that that commodity experiences prior to the expiration of a contract. If you have done any reading about peak oil, you are aware that the world's supply of oil is rapidly diminishing and that we have no suitable replacement. I can't explain why oil fell to a low of $10.65 per barrel in late 1998, though I'm sure there are some in the oil business who could. That price and the $17.12 price in 2001 represent two of the greatest buying opportunities in our lifetimes.

Futures contracts pay no dividends. Exxon Mobil stock does and has done so consistently for many years. Keep in mind that no company has any assurance it will make a profit. To be profitable, companies must overcome obsolescence, competition, regulation, economic turmoil, taxes, inflation, and many other things. You can calculate the book value of a share of Exxon Mobil stock, but the price you pay to buy that share of stock may be either lower or higher than its book value. Most of the time you will pay more for a share of Exxon Mobil stock than it is worth. When you buy a share of stock, you are buying the expectation of future profits and/or dividends.

What if Exxon Mobil decides to sell additional shares of its stock to the public? Each new share has the potential to dilute, however minutely, the value of every other share in existence. If Exxon Mobil's earnings fall, its stock price will fall, even though one quarter does not necessarily give any good indication about the future. If Exxon Mobil's management does not continue to discover and obtain new oil reserves, the company will have to find some other way of making money. Since oil is a scarce and dwindling resource, unless Exxon Mobil moves into some other business (such as alternative energy) its future is pretty bleak. In fact, Exxon Mobil and companies like it are buying their own shares back because they know there's no more oil to be found.

Do you begin to see the difference between a common stock and a commodities futures contract? In many ways a share of common stock is very similar to a piece of paper money; neither of them have any intrinsic value. Money without a precious metals backing and common stocks only have value if people believe they do.

A futures contract has the intrinsic value of the underlying commodity. Unless during the life of the contract a perfect and inexpensive replacement is found for that commodity, it is reasonable to expect that that commodity will retain some value. Contrast that with a stock, which can always go to zero.

• • •

Preventing Losses

The strategies we have been discussing are sophisticated and designed to give you a better opportunity to profit with reduced risk. There are similar strategies that attempt to do the same thing; let's look at a couple of them.

When you own a stock, at some point in time you may feel that the stock is about to decline. If you don't want to sell it at that moment—and I'm not particularly interested in trading options on it—you can simply put a "stop loss" order in on the stock. Generally speaking, stop-loss orders are not allowed on many stocks with four-letter symbols or on any stocks with five-letter symbols.

Let's say that you bought GM for $9.45 as we did in the previous examples. All you have to do now is place a "trailing stop loss" order in the same account. That order will specify an amount of, say, $.50 or $1.00. A trailing stop loss order starts out as a stop order and will not be changed to a market order until the stop is triggered. When you place the order, you set the stop. For example, you just bought the stock for $9.45 and placed a $.50 trailing stop loss order against it; $9.45 minus $.50 equals $8.95. If GM stock drops to $8.95, your stop is triggered, and your order becomes a market order. That order will be filled at the next available price.

That all sounds pretty good. You think you can limit your losses to the $.50 that you specified in the trailing stop loss order. Unfortunately, that's not the way it works.

The trailing stop loss order becomes a market order when the stop is triggered. Suppose that tomorrow morning GM announces bad earnings or there is some terrible news on the economic front and GM is expected to open down as much as $1.50 a share. If GM opens down $1.50, your $.50 stop will immediately be triggered—at $7.95. Your order is now a market order and will be filled at whatever price it is filled at. You have no way of knowing what price you will actually receive, but it could be much less than what you anticipated.

There is another form of trailing stop order that, in theory, can enable you to get out of the price you expect to. This is called the trailing stop limit order. With this type of order, when your stop is triggered your order will be filled at the limit price established by that stop. The problem is with this type of order you may never get out at all because the price may never come back to your stop-limit price.

This is why I generally favor the use of options. Options are more complex, and they add to your costs and your commissions; but they give you a greater degree of control over your investments. There may be no better tool available in limiting losses than the protective put with a covered call we discussed previously.

Chapter Twelve

Making It Grow: Precious Metals, Gems, Real Estate, Art, and Collectibles

Precious Metals
"Gold pays no dividends."

Here's an opinion for you:

If you invest in nothing else, you should buy some gold and silver— especially silver.

Why? Because nothing but the precious metals and other tangible, valuable commodities will survive a currency collapse. The "slow-motion" collapse of the dollar that began in 1913 has accelerated, and there is a very good chance that the U.S. dollar will go the way of the Reichsmark.

Many people believe that real estate is an inflation hedge. Residential real estate may seem to do well in inflationary times because in the past forty years housing prices have generally kept pace with inflation. This, however, is deceptive for many reasons. Real estate is not the store of value precious metals are. Real estate is subject to property taxes, requires regular maintenance and upkeep, is affected by occupancy and vacancy, must be insured against much more than theft, and can lose value rapidly for a multitude of reasons.

Precious metals, on the other hand, are not subject to the whims of government or the economy. They simply are, and throughout the history of mankind have been treated as a store of value. When your currency is subject to the whims of a central bank like our Federal Reserve, you always want to have some gold and silver because they are the real money. Pieces of paper with pictures of dead presidents on them have no value. We only think they are valuable because of the confidence game our government plays.

There are many ways to purchase precious metals. Sometimes you do not purchase the physical metal itself but merely a representative of the physical metal. Sometimes you have "your" metals stored in a vault somewhere, and all you ever see is a receipt. (Note: I think that's a bad idea.) You may also purchase a "proxy" for the precious metals by buying mining stocks or mutual funds that purchase mining stocks. There are now ETFs that invest in silver or gold bullion, and these have proven to be immensely popular.

Here are some of the things you should be concerned about:

- Until alchemy becomes a science and we are able to transmute the elements—and that day may not be too far off—gold will be gold. It cannot be created by government decree. It is "scarce" in the sense that there is a finite amount available to us that can be economically extracted from the earth. For millennia it has been sought after, fought over, and traded as the world's primary store of value. Minted into appropriate shapes and sizes, it is accepted as money, the kind of money that transcends national or imperial boundaries. It has value because we attach value to it and because it is scarce relative to other things.

- Gold is beautiful, durable, non-corrosive, a good conductor of electricity, and has numerous chemical and physical properties that make it useful both in industry and as jewelry.

- Despite its use in industry, almost all the gold ever mined is still available to us. It is frequently recycled from its industrial applications, and since it never tarnishes or combines with other elements, it remains in its elemental form indefinitely. There may be some five billion ounces of silver available today, whether in large bars or ingots stored in bank vaults or as jewelry, coinage, or dental work. This figure of five billion ounces means that not every person in the world may own one ounce at the same time.

- Gold cannot be manipulated by governments or other entities, though efforts are frequently made to manipulate the trading and the price of gold. At the end of the day, you either own gold or you don't; a government that owns little or none is more subject to economic upheaval and uncertainty.

- No currency in the world today is backed by gold. We live in a world of central banking and "full faith and credit." Throughout the history of mankind, *every* state, country, kingdom, or empire that removed the gold or other precious metals backing from its currency saw their currency fail, leading to chaos and destruction.

- The United States government has confiscated gold twice, during the Civil War and in 1933, when Franklin D. Roosevelt made it illegal to own gold. His edict was not repealed until 1968, thirty-five years later. In 1933 numismatic (collectible or rare) gold was not confiscated nor were most forms of jewelry.

Let's examine the most common forms of precious metals ownership, listed in my order of preference. This list pertains to someone who will invest up to $250,000 in precious metals. You will find pictures of some of these items in the color section.

• • •

Gold

1. $20 Gold St. Gaudens "Double Eagles," certified by NGC or PCGS

Double Eagle refers to the coin many people believe is the most beautiful ever minted, the $20 U.S. gold coin designed by Augustus St. Gaudens. It weighs just under a troy ounce of gold and is fairly common. Hundreds of thousands of these "saints" have come back into the United States in recent years once it became legal to own them again. Some of them were owned by Egypt's King Farouk, who was an avid collector.

When these coins were sent overseas—many of the rest were confiscated and melted by the U.S. government—they were circulation coins, not numismatic coins. They were not graded by a grading service—in fact, there were no grading services in the 1930s. Grading services exist today in the dozens, but only two of them are considered thoroughly reliable. They are the Professional Collector's Grading Service (PCGS) and the Numismatic Guarantee Corporation (NGC). They have developed grading standards that make it possible to assign a numeric grade to a coin. The grading decision will never be entirely objective, but it is critical because the grade has a tremendous effect on the value of a coin. When a coin is graded by most services, it is encased in a clear plastic "slab" that is tamper evident and designed to protect the coin while permitting almost full view. You can see what this looks like in Image 6 in the center section.

The grading system in common use for coins is a seventy-point system. There are two types of coins, proof and regular strike. Regular strike coins are those we use in change every day; *proof* coins are struck from specially polished dyes and are not intended to be circulated. In both cases a perfect coin receives a numeric grade of seventy; there are very few coins that receive the grade of seventy because as coins are released from the dies they fall into a bag with other coins and can receive dings and scratches. These "bag marks" quickly downgrade a coin.

In recent years coins have been struck and treated very carefully after coming out the dies, so that PCGS and NGC have graded a very few of them MS70 (Mint State—for regular strike coins) and PF 70 for proof coins. This has created new coins with immediate scarcity, and the difference in value between a coin graded MS69 and one graded MS70 can be very significant.

For example, one of the rarest coins in the world is the 1933 $20 Saint Gaudens, because most of them were melted and none were "legally" removed from the mint where they were struck. Several were taken away, probably by mint employees. Until recently only two were known to exist, and though they had never been in circulation one was graded MS64 and the other MS65. PCSGS currently values them at $4 million and $6 million respectively—which gives you a good idea how important accurate grading is.

A couple of years ago the daughter of a former mint employee came forward with several more

1933s, and they were immediately seized by the Treasury Department. I don't know what their fate will be, but at least one will probably end up in the Smithsonian.

A typical "numismatic" $20 Saint would be a 1924 graded MS60, MS61, MS62, or MS63, the four lowest "uncirculated" grades. This is a common date coin, readily available at dealers, coin shows, and on eBay. If graded by NGC or PCGS, their value as of February 2007 and February 2009 is as follows:

February 2007		February 2009
Gold price: $640.00 per ounce		$940.00 per ounce
MS60 Saint:	$890.00	$1,460.00
MS62 Saint:	$900.00	$1,565.00
MS63 Saint:	$960.00	$1,685.00

Note that there is little or no "spread" between these grades. When gold resumes its bull market, I expect those spreads to widen considerably. You can purchase these coins on eBay or other Internet auction sites for about 80 percent of the prices above, which means that you are paying a relatively low premium for a coin with numismatic value. Just grading the coin costs at least $25; grading by the right company adds value to any coin.

No one can say whether our government will ever confiscate gold again or whether numismatic gold or jewelry will be exempted from confiscation if it does. With the relatively low premiums associated with purchasing these Saints instead of one-ounce bullion coins, the additional cost is justified.

2. American "Eagle" $50 gold coins

These coins were first minted in 1986 in one-tenth, one-fourth, one-half and one-ounce sizes, and they have become immensely popular. You pay a premium over the gold price to purchase each of them; the smaller the coin, the higher the premium as a percentage of the coin's gold value. That's why I prefer the $50, 1-ounce coins.

The "$50" associated with the coin is a misnomer, for these coins contain a full ounce of gold and are priced accordingly. The $20 Saints, on the other hand, were minted for circulation and were worth $20 when they were used as coinage. The fact that these coins now sell for $900 and more gives you some idea about how much inflation we have had since 1933, though the value of gold fluctuates daily and does not closely correlate with inflation.

Other countries and entities mint their own gold coins, but I prefer Eagles because they are the most widely recognized and will command the highest price upon sale in the U.S. The Canadian Maple Leaf is a beautiful coin and has a purity of .9999. The South African Krugerrand sports a reddish color because it contains 5 percent copper. Mexico's gold coins contain more than an ounce of gold. The Chinese Pandas have different images each year and have not gained wide acceptance in the U.S.

Counterfeit Chinese Pandas are appearing in ever-increasing numbers. Even the Austrian Philharmonic issues its own gold coins.

Twenty-five years ago none of these coins existed, with the exception of the Krugerrand. Since then, due to the legalization of gold ownership in the U.S. and some aggressive marketing, these coins are owned ("hoarded" is the technical if impolite term) by millions of people all over the world.

Eagles and their counterparts are "bullion" coins, designed to sell based upon the value of gold. Aggressive marketing and investor interest has created a new form of collectible in graded bullion coins. For these coins you can forget the first sixty-nine points of the seventy-point scale; if PCGS or NGC certifies an Eagle at any grade less than MS70 or PR70 you have a bullion coin in an expensive plastic slab.

3.   Graded American "Eagle" $50 gold coins

These coins are new, having been first minted in 1986, but what gives some of these coins numismatic value is the relative scarcity of coins that will grade MS70 or PF70. In some cases, such as the 1989 $25 (half ounce) gold Eagle, PCGS has graded only one MS70 and NGC has graded none. For that reason PSCGS on its retail price sheet has listed the 1989 $25 MS70 at $6,950.00, well above its current gold value.

Let's step back for a moment. I recommend numismatic-value graded $20 gold Saints above all other forms of physical gold because of their scarcity and the remote possibility of another government gold confiscation. I place American gold eagles next on the list, a coin minted by that same government that just might confiscate all your Eagles and all the rest of your gold. There is a seeming disconnect in the logic of that argument.

Numismatic-value-certified Saints are a piece of history, and their value will increase faster than any increase in the price of gold. Greater scarcity yields higher prices and better profit potential—to a certain point. I won't pay more than $2000 for a Saint, so I will never have a complete set. Saints that sell for more than $2000 today are more subject to the whims of bidders at auctions, and the market thins quickly.

There is an economic justification to giving Saints preference over non-numismatic Eagles. However, if you are more concerned about government confiscation than I am, you might want to make your second choice (after Saints) MS70 Eagles. If you go that route, I would recommend that you stick to the $50 coins, for the same reasons I stick to Saints; the gold value/scarcity value ratio is higher than for the smaller coins. The premium over the spot price of gold for a common date MS70 $50 Eagle is about the same as the premium for an MS62 or MS63 Saint, though PCGS lists the 1994 and 1996 $50 MS70 Eagles at $6,500 because PCGS has graded only one of each. There may be others as yet ungraded.

4.   Other gold "bullion" coins

The Krugerrand (Image 7 in the center section) introduced Americans to bullion gold in 1967, decades after FDR made gold ownership illegal. To this day many Americans are not aware that they are allowed to own gold in any form. However, once the Krugerrand had become successful, numerous copycats were created.

My recommendation is the same. Unless these are coins are graded MS 70 by PCGS or NGC, they are nothing more than bullion and should not be considered numismatic or collectible coins. Since they are bullion, they are an investment, and your investments should always be as marketable as possible. If you plan to continue to live in the United States, for example, you would probably do well to focus solely on the Eagle coins produced by the U.S. Mint. I specifically recommend against the Mexican coins because of their odd weight; a fifty-peso Mexican gold coin weighs about 1.2 ounces.

Assuming that you do not anticipate a breakdown of the economy that would necessitate using your gold coins for barter, you should probably focus on the larger-sized coins instead of the one-tenth-ounce, one-fourth-ounce, and one-half-ounce gold coins.

I also recommend against many of the coins sold on the shopping channels, particularly those which are made of silver plated with gold, reproductions of old coins, proof sets, and mint sets. There is a huge markup in these coins, and most of the time their numismatic value is significantly less than what you are told.

5. Gold futures

Commodity futures are quite different from stocks. You can hold onto shares of AT&T until the cows come home, and basically nothing will happen to them. However, if you fail to sell your corn contract by the deadline, someone will knock on your door and try to deliver five thousand bushels of corn. Most of those who trade commodity futures never take delivery on those commodities; they are speculating in anticipated price changes. On the other hand, the Nestlé Company trades heavily in cocoa futures, and frequently takes delivery for its own manufacturing.

You can purchase gold futures contracts with the intent of having the gold delivered to you at the end of the contract. Unlike stocks, futures contracts have an ending date. At any moment there are more than a dozen open contracts for gold. There is the April 2009, the June 2009, the October 2009, the December 2009, and so on. The "nearer date" contracts are more heavily traded than those with a later expiration; much of the time the later-dated contracts trade at higher prices than those expiring sooner. For example, on 6 February 2007, the April 2007 gold futures contract closed at $646.20, while the June 2007 gold contract closed at $652.40 and the December 2007 gold contract closed at $673.70. By purchasing a futures contract instead of the physical metal, you save yourself the storage and handling charges until such time as you take physical delivery. For that reason you generally pay less for a contract that is going to end soon.

Trading gold futures contracts has some significant benefits, and I see no reason why they cannot be a part of a normal precious-metals investment portfolio. There are those who are concerned that some day the financial markets will collapse or do something that will make it impossible to obtain delivery, and they see that as an unacceptable risk.

There was an instance recently in which an exchange was unable to enforce its rules for physical delivery. That occurred in the London metals exchange in 2006, and the commodity was zinc. It is possible that there will be other similar failures to deliver in the future, for these are indeed free markets. Though they are regulated, they are largely self-governing and subject to the whims of their larger participants.

One of the benefits of trading futures contracts is that you do not have to make physical delivery when you sell or accept delivery when you buy. You can quickly move into and out of both long and short positions in one or more commodities.

There are also options against most futures contracts. You can use them to help hedge your futures position or your physical metals holdings. For instance, you can use a covered-call strategy during times when you feel that the price of gold is going to fall or at least remain in a fairly tight trading range. The premium you receive when you sell the call option can reduce the net cost of purchasing the physical gold or futures contract that you own.

As we have discussed previously, commodities trading can involve a very significant degree of risk because of leverage. As with all other investments, you only want to trade commodity futures when you have an opinion about the future trend of the commodity you are trading. You can always pay cash for your futures contracts; you do not need to borrow 90 percent of the money to pay for them.

There are two types of gold futures contracts: the regular contract is for one hundred ounces of gold, and the mini gold contract is for 33.2 ounces. I generally use the mini contracts; those who own or wish to control larger amounts of gold gravitate toward the full-size contracts.

Many more people will enter the commodities market over the next several years, particularly people with experience in the stock market. We are entering a period of scarcity when the competition for certain commodities will become intense. Commodities will regain some of the prestige and interest they used to enjoy years ago, especially when the stock markets are no longer providing the stellar returns they have shown us most of the time since 1987.

I also believe that more and more people will become aware of and begin investing in physical gold, particularly the gold eagles and other bullion coins I mentioned previously. Gold has always held a certain appeal. It will regain that appeal among the American people in the near future.

6. Gold ETFs

Financial types all over the world are jumping on the bandwagon of securitizing commodities. There are now several ETFs that purchase and hold physical gold. Their share prices track the price of gold and are usually valued at one-tenth of one ounce of the spot price of gold. These ETFs have become popular very quickly, perhaps even more so than the gold certificates mentioned below.

As an investment vehicle, I cannot fault gold ETFs. They seem to be viable, and there are numerous means of independent verification that the physical gold is actually stored for the benefit of the shareholders. As long as you are not worried about a breakdown of society and the need to take your gold coins to the grocery store, gold ETFs are probably as good as any other investment in gold. In some cases options are available for commodity ETFs.

The primary difference between gold ETFs and gold futures contracts is their pricing and the amount of leverage you can use to purchase and sell them. You can generally borrow half the price of an ETF share from your broker; you can borrow 90 percent of the cost of a futures contract. Otherwise the two are similar in several ways. You might want to investigate both to see which one you are more comfortable with.

7.   Gold Bars

It is true of all the precious metals that the larger the unit purchased, the smaller the premium per ounce. You might pay a premium of $35 an ounce or 5.5 percent to buy the one-ounce gold eagles but only a $120 premium or 1.8 percent for a ten-ounce bar. Most of us will never own a ten-ounce or a one-hundred-ounce bar of gold, but some of us will own one-hundred-ounce and possibly even one-thousand-ounce bars of silver. If you are a big investor, you will do well to take advantage of the lower premiums available in the higher unit sizes.

Please avoid the tiny gold bars, the one gram, ten gram, and even the one-ounce bars of gold, along with all the other miscellaneous sizes that exist today. These are not as common as an American gold Eagle or a Gold Canadian maple leaf.

8.   Gold Certificates

Despite the costs of holding physical gold and retaining it in your possession, I always prefer that to holding any of the different types of certificates available today as proxies for gold. The best of them, the Perth mint gold certificate, is issued by an institution located in one of the most remote places on earth.

A few certificate programs tell you of the numbers on the bars of gold or silver that you own; I would never send money to one that did not. In a certificate program, you purchase a certain number of ounces of gold, usually over the phone, from the company issuing a certificate. When they receive your money, they send you a certificate, and you have to hope that there is actual gold on deposit at their firm to back it up. Otherwise, you have just paid a lot of money for a piece of paper, one whose value could well approximate that of those pieces of paper with pictures of dead presidents. The rule of thumb for certificates is simple: if you can't verify, don't buy. The Perth Mint Certificate program is fully backed by the government of Western Australia; I know of no other syndicate programs with any backing from any government.

9.   Gold Jewelry

Jewelry is the obvious last choice for three reasons: first, the premium you pay for workmanship is huge. Second, most jewelry gold is less than 100 percent pure gold. Only 24k gold is pure gold, and because it is so soft, it is seldom used in jewelry. Third, the market for jewelry is very different than the market for easily-identified bullion coins or numismatic coins graded by PCGS or NGC. You can forget about gold-plated or gold-filled jewelry, too; it sells very cheaply for a good reason. It's just not a good idea to invest in something that cannot be instantly and accurately valued by a potential buyers.

10. Everything else

You can find an amazing variety of items that purport to be gold or to have value related to gold. They include trading cards made of gold foil, gold "dust," reproductions of numismatic coins, figurines and statuettes, and things you probably can't even imagine. Please avoid them all as investments.

• • •

Silver

Almost everything I have said about gold also applies to silver. Silver, however, has many industrial uses gold does not have, such as film photography (including X-rays), electrical contacts and wiring, antibacterial applications, mirrors, and much more. Silver is the world's best conductor and is finding application in superconducting high-tension lines that can "carry" electricity many miles without losses.

Unlike gold, which is used primarily as a store of value or as jewelry, when silver is utilized in most industrial applications it becomes very difficult and expensive to recover. There are credible statistics to the effect that the remaining supply of silver both above and below ground is much smaller than most people imagine. One such statistic claims that there are five billion ounces of gold available in the world today in all forms, but only one billion ounces of silver. Based upon scarcity alone, that fact would make silver significantly more valuable than gold, particularly because it is irreplaceable in many of its uses.

Throughout history gold has almost always been more expensive than silver. The ratio between the prices of gold and silver was once pegged at sixteen to one. Today, with gold at $922 and silver at $17, the ratio is about fifty-four to one. That ratio is much too high and either the price of gold should come down or the price of silver should go up. I think it will be the latter.

In recent years some have argued that the world has used more silver than it has produced for as many as sixty years. This is what is meant by a structural deficit; the shortfall between current demand and current supply must be made up from reserves, usually central-bank holdings. The same people who make the argument about deficits also declare that the price of silver is heavily manipulated using sophisticated options strategies. I believe that the price of silver ought to be much higher today than it is, manipulation or no manipulation.

Following are my recommendations concerning the purchase of silver as an investment.

1. I do not recommend the purchase of graded and certified rare silver coins. When you purchase common date-graded and certified $20 gold Double Eagles, you are paying a relatively small premium over their intrinsic gold value. The same is not true with silver coins. You are better off

buying circulated or "junk" silver dollars at a small premium over their melt value than you are by buying certified rare coins. Also, silver tarnishes. The process of oxidation can produce beautiful toning on a coin, and some collectors consider the toning to be valuable, but in other instances the tarnish simply cuts the value of the coin.

2. If you are going to buy "junk" silver coins, I recommend that you buy only American coins and that you try to pay the lowest premium possible. U.S. dimes, quarters, and half dollars minted prior to 1965 are all 90 percent silver. Dealers sell them in bags holding a certain numerical face value of silver. For example, a regular bag would have $1000 face value of coins, which is four thousand quarters, ten thousand dimes, or two thousand half dollars (Image 8 in the center photo section). Smaller bags are also available.

3. "Junk" silver coins are recognized worldwide. If the United States government ever declared a bank holiday, as was done during the Great Depression, people could use their silver coins as real money. (See Image 9, the 1921 Morgan Dollar.) Today these silver coins are worth much more than their face value. If the time came that you needed to spend them, you might have to barter in order to get the best value for your silver. "Junk" silver coins are a highly marketable form of silver.

4. When you are buying silver bullion, you should compare the prices of recently minted one-ounce silver Eagles (Image 10) against those of "junk" silver coins, for the premium over the silver value in each type of coin constantly fluctuates. For more than twenty years, several mints all over the world have produced attractive one-ounce silver coins. The price per ounce for these coins is usually more than the price per ounce of ten-ounce silver bars; the price per ounce of ten-ounce silver bars is usually higher than the price per ounce of one-hundred-ounce silver bars. Depending upon how long you intend to hold your silver and whom you intend to sell it to when you are ready, you might lean toward one or the other. Whenever you sell silver bullion or coins, you will probably do better selling them in an online auction than you will selling to a dealer.

5. Just as there are gold certificates issued by institutions like the Perth mint, there are also silver certificates available. The same cautions apply.

6. I recommend against buying silver jewelry as an investment in silver. The premium over the silver value is even higher than it is for gold.

Precious Stones
Are diamonds an investor's best friend?

There are many more types of precious stones available for jewelry and investment today than there were even fifty years ago. Back then the absence of color in a diamond made it more valuable; today colored diamonds can be more valuable than colorless diamonds. Today there are many treated stones, many synthetic stones, and not a few varieties of stones that were not popular previously. Sorting them all out and attempting to decide which will grow in value the quickest requires education, time, and patience. Coming up with the right answers will also require some luck, for the precious gem markets are every bit as fickle as the stock markets.

Precious gems have been prized for millennia and have even been the cause of war and rebellion. The demand for them is so great that there is a multibillion dollar industry in imitations. As with any other category of investment, their emotional appeal can affect our judgment, so that we may rationalize the purchase of a piece of jewelry as an investment when it is not.

High-quality precious gems tend to do well as investments. Demand is strong most of the time, and the supply is always limited, whether determined by a cartel or by the playing out of mines. They are also very portable and often manage to find their way across borders with relative ease. Here are some of what I perceive to be the negative aspects of precious gems.

1. Precious gems are not liquid; that is, you can never have a guarantee of getting your full purchase price back.

2. In fact, because of the way they are priced, there is usually a huge spread between what a dealer will charge you or pay you for the same gem. The spread can be 50 percent of the full retail value or even more.

3. The supply of precious gems can fluctuate dramatically as old mines close or new ones are discovered.

4. The value of precious gems is not directly linked to inflation.

5. Every so often a new category of precious stones becomes popular, and people flock to them for a time until the next "fad" appears.

6. You need to be very careful about what you buy. Too many people buy something on the advice of a broker only to find that the item is not what they were told it was or that it is not the quality it was represented to be or that the actual market for such things is small.

7. If you pay only a 25 percent markup to buy your gems, you must wait until the price has risen 25 percent before you reach "breakeven" on your investment. But wait; if you sell your appreciated gem to a deal or at an auction, you can expect to pay at least another 10–25 percent in fees. In other words, your gem must rise in value at least 35 percent before you can reasonably expect to get your money back.

I don't like precious gems as an investment. They are more portable than real estate, but they are much too subject to the whims of finicky markets.

If you insist on investing in precious gems, my advice is similar to what I said about rare coins; buy the best you can afford and plan on holding for a long time.

Energy
Rapidly growing demand; rapidly decreasing supply

The outlook for energy is less certain than it is for the precious metals, particularly for silver. I am a firm believer in Peak Oil and Peak Coal. Peak Oil refers to the day on which the world will attain its highest-ever production of crude oil. That may not seem to make a lot of sense; after all, we have only used half of all the oil ever discovered, and it took over a century do so. Even though we are using oil faster than ever before, with modern technology, we should still be able to produce more and more oil each day. However, this is not the case. Oil production in the United States peaked in the 1970s and has been in terminal decline ever since. Our half a million remaining oil wells in the U.S. produce far less oil than a few hundred wells in Saudi Arabia. The actual numbers, as of 2005:

Table 7. Oil Production by Country, 2005

Country	Oil Production (barrels per day)	Number of Oil-producing Wells
Saudi Arabia	7,700,000	1,560
Russia	7,400,000	41,192
United States	5,800,000	521,070
Source: *Beyond Oil,* by Kenneth S. Deffeyes		

Investing in energy today is probably one of the best things you can do—if you invest wisely and have good timing. To my analytical mind, the production statistics offer sufficient proof that we either have already reached a peak in both or that we soon will.

On that basis, oil at $200 per barrel or even $300 is almost a given over the next few years, but what does it really mean? Can you find a way to make money in an essential commodity just because of its scarcity? Can you even make enough to offset the additional energy costs you will pay for your own transportation and climate control? What happens to your investment in "fossil fuels" if some new, viable alternative technology suddenly bursts upon the scene?

Let me give you some ideas that may help you to answer these questions.

1. Forget alternative technologies for now. None of the technologies that seem so promising when government or the media talk about them is going to be workable on any useful scale for years to come. Some, like ethanol produced from corn, are disastrous and useless because they utilize more energy than they produce. Others, like hydrogen, are merely a medium of energy transmission rather than an energy source in and of themselves. (Like ethanol from corn, hydrogen takes more energy to produce than it gives up when it converts back into water.)

There may be a reason for this. Early in the twentieth century the major automakers conspired to buy up interurban rail lines and bus lines and bankrupt them so that people would become more dependent on their own automobiles. The strategy was an environmental and resource disaster, but for decades it proved extremely profitable for the automakers. Similarly, for years I have been hearing that the automakers or the energy companies or both have conspired to retard or prevent the development of many technologies, preferring to profit from industries they own that would otherwise be obsolete. I take a cynical view of American business; it's entirely possible that technological suppression is being widely practiced today.

Just look at ethanol. The farmers love it because it guarantees them a good price for all the corn they can grow. Our government has to heavily subsidize the production and sale of ethanol because at every stage it is uneconomic. While the subsidies remain, the industry will appear to flourish, but watch for numerous bankruptcies in the ethanol industry in the not-too-distant future.

2.   Hydroelectric isn't the answer. Most of the rivers and streams suitable for hydroelectric power generation already have numerous dams, all of which are silting up and will be useless in a few more years.

3.   Many technologies for recovering oil or oil equivalents (the "oil" we get from the tar sands of Athabasca, for example, isn't really oil: it's a related product called bitumen, which can be used as a component of oil) utilize enormous amounts of other scarce commodities, such as natural gas and water. According to a recent study, Canadian oil sands producers will utilize every remaining molecule of natural gas in Canada by the year 2015.

4.   Even if we were to come up with some amazing new technology that would replace oil and natural gas for transportation and power generation, we still need both those hydrocarbons as feedstocks for industry. You would be hard pressed to find any manufactured product in the world today that does not have one or more components that are derived from oil. The fertilizers most farmers use in the United States today are derived from natural gas.

5.   If we are indeed faced with peak coal, contrary to what so many have been telling us about the U.S. having enough coal to last two hundred years or more, coal will probably be a good investment despite its environmental drawbacks.

You may make appropriate investments in energy and have a reasonable expectation that they will be in demand well past our lifetimes. The question is, what do you buy?

I avoid oil exploration companies. There is significant agreement among oil people that there is little more oil or natural gas to find. Oil drillers are a different matter, as long as they take an equity position in their discoveries.

I also avoid the major oil companies for reasons mentioned above. BP may have changed its name to "Beyond Petroleum," but whether they can survive as a corporate giant once the oil and natural gas run out remains to be seen. I wouldn't want to own stock in a dying industry. That's why I don't buy the automakers.

My favorite energy strategy involves royalty trusts, especially those that have options. As with all stocks, you should buy low and sell high, while enjoying significant dividends along the way. Here's a hypothetical example of Advantage Energy, a Canadian royalty trust I believe is quite undervalued:

AAV common stock	$ 8.23 per share
Current yield	$ 1.35 per year or 16.4 percent
Sell 1 $10.00 covered call	$ 0.25 every six months

If AAV stays between $8.00 and $10.00, your return (ignoring stock gains) will be over 20 percent per year.

• • •

Residential Real Estate

If you know your market inside and out, can get a significant break on commissions, have numerous well-placed contacts in the mortgage business, and can afford to take a great deal of risk, you might consider residential real estate. I stay away from it because it is unmarketable, not to mention illiquid, and properties cost money to maintain when they are vacant. I have numerous personal biases against residential real estate, but don't let that get in your way. Many people have made a great deal of money in this sector, but it recently became much more difficult to do so.

• • •

Commercial Real Estate

Commercial real-estate prices are subject to numerous factors including the rate of inflation, the general level of interest rates, the direction in which the economy is heading, supply and demand, the level of speculation in the marketplace, and location. Usually commercial real estate is traded in very large transactions conducted by large investment firms and financial institutions; the only way the most people can invest in commercial real estate is to purchase Real Estate Investment Trusts (REITs). REITs trade like stocks and operate like ETFs. You can evaluate them based upon their holdings, the discount or premium to net-asset value they are selling at, the most recent dividends paid, and other fundamental and technical factors. Unlike most real estate, REITs, like all ETFs, are fully marketable. You can buy and sell them any day the market is open.

The great appeal of real estate has been the investor's ability to purchase it using other people's money. Some REITs purchase partnerships that utilize debt and individual properties utilizing borrowing, and thus they enjoy the same leverage as any other real estate purchase made with borrowed funds. Other REITs are "cash only" programs, and they have been known to pay higher dividends than the leverage programs. You have a choice: greater potential for growth in the leveraged programs or higher current yields in the "cash" programs.

Like everything else, there is a time to buy and a time to sell commercial real estate. Since real estate is generally outside my area of expertise and analysis, I must resort to prominent indicators to get a feel for what's going on in the commercial real-estate market. In the latter part of 2006, I closed all of my clients' positions in both residential and commercial real estate. I correctly anticipated the bursting of the residential real estate bubble and expected it to affect commercial real estate as well. We have seen massive damage to the residential market and the peak of the commercial market as well. In 2006 my clients took very nice profits in real estate and shifted most of the proceeds to the commodity funds, including precious metals and energy.

I believe that the risks outweigh the potential rewards in commercial real estate, and will continue to do so indefinitely. That does not mean that there are not certain segments and sectors of the market that can be very profitable for you even now. Storage units have had a great run, as have certain motel chains, strip malls, and some office buildings. You just need to be very selective and knowledgeable.

• • •

Limited Partnerships

In the mid-seventies a new concept arose on the American financial scene. The limited partnership was endorsed and enhanced by the United States Congress at the request of lobbyists for the real-estate industry and others. Limited partnerships of various sorts had been available for a long time, but now under the new laws they were popularized and made available to the general public. For the first time a person could tie up his money in an illiquid and unmarketable investment for up to thirty years if he had three things: 1) money to tie up, 2) an income of at least $30,000 per year, and 3) a net worth of at least $100,000 (sometimes less).

What was the purpose of these limited partnerships? They were designed to provide long-term funding of certain projects so as to provide tax benefits to the limited partners, possibly as a substitute for the income they might be receiving from dividend-paying stocks. Much was said about how the legislation would give the "little guy" access to the real-estate investment market, which formerly had been open only to large investment pools and insurance companies. However, many of the partnerships that were created under these laws tended to benefit only their promoters.

I speak from personal experience; of the approximately $250,000 of my clients' money that went into limited partnerships in 1980 and 1981, less than half of it ever came back to the limited partners. They did receive some tax write-offs, but not nearly enough to offset their capital losses. I was somewhat amused when limited partnerships began to be created that were specifically designed for IRA and other retirement accounts; in these programs the promoter or the general partner got to keep even the tax benefits because the limited partner couldn't use them.

There was one category of limited partnership that generally did better than the others, and that was cable TV. At that time cable TV was in its infancy, and those who got on board generally did quite well.

From what I saw, the best performing category of real-estate limited partnership was the storage unit. In this case the logic was almost compelling; if you can get people to pay roughly the same rent per square foot for a storage unit as they were paying for their home or apartment and the cost of building and operating the storage unit was significantly less than that of an apartment or home, you should have a profitable business. Also, storage units were completed quickly, did not raise environmental issues and almost instantly begin to generate cash flow.

On the other hand, those who invested in commercial real estate, which included apartment complexes, strip malls, motels, hotels and resorts, and small office buildings, did not do particularly well. I remember all too well some spectacular bankruptcies, foreclosures, accounting shenanigans, and other events that all too often took away the limited partners' investment dollars.

Why did these programs generally perform so poorly? Not all of the answers have to do with the greed of the general partner. On paper most of the programs looked reasonably good, as long as you were willing to make one basic assumption; that real estate would be worth more in thirty years than it was then. Clearly, real estate of all types has been, generally speaking, a good investment over the past thirty years, so what's the problem?

Part of the problem may have come from the lack of accountability on the part of the general partners. Of course, they published their quarterly reports on time, but who was reading them? Who was monitoring the performance of the program? The stocks of Fortune 500 companies are monitored by many analysts, and their opinions regarding those stocks and those companies are a matter of public record. The markets seem to turn on quarterly reports, which means that every ninety days a publicly held company discloses its results and the investing public responds.

With a limited partnership, the general assumption is that the partnership will be in operation for as long as thirty years. Investors in stocks can "vote with their feet"; investors in limited partnerships don't vote at all. The general partner has been chosen for the duration and barring significant criminal malfeasance or death will not be replaced. Many of the individuals and institutions that placed their money into these limited partnerships placed a relatively small portion of their investment capital into them. That does not mean that they were not as concerned about the performance of that money, but given the lengthy time span of the partnership and the fact that none of them had any opportunity to bail out, there isn't really much reason to monitor the actions of the general partner.

In addition, some of the premises on which these partnerships were sold may have sounded good to the uninitiated but really didn't add value to the program. I remember all too well a presentation given at a national conference of one of the broker/dealer firms with which I was associated. This conference took place in the early nineties, by which time I had stopped offering all forms of limited partnerships to my clients. The promoter bragged about how his partnership could walk away from their debt obligations, thus reducing the risk of default by the general partner and losses on the part of the limited partners. He was making the point that the partnership had taken on "non-recourse" loans so that if certain things went wrong the loans would not have to be repaid.

Now, I have always been taught that if you borrow money from someone you do whatever it takes to pay it back. I wondered to myself how I would go about selling my clients on a program that was designed to leave someone holding the bag. I also wondered what it was about the partnership that made it so weak financially that default would even be a consideration.

I like my money to be under my control as much as possible. One of the greatest attractions of the financial markets is the marketability of securities. Unlike a car, a boat, a house, or other valuable property, you don't need to find a seller or a buyer when you want to make a trade in the financial markets. The other side of the transaction is always available to you, provided by someone who was either another investor or a "market maker." Whenever the market for your security is open, you may buy and sell that security. There are thinly traded securities, of course, but you buy them with an understanding of that limitation.

Limited partnerships, however, are illiquid and unmarketable. By purchasing units in a limited partnership, you have made a very long-term commitment. If you need to get your money out before the program has been terminated by the general partner, you usually have only two choices: you sell your units back to the general partner or you sell them to the securities equivalent of a pawnbroker. If the general partner has been successful in increasing the value of the units, he might well purchase your units from you, although at a discounted price. The securities "pawnbroker," on the other hand, is simply looking for bargains. You can expect to receive as little as five cents on the dollar of your initial investment from him, after which you attempt to assuage your hurt feelings by tallying the dollar value of whatever tax deductions you received plus any cash distributions that may have been made to date.

There is one exception to my rule about limited partnerships today, and that is the real-estate tax credit program. Hopwever, as their benefits have declined and the real estate market has become much less stable, I have ceased recommending them as well.

Tax law has changed significantly since the heyday of the limited partnership, and there are far fewer programs available today. I continue to talk to promoters of various programs and generally find very little to recommend them. From the beginning these programs have been loaded down with marketing costs, operating costs, and other fees and expenses, most of which have ended up in the pockets of the promoters and the general partners. To me, that means that the playing field is not level and that the odds of getting a decent return are better elsewhere. Besides, do you know of anything that will be more valuable in real dollars fifteen to thirty years from now? I don't.

If you own a limited partnership be aware that there are vultures circling. They are people who will write to all the owners of a particular partnership and try to create doubt in their minds about the potential of their program. They then proceed to offer some pittance for the units, claiming that you have already received all the tax benefits that will ever come to you through this partnership, and now you have little expectation of getting your money back. I have seen letters like these offering as little as 1 percent of the initial purchase price of the partnership units. My advice to you is don't allow them to scare you. They wouldn't buy at any price unless they knew the partnership was still valuable.

Here's a partial list of industries in which limited partnerships are available:

- Commercial real estate

- Vacation time shares

- Storage units

- Oil and gas exploration, developmental drilling, and completion programs

- Container, aircraft, and locomotive leasing

- Fast food franchising

- Resort development

- Cattle feeding

• • •

Art

Not being a fan of "modern" art, I am hard pressed to understand why it is so very expensive these days; however, it is obvious if you look at some recent auctions that certain pieces of art, from the old masters to artists living today, have appreciated at a tremendous rate in recent years. New records are being set and broken all the time for various paintings and sculptures at auctions in places like New York and England. I attribute the increases to two primary reasons: first, the increase in the number of collectors and second, my belief that some people have way too much money.

Art, antiques, and collectibles all fall into the same category, the one I call the "greater-fool theory." When you buy Beanie Babies or Barbie dolls at a time when they are "hot" collectibles, when you are ready to sell—or when you need to sell—you need to find someone more "foolish" than you were who will take them off your hands at a higher price than you paid. As is the case with every form of investment, value is in the eye of the beholder. Just because you are willing to pay $1,000 for that original print does not mean that anyone else will ever see that much value in it. Of course, if you sell to a dealer rather than to a fellow collector or at an auction, you know you will lose some of your potential profit to the "spread."

There are numerous other considerations involved when you invest in art. You must protect and preserve your purchases against theft, weather, humidity, deterioration, sunlight, and a host of other things that can decrease the value of your collection. You must purchase insurance on your collection, and insurance is usually quite expensive. Of course, you have to be careful not to purchase forgeries, and what you do buy needs to be authenticated by expert appraisers. You must buy right, which means that you shouldn't buy just because the market is hot and it seems as though everybody wants the same item you do.

In addition, you probably ought to have a trained eye for those things that will rise in value. Much of what sells for tens of millions of dollars in these days is art I wouldn't go to a museum to look at.

• • •

Antiques
One Man's Trash . . .

Antiques are in a different category than art, for antiques can incorporate art as well as history and craftsmanship. As with art, you need to be well-educated and have cultivated tastes to be able to make money in this area of investment. Forgeries, reproductions, and copies are common and becoming more common as more and more people seek out the choicest pieces. Antiques may be more subject to cycles than art, though I have no particular evidence to support that contention.

Antiques need to be preserved, restored, insured, protected, and kept under climate control to retain their value. After all is said and done, the odds of you coming up with a piece that will be presented on Antiques Roadshow is pretty remote. That doesn't mean you can't be one of the lucky few, like the person who bought a painting for $10 at a flea market intending to toss out the painting and keep the frame. When he cut the picture out, he found one of the very few original copies of the Declaration of Independence, which he then sold at auction for several hundred thousand dollars.

With art, antiques, and collectibles, your enjoyment of your holdings matters a great deal. That enjoyment is intangible, but if you can afford to do so, there is absolutely nothing wrong with paying a large sum of money for something that you value highly, something that you have no intention of selling a later date. Such an item would *not* be considered an investment.

• • •

"Collectibles"

People love an investment mania every bit as much as they love chain letters and Ponzi schemes.

Collectibles tend to trade in cycles, and they tend to run hot and cold. There was that time when Ming Dynasty porcelain was all the rage, and it was selling for unbelievable prices. Today the baby boomers seem to express significant but fleeting interest in some of the things they grew up with, and now that they have the wherewithal to spend on collectibles they do so.

There are thousands of things you can collect; not all of them will qualify as investments, because many of them are not considered valuable by others, have no collectors' associations, nor are sought after by collectors. It is often difficult to judge what items will become valuable as collectibles or how long it will take for them to become valuable.

If you have purchased your collectibles with the intent of selling them at a profit, you have to be careful not to get attached to them, and you have to watch the markets pretty closely. Opportunities for profitable sale can be very fleeting, as we saw in the very rapid decline in value of beanie babies a few years ago.

I used to think that postage stamps, particularly old and high-quality U.S. regular issues and commemoratives, would appreciate in value for several reasons: they are scarce, their quality is determinable, they are sought after by collectors, there is a well-established market, and there is significant collector and investor interest in them. When I was buying rare stamps back in the early 1980s, I was buying at the peak of the market. Very few people my age had become interested in stamp collecting, and the few of us who were interested were not passing that interest on to our children. I talked to a stamp and coin dealer a few years ago about the decline in stamp collecting, and he told me that the average age of the members of the philatelic club to which he belonged was in the mid-sixties.

I stopped buying rare stamps in the 1980s, and twenty years later my collection is still worth only a fraction of what I paid for it. Fewer collectors means less demand. Much of the demand that existed in the early eighties was driven by inflation and speculation.

That experience taught me an important lesson: any collectibles I buy must have an intrinsic value. Following that principle significantly reduces the universe of collectibles I will look at. In addition, I'm only willing to pay a certain premium over that intrinsic value.

The only category of collectible I purchase today is graded $20 gold St. Gaudens double eagles. Each has the intrinsic value of roughly one ounce of gold, while the guaranteed grading ensures the coin's quality and scarcity. There is a large and growing market for this type of collectible. The coins themselves are beautiful, for the $20 Saint Gaudens is considered by many to be the most beautiful coin ever minted.

On the other hand, the likelihood of my "making a killing" on the sale of one of my $20 Saints is low, for unlike a one-of-a-kind piece of art, there are thousands of Saints in the more common dates and grades. Over the long term, I would be almost certain to make more money from my coins if I were purchasing the scarcer dates and grades, but I choose not to do so because of my rule about intrinsic value and small premiums. That does not mean that I cannot profit from "grade expansion" as the mania builds for rare gold coins. There was a mania in numismatic coins back in 1980, and it took years for it to fade as gold lost its value and took the rare coins down with it. Even with gold at an all-time high in 2008, many common date-graded Saints sold for much more in 1979 and 1980 than they do now. I expect history to repeat and graded coins to widen the gap between their value and the value of bullion.

Like art and antiques, all collectibles need to be carefully preserved and stored securely. They must be insured and kept in such a way as to avoid deterioration. I admire antiques dealers because they have to know so much about the things they look at all the time. Their knowledge has to be kept current by regular communication with others in their field.

• • •

Other Types of Investments

The list of things that could qualify as investments is almost endless. These days there are futures and options on everything from pollution credits to the results of sporting events and elections. Investments can be tangible or intangible; the intangible group would include patents and copyrights and intellectual property, all of which can be valuable.

My personal preference in investing is to buy only those things I can liquidate quickly, easily, and at low cost. That's why I have a personal bias against real estate; regardless of the type, it usually takes a long time to sell, its buyers can be fickle, and the transaction costs can be very substantial. I also prefer to work with investments that are widely recognized and popular. However, if there is something that you do as a hobby that could double as an investment and you have the knowledge, interest, and ability to make money at it, feel free to pursue its investment potential.

Never let your broker or other financial advisor convince you that your hobby or your "non-traditional" investments are not appropriate and worthwhile for you. It is the mindset of my industry and part of our training that we want to be able to control all of our clients' assets. Of course, we also want to be able to make a commission from all of our clients' investments. That approach can motivate a financial professional to try to move you away from what *you* know to something that *he or she* knows. Sometimes the professional is right, especially if they discover that you are one of those who stuck to a fad long after its day was past. Ostriches, emus, sheep farms, and uncertified rare coins all fall into this category. A once-valuable investment can become an albatross around your neck.

Now that you have a brief overview of what you can buy, let's look at how you should go about buying it.

Chapter Thirteen

SIR (Savings, Investment, Retirement)

The simplest and most effective method I have found of organizing our disposable income is to divide it into these three categories:

- S–Savings–no *perceived* risk of principal

- I–Investment–funds not needed soon but available prior to retirement

- R–Retirement–funds accruing tax-deferred (or, in a Roth IRA, available tax-free during retirement)

These categories are not set in stone, but they do provide useful guidelines. Savings money you won't need in less than two years ought to be allocated elsewhere, probably into investments. Things considered to fall into the savings category may be used in a retirement account, as can most of those items described under investments. Understanding and utilizing these categories properly will help you to make better informed financial decisions.

• • •

Savings

- Savings is the simplest part of S-I-R. Savings vehicles include:

- Passbook savings accounts

- Interest-bearing checking accounts

- Online bank accounts that pay interest

- Certificates of deposit

- Money-market funds

- Fixed annuities

These are not investments because they have no risk. They also tend not to keep up with inflation and taxes.

All of the above must be denominated in U.S. dollars. Any savings account denominated in any *other* currency is deemed an investment because it has currency risk. Of course, there is risk in everything we do, but in the case of a savings account, any risk of principal is insured by someone other than you. At a bank, savings accounts and certificates of deposit are usually guaranteed by the Federal Deposit Insurance Corporation (FDIC).

Money-market funds, available singly or as part of a family of mutual funds, usually pay a higher rate of interest than passbook savings accounts. They are deemed to be riskless only because money market fund managers have seldom "broken the buck," which means that money market funds have always maintained a value of $1.00 per share. However, because of the subprime mortgage mess, we found out that money market funds have more risk than we thought.

If you want a "safe" money-market fund, you can usually turn to U.S. government short-term securities money-market funds, which are backed by the full faith and credit of the U.S. government, or, in the event that the money market fund owns "agency" securities such as soon-to-mature GNMAs, you have to hope that the U.S. government will always be there to bail out its poorly run agencies. In recent months U.S. Treasury bills (also called T-bills) have paid as little as 0% interest, which is not a return I recommend. Most U.S. government money market funds own mostly T-bills.

Fixed annuities, which technically are not savings accounts because they can have significant penalties and tax consequences for early withdrawals, are insured by the insurance company that issues them. The insurance company is rated by one or more of several ratings agencies, any or all of which can be—and often are—blindsided by "unanticipated events." The annuity contract is very specific in laying out the length of the contract, the interest rate it will pay, any withdrawal privileges, and applicable surrender charges. All annuities offer tax-deferred accumulation of interest.

The savings component of S-I-R is simple enough. Since our savings do not keep up with inflation, taxes, and the declining dollar, they are kept to a minimum *as long as better opportunities are available.*

Everyone ought to have an emergency fund and a savings program that enables them to pay cash for major planned purchases instead of paying heavy credit-card interest charges. Most of my clients will always pay interest on mortgages and car loans but should not have to do so on appliances and maintenance.

Under ordinary circumstances your savings ought to be in a money-market fund rather than in a bank. Many people keep savings accounts at a local bank to avoid monthly fees on their checking accounts, and this can be a valid strategy. A better strategy might be to find a bank that offers no-fee checking accounts.

With an account at a money-market fund, you may be able to earn better interest than the banks pay and, if you wish, utilize professional management of your account to attempt to improve your return even more. In a money-market fund, your money is always accessible to you without any commissions or contingent deferred sales charges (CDSCs). You ought to have one.

• • •

Investment

This is the area many people neglect. We focus on our savings and our retirement plans, but for one reason or another we neglect the middle-term program. Many people feel they cannot afford to fund an investment program in addition to a retirement plan. However, your investment program usually has the greatest flexibility of all the components of your personal financial plan. Silver, stocks, bonds, Swiss francs, tax credit limited partnerships, oil and gas properties, and much more belong exclusively to your investment program. For this reason your investment program must be carefully designed and reviewed regularly.

An investment program is usually built gradually. The risk level is determined in part by the timeframe available for investment. Will the money be used to buy a vehicle, send a child to college, or start your own business? The timeframe should be at least two and preferably three to five years at a minimum. Investments need time. At some point most of the investments you will own will probably be worth less than you paid for them.

Why have an investment program? Among other reasons, your retirement program probably will not be sufficient to meet your financial needs during retirement. For many Americans their investment program will provide a significant supplement to their retirement income and may make all the difference in the quality of their lives.

We have discussed at length the types of investments available for an investment program. Let's be sure to add one more: foreign currency savings accounts and certificates of deposit. These accounts have risk of principal as long as the currency in which they are denominated fluctuate against the U.S. dollar, your primary currency.

• • •

Retirement

This is the area of greatest emphasis. Most of my clients have some sort of retirement program, and many of them have made good and informed decisions about the positioning and the management of their retirement funds. I still spend a lot of time moving people away from inferior products, but the trend toward quality is encouraging.

Retirement programs include corporate and government-sponsored 401(k) plans, SEP-IRAs for small companies, 403(b) TSA and ORP accounts (DCRP in Colorado) for educational and charitable institutions, and IRAs for those not eligible to participate in an employer-sponsored plan. The law has recently changed again. The new "SIMPLE" IRA became effective on 1 January 1997. The Roth IRA and others were added later in 1997. The laws concerning 401(k) accounts and 403(b) accounts was modified in 2007, and more changes are expected that will impact all types of retirement accounts.

I offer my clients any or all of the plans listed above. Congress has simplified some of the rules regarding retirement plans and made it a little easier for us to understand what our options are. Most Americans are limited to two choices: their own IRA account and/or their employer's account. Whenever possible you should take advantage of your employer-sponsored account, particularly when the employer makes a contribution based upon the amount you have withheld from your paycheck to put into the retirement account. Psychologically that money has a very good effect. It is the best type of "forced savings" program because we allow money to be deducted from each paycheck. We never see that money except in our retirement statements, where it is accumulating (and, hopefully, growing) tax-deferred.

Unfortunately, most Americans fail to accumulate enough money in their retirement plans to adequately provide for them during their retirement. This is partially due to the fact that we are living longer and many people will spend as many years in retirement as they spent working.

• • •

"Safe" Investments

Every investment carries an arbitrary risk level. A bank account or a fixed annuity in reality has the highest risk level of all because such accounts frequently fall victim to inflation and taxes; however, they are considered "safe" because they have no perceived risk of principal.

I have devoted my career to helping Americans move money from such "safe" guaranteed losers into investments that have some risk of principal and that offer some means to protect yourself from inflation and taxes. I call them guaranteed losers because history indicates that money in banks and fixed annuities has generally lost purchasing power to inflation and taxes for decades. For example, if you had put $100,000 into a six-month CD in 1984 and renewed it at competitive rates through 2008, after inflation and taxes the purchasing power of your $100,000 would have fallen to about $59,250 even though you would have been compounding your interest.

• • •

What does a typical client do?

Here is a sample:

Savings

Savings: An account at an online bank or a no-load mutual fund that holds funds for emergencies and major purchases. This account can be stable or funds can be added and withdrawn frequently. Some or all of the account can be managed using the high yield strategy described below.

Investment

Investment: An account in a mutual fund family that is managed at a risk level of type one or type two in most cases. Also, if tax relief is needed, a tax-credit limited partnership might be part of the investment program. For those concerned about inflation and the falling dollar, a regular investment program into Swiss francs and/or silver could also be part of the program.

Today you have more options than ever. The choices are suficiently diversified that you can formulate an effective strategy without having your money scattered all over the place. These days I utilize my "stocks at a discount" program for both investment money and retirement money; the only difference is that the retirement money is in an IRA or other retirement account. We use, wherever possible, a discount brokerage firm with its own no-load mutual funds so that we pay as little as possible in commissions and fees.

In this account we purchase high-yielding closed-end mutual funds, energy trusts, open-end mutual funds, and ETFs. The ETFs include funds that invest solely in a particular foreign currency or precious metal.

Retirement

Retirement: This account is generally the recipient of the largest chunk of your disposable income after expenses. Whether you use a 403(b), a 401(k), an IRA, a SIMPLE plan or something else, you need to set this program up to maximize the tax benefits to you both now and in the future. Most of my clients add to their retirement accounts with each paycheck. You should evaluate the level of your contributions each year and increase them as appropriate. Some people utilize a form of life insurance with growth potential instead of a standard retirement program because of the special tax benefits available to life insurance.

• • •

The High Yield Strategy

Most Americans prefer the guarantees offered by a bank or insurance company even if deep down they realize that they are losing ground to inflation and taxes year after year. I am constantly on the lookout for conservative ways to invest in a way to beat inflation and taxes without taking a high level of risk. This strategy has been a good solution.

In 1996 I developed a strategy for my more risk-averse clients. This strategy utilizes a combination of four different bond funds. They are:

- High Yield or "junk" bond funds

- High Quality Corporate Bond Funds

- U.S. Government Bond funds

- Money Market Funds

This strategy requires market timing and active management. The idea is to have all your money in one of the four fund types at any moment, the type with the best potential for total return in the immediate future. By following the trends in interest rates and credit quality this strategy can be maintained with few exchanges.

For example, as credit quality began to deteriorate we moved out of High Yield Bond funds in early 2008, exchanging that money into U.S. Government Bond Funds. When Governments peaked in late 2008 we moved to High Quality Corporate bond funds.

There is one other nice feature related to the High Yield strategy; you can reinvest your dividends each month into one of the other mutual funds available in the fund family. This is what I call a "have your cake and eat it too" strategy. Your principal remains in the four bond funds, and you pay no fees or commissions to switch from one fund to another. Your interest (dividends) are paid into a mutual fund with significant growth potential, and though that fund has risk it is mitigated by the fact that you are "dollar-cost averaging" by investing money into it each month.

Now that you have a better idea of how I categorize disposable income, let's get serious about risk and how we can both avoid excessive risk and utilize risk to our advantage.

Part IV

Risk and Reward

Chapter Fourteen

Understanding and Managing Risk

Over the years I have spoken to thousands of people about risk, and have found that both the general public and many financial professionals do not fully understand it. I'm not just talking about investment risk; I'm talking about all the risks we encounter in life. Some are quantifiable and can be offset, and others cannot. Our understanding of risk must consider our environment, for risk is relative to our situation.

For example, insurance contracts of various types have been invented so that we may share different types of risks. We share the risk of a particular event—death, disability, fire, theft—with the insurance company, and the company takes on all or a portion of the risk in return for the premium we pay. You probably keep a deductible on your homeowner's insurance of $500 or so. By doing so you are self-insured against the first $500 of any claim that may arise, which is covered by your insurance; the remainder will be paid up to the policy maximums, at which point you will once again be self-insured. The same is true of your car. If you do not own a car, you do not need to insure a car, for you incur none of the risks that car owners assume.

You probably have some life insurance, whether it is the kind you purchase yourself or coverage provided by your employer. Your insurable risk is the cost of replacing yourself, the net benefit you provide to your beneficiaries.

One form of insurance that is quite unpopular is disability-income insurance, which to a limited extent replaces your income when you are unable to work. It is unpopular because it is expensive; it is expensive because more people suffer disabilities than you may realize. Disability income insurance is an important tool in your financial plan, for without it an accident or illness could prevent you from accomplishing any of your financial objectives. In addition to the loss of income, disability might mean the inability to properly manage your assets.

There are other risks that we ought to quantify as part of our planning process. Each real or potential risk should be quantified and evaluated. This task is made more difficult because each decision along the way is subjective. For instance:

If you have a family history of cancer or cardiac disease you may want to purchase specific insurance to help share those risks.

If you hand your credit card to a waiter in a restaurant, you are taking a specific risk regarding the integrity of your financial data. Likewise, when you conduct financial transactions over the Internet, you subject yourself to risks far more significant than that particular purchase.

Some of us choose our motor vehicles based upon our feelings about risk and safety, even though most accidents can be prevented by remaining awake and alert and by driving defensively. If we choose to use a cell phone while we drive, we are making a trip just a little more dangerous.

If we take illegal drugs, we run the risks of public humiliation, imprisonment, loss of our job, alienation from our families, and much more. People take these risks when they either fail to consider or simply ignore the possible consequences.

Smokers take a particular risk by continuing their habit. It's not as much of a risk as it is a foregone conclusion that they will experience poorer health over a shorter life span. Some recent research suggests that although just about everyone tries cigarettes in their youth, only those with a genetic proclivity toward nicotine addiction stay with it and develop a lifelong habit.

Many of the choices we make involve a degree of risk. Did we choose the right college? Did we get the right degree? Are we in a profession and on a career path for which we are well suited? Did we buy the right home at a good price? Will our children obtain an adequate education through the local public schools? Will we be able to set enough aside to provide for ourselves during a lengthy retirement? Will we look back upon our lives and be satisfied that the world is a better place for our having occupied it these many years? The risk is that our life might have been "better" if we had decided or acted differently.

Managing risk and making appropriate plans and decisions involves weighing the possible consequences of our actions as best we can, then closing the door to the paths we do not want to follow. This way can we begin with the end in mind and have a good chance of achieving our goal.

I have never met a person for whom money was not a dominant aspect of his life. Whether we are striving to obtain it, already have it, have too much, or never have enough, our lives and our futures are largely determined by money. You would think that something so vitally important would be a mandatory portion of our public education, but it is not.

• • •

Risks in Investing

When we consider an investment, our first concern should not be the potential return *on* our money but rather the return *of* our money. If your investment is paying a 12 percent dividend and its prices are sliding by 20 percent per year, you're losing principal. An investment that guarantees principal and has no surrender penalty is said to be liquid. A stock whose principal value fluctuates every trading day is marketable but not liquid. A liquid investment is one where you can get your principal back at any time.

Getting your principal back is the most important risk. You must decide how much risk a particular investment holds. Are you willing to accept that risk, or is it too great for the anticipated return? It's your decision. As you make those decisions, you are setting up your own risk/reward profile.

We evaluate several prospective investments side by side, examining characteristics like liquidity, guaranteed rate of return, suitability, and risk factors. Some risks have names like market risk, interest-rate risk, industry risk, and so on. Each has its place in our analysis, and each will be discussed here. However, the most important risk may be your own risk tolerance. By that I mean the way you will feel and what you will think as the value of your investment rises or falls. If you manage your own investments, you will always have opinions about what you own. If you allow your opinions to affect your investment decisions—if you constantly second-guess yourself, for example—you can significantly *reduce* the return on your investments. You will seldom improve it. You will be better off finding a methodology that works and leaving your opinions out of it.

Maintaining objectivity with our investments is difficult because it requires us to suspend both emotion and intuition. That is difficult for most people to do, which is why many systems and "black boxes" have been developed to try to eliminate the effect of flawed judgment. Unfortunately, as we shall see later, most of them ultimately fail—and some never work at all.

Let's look at this process of evaluation as a series of questions we ask ourselves about each investment we are considering. Let's use a bank certificate of deposit as an example:

1. Is this investment guaranteed as to principal and interest?

2. Is the guaranteed interest rate likely to be raised by the bank in the near future, and will I miss out if I lock in a rate today?

3. How long is the term of the investment?

4. Are there penalties for early termination?

5. Are there commissions charged at the time of purchase or sale?

6. What will my net after-tax return be?

7. May I reinvest my dividends or interest?

8. What will the tax consequences be of this investment each year? At maturity?

9. Will I be required to roll my CD into another at maturity?

10. Is this investment appropriate and suitable for me?

11. What is my *opportunity cost* of buying this CD versus probable alternative uses of this money? To answer that we must ask:

12. Is the guaranteed interest rate competitive?

13. Are there comparable investments paying a higher guaranteed rate with a similar risk level?

14. Will I still be happy with this investment if interest rates rise shortly after I make my purchase?

15. Is this investment appropriate and suitable for me? (This question combines questions two, eight, ten, and thirteen.)

A certificate of deposit (CD) is easy to evaluate, because most of what we need to know about it is guaranteed by the certificate and backed by the FDIC. It is a simple product with only a few variables: interest rate, term, and whether we will pay income taxes on our interest. If we purchase a CD in an IRA, for example, the taxes are deferred until we withdraw the money from the IRA.

Fixed annuities are similar to CDs because they offer an interest rate with a minimum guarantee. Annuities offer tax-deferral of interest. Money-market funds offer relative safety of principal and a fluctuating rate of return. An annuity has the advantage of tax deferral, but an annuity may pay less than a CD.

CDs, annuities, and money-market funds usually fail to provide a return sufficient to keep you ahead of inflation and taxes. I use money-market funds all the time as a "parking place" for cash that is "between investments." CDs and annuities can be very useful when an inflationary cycle is ending because you can lock in an interest rate for serval years. Once Paul Volcker got inflation under control in the early 1980s, thirty-year Treasury bonds and multi-year guarantee (MYG) annuities purchased in 1980 were particularly attractive. We didn't know how attractive they were at the time because it looked like high inflation was here to stay.

If CDs and annuities, savings accounts, and money-market funds all fail to keep up with inflation and taxes, why do people put so much money into them? We do it because we are afraid of risk. We are no more than two generations removed from the Great Depression, an event that significantly changed the attitudes of millions of people. Fear and panic drove many away from the stock market, never to return. It wasn't until the early 1980s that people finally overcame that fear and began to invest in the stock market once again. If only we had been fearful and cautious when we were optimistic and fearless, and vice versa, Americans would be much more successful investors.

A real investment has risk of principal and no guarantees regarding interest or dividends. When we evaluate an investment, we must ask a larger set of questions. Let's look at a stock mutual fund. You can ask the same questions about an ETF.

- Is this investment guaranteed as to principal and interest? *No, by definition.*

- How long is the term of the investment? *Limited partnerships have a maximum life of twenty-five or thirty years, and bonds have a maturity date; but stocks and most other investments have no specific term.*

- How long do I plan to keep this investment? *Something we purchase for the short term often becomes a long-term holding after it falls in value.*

- Are there penalties for early termination? *That depends on the mutual fund.*

- Will I pay commission for this investment? *Except for true no-load funds, you will almost always pay a commission at the time of purchase or possibly at the sale. Many mutual funds today charge a quarterly fee called a 12(b)(1) fee as well.*

- What will my net after-tax return be? *Cannot be accurately predicted in advance.*

- May I reinvest my dividends or interest? *Some investments have a reinvestment privilege.*

- Will I still be happy with this investment if interest rates rise shortly after I make my purchase? *If the investment is a fixed-income security like a bond, the answer is probably no.*

- What will the tax consequences be of this investment each year? At maturity? *That depends on the investment.*

- Is this investment appropriate and suitable for me? *That decision is based upon your risk tolerance and other factors after you have done your analysis.*

- What are the risks posed by this investment? How may I lose my money?

- How will I determine whether this investment has been successful?

Let's focus on those last three questions. With a stock mutual fund, there are several things to evaluate before you make a decision to buy. Let's list them in a careful order:

- How much money do I wish to invest?

- What percentage of my total net worth does this amount represent?

- How is the rest of my net worth positioned in terms of liquidity, risk, and anticipated return?

- What portion of my annual total return should this investment represent?

- Does the investment have the *potential* to fulfill the purpose for which I would buy it?

- What are the optimistic, pessimistic, and average scenarios for this investment over the period during which I would hold it?

I'm sure by now you have said to yourself at least once, "Does anyone ask all these questions before he makes an investment?" Very few people do their homework to this extent, which is why so many people lose money when they invest. We're not done yet; we haven't identified all the potential risks that can cause our investment to underperform our expectations. Let's look at them.

- Am I buying at the right time? Where is the fund's price today relative to its [recent] history?

- What is the trend of the fund?

- What industry sectors does the fund emphasize?

- What major changes have been made in the portfolio in recent months?

- Has the fund had recent management changes?

- How does the fund's net after-fees historic performance measure up against its peers?

If you attempt to sift through any of the thousands upon thousands of stock mutual funds available today, you're going to be hard-pressed to answer these questions. There are resources available to help you in your screening process, but all the information you will find is literally "old news." People assume that you can project a trend indefinitely into the future, and that a fund that has done well in the past will continue to so. Unfortunately, that kind of thinking will usually get you into trouble, especially with sector funds that focus on specific industries. That's why I like to begin with "top-down analysis" and try to identify sectors or investment categories that are cheap because they have been in a downtrend. I want to buy them before they begin their next major move upward. You are more likely to buy value that way and avoid chasing overpriced securities.

Most of us hate to lose money. Most people don't like to feel as if they have made a mistake. Some are concerned that their friends and associates might think less of them or even make fun of them for having made a bad investment.

You often hear people talk about their successful investments, but very few talk about their losers. Just about anyone who has invested has experienced losses at one time or another.

When I lose money in an investment, it means that my method of selecting investments failed me. Since I manage money professionally, it also means that I have lost money for some of my clients. I often put my own money into a particular investment to get some experience in it before I offer it to my clients. By taking a position ahead of my clients, I often find that the stock has not yet bottomed, and I experience a loss in the stock before I ever put my clients into it.

It's time to talk about the two primary methods you should use to evaluate an investment.

Chapter Fifteen

Analyzing Investments

To answer the questions we posed in the previous chapter, you should perform two types of analysis. They are called *fundamental analysis* and *technical analysis*. You cannot use both techniques on some investments. Finding a company with great prospects requires fundamental analysis. Determining that its stock is trading for less than it is worth requires technical analysis. Very few financial professionals besides myself apply *both* methods. It's rare, and it is an important part of the *Wealth Creation Way*. Since there are several good books available today on one method or the other, I will not spend a lot of time describing either.

Please note that the following discussion applies primarily to common stocks. You can perform a limited form of *fundamental* analysis on mutual funds, but they are not at all susceptible to *technical* analysis. The reason for this is simple; most technical analysis requires *volume* (the number of shares traded per time period). Mutual funds have no volume.

ETFs, on the other hand, are about as susceptible to fundamental analysis as mutual funds, but because they have volume, you can use technical analysis.

Some stocks are not good candidates for fundamental analysis. It's difficult to evaluate the prospects of a company faced with bankruptcy, for example. A stock's trading range can also be significant; "penny" stocks can make tremendous percentage gains and losses relative to stocks selling for more than a dollar per share. However, stocks trading below $10 a share demonstrate different technical characteristics than more expensive stocks. Remember these exceptions when you start to apply the analysis.

• • •

Fundamental Analysis

The job of the fundamental analysts—which includes most of the analysts on Wall Street—is to find hidden value. Value is always the name of the game, because in the long run it is the perceived value of an investment that has the greatest effect on its price. When you are looking for value, you are looking for a profitable company that has not been "noticed" by the Wall Street crowd. It may surprise you to learn that it's not too hard for a company to go unnoticed, for most analysts are focused on the same few stocks.

What do we mean by value? A value stock is selling for less than it is worth based upon the company's fundamentals. Perhaps its earnings give the stock a very favorable price/earnings (P/E) ratio that has gone unnoticed. Perhaps the company has just been granted a patent that will open up a new and profitable division of the company. Perhaps the company is flush with cash and its directors are debating whether to repurchase the company's shares because they are cheap or go on the acquisition trail and buy other businesses. Maybe the company is brand new and has a fabulous product that will sweep the earth—the way Google did.

On the flip side, a company's stock can be overpriced because some of its negatives have gone unnoticed. Perhaps that new patent was not granted, or the company is about to be embroiled in a major lawsuit. Perhaps the company has lost one of its biggest customers, or an important product line is about to become obsolete. Overvalued stocks can be candidates for "short selling" or put buying, but those strategies can be risky.

Markets have cycles that are affected by government intervention in the markets and the economy. Also, the business cycle has not been repealed. A new company begins a business cycle at the bottom of the chart. The company moves up the growth cycle as it meets ever-increasing demand. Then the company peaks at the top of the cycle when it has become a "mature" company. At that point the product has been "commoditized"; competitors have stepped in to sell less expensive or better versions of the product. Finally, the company declines as the product becomes obsolete.

Today there are relatively few one-product companies; companies and corporations prolong their existence by diversifying into additional product lines, buying and selling other companies, and performing ongoing R&D in order to improve their existing products and create new ones. It is perhaps for this reason that the United States government saw fit to treat the corporation like an individual, though one with a potentially unlimited lifespan.

This is what fundamental analysis is all about. You may be searching for value stocks or overpriced stocks; in either event you're trying to find valuable information that the rest of the crowd doesn't know about. That is a short- and intermediate-term approach to investing. Investing for the long term has largely gone out of fashion, except perhaps for institutional investors like insurance companies and pension plans. Your broker does not want to sell you a stock that you plan to pass on to your grandchildren. Very few of us can predict that a particular stock will beat the averages for the long term. Warren Buffet is one of the few, and he has built a highly successful career out of seeking undervalued investments that will produce significant returns over the long term.

• • •

Getting Started in Fundamental Analysis

How do you get started in fundamental analysis? You do your homework. You look at the company from numerous points of view. I used to start with the P/E ratio, but that indicator can be highly misleading. You need to focus on the financials and look at the debt to equity ratio, the liquidity ratios, the cash flow numbers, return on equity and the more recent EBITDA (earnings before interest, taxes, depreciation, and amortization). These numbers will give you a feel for where the company is today, and by looking at the history you can get some sense of the trends.

You also have to get a feel for the company's cost of doing business. Are a significant portion of revenues plowed back into the company for R&D? What are the profit margins like for the various products or services the company sells? Are there new and potentially profitable products in the company's pipeline? Is the company developing new markets for its products? Of course, you must never forget about the company's cost of compliance with government regulations. I have seen both small and large businesses fail because they could not afford to comply with all the regulations.

Another step in fundamental analysis involves looking at the company's "team." For this information you probably have to rely on either the annual reports or the company's 10K reports. Do you find competent, experienced people who have been in place for a while? Has the company seen recent turnover in the executive suite? How much of the company's stock do the insiders hold, and are they buying or selling? Unless you find something glaring here, you will probably find your time to be better spent elsewhere because that sort of information may not be actionable.

All of this probably sounds pretty difficult, but it really isn't. With practice you will quickly discover what you need to know. I recommend that you spend some time on the CNBC Web site and the business section of the MSNBC Web site. On the latter you will see the stock scouter, a valuable introduction to how the professionals do fundamental analysis. Remember that you are looking for value and that you want to buy stocks that are currently out of favor.

How will you know when you have found a good investment? You want to find an undervalued company with great prospects, one that is currently trading for less than it is worth. What you think a stock is worth is your target price, the price at which you will sell. I don't buy stocks that I will need to hold onto for several years to see a meaningful gain; I buy stocks that I expect to have recently bottomed and are now in a new uptrend. Stocks like that have a better chance of making money for you both in the short-term and the long-term.

Once you have found a stock you want to buy, you should decide how long you plan to hold it. Do you expect the stock to perform like a "clear-the-bases" homerun, or is this a "single" or "double"? Do you expect the stock to return to a previous high? If so, you should predict how long that will take. In fundamental analysis, you look at how the company's actions will make investors feel the stock is more valuable. You should also consider some of the factors external to the company, such as the performance of the stock market, the trends in interest rates and inflation, and the company's competitors.

As I mentioned previously, I am definitely not a "momentum trader." Momentum traders can get themselves into all sorts of trouble when they buy something simply because it is going up. Nothing goes straight up forever (or straight down, for that matter). Whenever I have bought something because it was going up, it usually goes flat or begins to decline.

I prefer to buy value, especially when it has traded off from its momentum highs and has moved lower temporarily. How do you know the decline is temporary? With fundamental analysis, you don't. You may know everything there is to know about that company, but the one thing you cannot deal with is the market itself. The market is a great humbler, and all of us find ourselves deflated and brought down to earth once in a while. That's one of my gripes about the financial media; they always want to give you a reason why a stock did what it did. There is never a reason, because the market will do what the market is going to do. Or, as my assistant used to say, "There are more buyers than sellers."

Here are some useful screens you can use as part of your fundamental analysis:

- Stocks that are selling beneath their book value

- Companies that are awash in cash, where their liquidation value is greater than their current share price

- High-dividend or high-yield stocks

- Stocks achieving fifty-two-week highs or lows

- Stocks selling at a discount to their book value

You can use any of the dozens of stock search tools on the Internet to find these stocks. Some of them are literally "selling at a discount."

Closed-end mutual funds and ETF's usually sell at a premium or a discount to their net asset value. Fundamental analysis can help you to see a few stocks according to the screens you design yourself. You can search thousands of stocks, funds, and ETFs in seconds using these tools.

In chapter eighteen I will describe the "stocks at a discount" program I have used effectively to pick stocks for more than a dozen years. Like everything I do to find good investments, this program utilizes both fundamental and technical analysis.

• • •

Technical Analysis

The other major school of investment analysis is called technical analysis. Most of its proponents largely ignore the fundamental data we have just discussed and focus on an investment's trends, patterns, and trading history. Much of technical analysis involves identifying repeating patterns. Millions of man-hours have been devoted to creating statistical tools to help identify, isolate, and predict these patterns. The advent of high-speed computing has been a boon to technical analysts, freeing them from endless redrawing of charts and number crunching.

There are many books available written by proponents of technical analysis. Most of them have developed their own methodologies and, they claim, become successful at investing because their methodology works. Some of the methods are valid; others are not. Some of these people have developed a software package you can buy that may help you make your investment decisions.

I have purchased more than one "black box" software package and numerous books on investment analysis. After reading and studying the books and applying the recommendations of the "black box" software, I have found many ways to lose money quickly.

Technical analysis uses innumerable hypotheses and suspected correlations to try to "fit" trading data into models. Some stocks are believed to trade relative to the business cycle; some commodities, particularly agricultural crops, are thought to be priced in accordance with the seasons. When harvest is at hand, prices should be the lowest of the year and so on. There are supposed inverse correlations, where if one thing rises another should fall. One inverse correlation is the U.S dollar versus a foreign currency like the euro.

One example of non-agricultural seasonality has to do with the S&P 500. Since 1990 the three best months of S&P 500 performance have been October through December; the worst four are June through September. Is this information useful in predicting future performance? To answer that question we must find out why that particular history came to be. Was it a continuation of a previous trend? Was it the traders' response to a perceived pattern? We often hear that the stock market rises right at year end because of institutional managers' "window dressing." If a money manager is buying, he is usually selling at the same time. Why would that type of activity caused the stock market to rise?

• • •

A Valid Premise

Both types of analysis require a basic premise upon which a hypothesis is based. a premise is an underlying principle that explains why things happen. For example, one premise of fundamental analysis is that when a company's earnings increase, its stock price will rise. This notion is true enough of the time to be a useful premise.

We tend to call things premises when they aren't. Technical analysts like to think that patterns will repeat simply because they are found in the historical record, but that is not true. On Wall Street they say, "Sell in May and go away," but that is drawn from statistics and is not a valid premise. Most of the time we are merely guessing, and we haven't found a true, repeatable pattern.

What is a valid premise? In fundamental analysis, it has a high correlation with a predictable outcome. In technical analysis, it accurately reflects the (human) psychology behind the trends. There are hundreds of statistical tools you can use to try to determine where the market is headed, but most of them are not predictive because they do not have a valid premise.

• • •

Stochastics and Elliott Wave Analysis

I spent a great deal of time and money studying stochastics from its inventor, George Lane, only to find out after several years of study that stochastics has no valid premise. In fact, some traders use stochastics in exactly the reverse of George's approach, and they have more success that way than I did. George taught that stochastics indicate when something is "overbought" or "oversold" and due for a change of trend. Most of the people I read about today look at an overbought condition as an indication that that market is going to *continue* to move in the same direction rather than change.

The only technical method I have found that *may* actually have a valid premise is the Elliott wave theory. Ralph Elliott came up with his theory in the later part of his life and didn't live long enough to refine it and profit from it. Because it had not been well publicized by the time of his death, the theory languished for decades until finally it was resurrected by Robert Prechter, who formed the company Elliott Wave International.

Elliott wave theory attempts to quantify human behavior. Ralph Elliott believed that all trends had either three or five components and that economic, market, social, and others types of activity fitted the various patterns he developed. I think that Elliott believed that all activity can be fitted into one of his patterns at any point in time. However, more modern research on Elliott waves seems to reveal that waves are where you find them, and that any short-term pattern does not need to sit neatly into a longer-term pattern but can stand on its own. This belief both simplifies Elliott wave analysis and may help to invalidate its fundamental premise. You can perform Elliott wave analysis on many investment charts and never identify any Elliott patterns. Does this mean that the Elliott wave method is wrong because it does not apply universally? Possibly. I still find it more useful than the others I have worked with.

There may be other methods with valid premises. Methods come and go because markets change. Stocks no longer trade in one-eighth increments. Commissions are lower than ever before. Technology continues to change the way markets work and the way traders think. All these changes can invalidate any analytical method.

All we are trying to do is to predict the future based upon the past. Elliott wave analysis does that for us. If the pattern it has derived from its analysis of the investment is valid, we gain a high-probability prediction of how that investment will trade in the future.

As they say, you only have to be right 51 percent of the time to make money, as long as you make as much with your winners as you lose with your losers. Put another way, if you let your gains run and cut your losses short, you don't even have to be right 50 percent of the time. Elliott wave analysis is simply the best pattern recognition tool I have ever found, but you have to interpret the patterns correctly.

A few years ago I found the *Refined Elliott Trader* (RET) software, which is available at www.elliottician.com. I like to use Elliott wave analysis to find whatever types of patterns may exist in the investments I want to work with. Sometimes there are no recognizable patterns or at least none that the software can find. If the fundamentals look good, I may buy an investment even if the technicals do not confirm. There are times when technical analysis may not contribute to the decision-making process.

For example, in recent years my fundamental analysis has focused on real estate, energy, base metals, precious metals, and interest rates. It has become clear to me that certain situations were developing that could make for very profitable investments.

I then applied technical analysis to find what might be the best-performing investments in each sector. The combination of fundamental and technical analysis has gotten us in and out of the real estate sector with significant profits. In 2007 and 2008, we had money in energy, precious metals, and other commodities, all of which we purchased in a regular brokerage account. These sectors were "the place to be" for three years, and my clients profited handsomely. During that time Elliott wave analysis was not much help.

• • •

Combining Fundamental and Technical Analysis

Unprecedented changes are taking place. The world is never the same from one day to the next; however, these changes are significant and far-reaching in their impact.

For example, global warming and climate change are real. What I have read indicates that it really doesn't matter whether humans have contributed to global warming or not. Many scientists believe that warming has already occurred to make the trend irreversible for the foreseeable future. Global warming affects all of us, and its negative effects will accelerate in the near future.

Next, I am quite convinced from my research that we are not only close to or at peak oil but that we are also close to or at peak coal. Even though there are still tremendous amounts of oil and coal in the ground waiting to be extracted and consumed, our ability to produce those commodities has reached or soon will reach an all-time peak. Our society is completely dependent upon cheap sources of energy; from now on their availability will only decrease. Since no meaningful alternatives have become commercially viable, what lies ahead is a future of shortages and economic disruption.

These two events, and others just as important, are "paradigm shifts." The way in which the human race relates to this planet will never be the same. Since fundamental and technical analysis enable us to project current trends into the future, we have to ask ourselves whether either method will apply in a world that has changed so dramatically.

I believe they will. Every investment decision we make looks into the future. We should be able to apply our analytical methods in much the same way as we always have. We will, however, need to be more *visionary* than ever before. For example, how will your investments respond if oil goes to $300 a barrel? How will they respond if a cheap substitute is found for gasoline and diesel oil?

• • •

How much risk should you take?

I manage a small amount of money for my clients. My clients don't expect me to beat the markets year after year. That's not my strategy. In recent years stock markets all over the world have moved to all-time highs, and some have gone "exponential." People get used to that type of performance and don't realize that a good year makes the next year more challenging for a fund manager.

I do not lure clients by showing them my past performance. I talk about the future in very realistic terms. I differentiate myself by doing exactly what a stockbroker does not do; I look at the big issues and try to figure out what effect they will have on my clients' money. That tends to make me rather unpopular when the stock market is "hot" and my clients are not in it. That happens whenever I believe the risks are too great to justify the potential reward. My job involves the future; I try to learn and heed the lessons of history and not repeat the mistakes of the past.

In recent years investors have become more interested in superstar fund managers and specialty products like hedge funds than in mutual funds. Should you follow the herd and send your life savings to someone with a great track record? No. Chasing performance usually turns out pretty poorly, especially with the higher-risk programs and funds.

I prefer to take less risk. My goal is to do better than the combined effects of inflation, taxes, and the declining dollar. Will we miss markets that rise 60 percent in one year, as China did in 2007? We may. Investing is an art and a science. No one really knows which investments are going to do well. That's the primary argument in favor of diversification; if you put enough money into enough investments you're bound to find one or two that will soar in value. I diversify my clients' investments, but I try to diversify *only* into sectors and investments that are expected to rise in value in the near future.

If you are asking yourself, "Doesn't everyone in the financial services industry do that?" you need to reread chapter four. Most financial professionals are salespeople with little knowledge of investments and markets. Professional money managers, on average, underperform their target market year after year. Only those who focus on specific sectors can significantly outperform the overall market.

Can you achieve above-average returns even though you are taking on less-than-average risk? I have proven that you can for almost fifteen years. My worst year as manager was 1994 when my average client lost about 1.5 percent; the best years saw average returns in excess of 18 percent.

You can pay commissions to a broker, you can hire a professional manager, or you can do it yourself. It's your money. It's up to you to make it grow.

Let's take a look at why some strategies that used to make people very wealthy may not work as well in the future.

Chapter Sixteen

"This Time It's Different"

Are there rules in investing that *always* apply? Were there any in the past?

What's different about the world today, and how do those differences affect your money?

One of the problems environmentalists face is that they see their job as preserving the *status quo,* though of course in nature, change is the only constant. Unless you live in a place like Singapore, where the year-round temperature remains in a very narrow band in the low nineties and where it rains for about thirty minutes almost every afternoon, each day brings different weather in most parts of the world. *Weather* changes, weather *patterns* change, and *climate* changes. Preserving the *status quo* is impossible, partly because we do not even understand all the forces that create weather.

Human nature generally does not change, but *behavior* does. Our behavior is conditioned by our upbringing and our environment. The way we view the world as individuals is determined by our past experience.

Just as environmentalists are always trying to nail down a moving target, investors are always trying to find the ultimate trading methodology, the "system" that will enable them to produce profitable trades day after day, year after year. This is usually not possible, but in reality it would not be desirable or appropriate. Humans are competitive, and trading is one of the most competitive "games" in existence. The challenge is to stay ahead of the curve by constantly upgrading the tools of the trade.

I remember taking a stochastics course taught by George Lane, the self-proclaimed founder of stochastics. As I considered what he was teaching us, I realized several things about George and about stochastics:

- First, George taught us how to use stochastics to pick market tops and bottoms, but by the time I took the course the method was no longer accurate or successful in that role. Today, many who use stochastics take what George would consider a turning point and label it the point from which the stock or commodity has much further to go in the same direction.

- Second, analytical methods like stochastics come and go, just like any other technology. There is always something newer or better, something that takes advantage of newly available technology.

- Third, despite the power of his method, George recognized that other tools were needed in conjunction with stochastics to make trading decisions, which is why he was such a successful trader.

Moving back to the environmentalist analogy, environmental scientists are much like the blind men and the elephant; each sees only a piece of the puzzle and usually a small one at that. Anyone can visit glacier after glacier around the world, as I have, and see that it is in a major, long-term retreat. That evidence may indicate global warming, and it may indicate climate change. To try to move the planet back to some prior state—akin to doing a system restore to a safe point on a computer but on a global scale—is simply impossible unless we understand all the relationships involved, and we probably never will.

Time marches on, and it is not our privilege to re-create the past. All we can do is mimic it.

• • •

Developing an Investing Model

Most human economic activity tends to be cyclical in nature. We have daily cycles and seasonal cycles, both of which operate upon us without our notice. We then have the business cycle and other cycles that come into being as a reflection of human nature and behavior. Our needs and desires change with the seasons, the trends, and the fads. The demand for goods and services is determined both by how much money we had to spend and by how much of a desire for those goods has been created through promotion and advertising.

If we invest in *things,* such as metals or grains or pork bellies, we are subject to relatively simple supply and demand dynamics. Supply can be manipulated when governments offer subsidies and producers respond by emphasizing certain commodities over others. Some increases in demand are traceable solely to population increases, while others are due to new technologies, lower production costs, the enactment or repeal of tariffs, seasonal changes, changes in style and fashion, and much more. Governments can affect demand just as easily as they affect supply by restricting the importation or sale of certain products.

Investing in *stocks* and stock mutual funds adds more factors that must be evaluated in order to choose one particular stock over another. Some companies have mediocre products but terrific marketing; others have superior technologies but are unable to bring their products to market. Stocks are designed to be long-term investments, but stocks are often pounded on news or even rumors. Stocks trade primarily on investor sentiment; when sentiment changes the stock's trend will also change, regardless of whether the company continues to perform well. By definition, the performance of most stocks determines the trend of the market. "A rising tide raises all boats," and if the market is in a downtrend even those companies that are doing well can see their stock fall.

If you are trying to develop a model strategy for your investments, you either have to develop a sophisticated model that will incorporate all of these factors and more, or you will have to do what most people do, which is to *identify repeating events in the markets*. A fundamental analysts, for example, might look for stocks with P/E ratios less than six with rising earnings, dividends greater than the 3 percent per year, and a price-to-book value of less than two. Modern technology has facilitated such analysis for use by almost anyone with a computer.

A technical analyst can try to identify tops or bottoms or momentum or any of millions of possible combinations of technical indicators to try to make investing decisions. One popular strategy, for example, is to find stocks that trade in a range. You buy at the bottom of the range and sell at the top.

In other words, the "game" changes constantly, and the rules of the game change as well. The only real constants in investing seem to be fear and greed.

• • •

The Changing Playing Field

For over two centuries America symbolized a land of unlimited opportunity to the rest of the world. Our nation was blessed with abundant natural resources, both the renewable kind and the kind that can be depleted. Our government was designed to ensure that Americans would be free to pursue their dreams. Millions have done just that.

Perhaps the middle class did not originate in America, but it can be said that the middle class truly came into its own here. We had no nobility or aristocracy, but we did have a class of people who believed they could improve their circumstances. They applied their energy and their ingenuity and created a nation without parallel in the history of the world. Some became wealthy, and many were able to live comfortably. Americans enjoyed the highest standard of living the world had ever seen.

Today we don't even seem to care that our 5 percent of the world's population owns, according to some statistics, almost half the world's wealth and consumes well over a quarter of its natural resources. After all, we are Americans. Doesn't the rest of the world envy us and want to be like us?

We are so sure that the government will take care of us when we get old and decrepit that we don't think we have to save for retirement. In fact, most of us don't even save for a rainy day or prepare for anything out of the ordinary. I remember overhearing a conversation in Colorado Springs just after a snowstorm. A young man was describing how he had to drive a couple of hours in his four-wheel drive vehicle to bring pizzas to his family. Because of the storm they couldn't get out, and they kept little or no food in the house.

Even more frightening, the majority of people I meet in America today have decided that their current expenses are far more important than saving for the future, and they pay only the minimum each month on their growing debt. They use their homes as if they were ATMs, drawing out precious equity and converting it into things they don't really need. In many respects we're not "keeping up with the Joneses" anymore; we're just trying to keep up with our parents.

There is a disconnect here. On one hand we pride ourselves in our independence and freedom, while on the other hand we gladly enslave ourselves to big government in order to get benefits that we hope will be paid by others. Most of the people I talk to believe that the United States is a democracy; they are almost always disappointed when I remind them of Benjamin Franklin's comment about this being a republic.

Here's another disconnect. We have been told that we can have the American Dream for ourselves because America is the mightiest and wealthiest nation on earth. What we don't realize is that all prosperous nations thrive because of their, industry and over the past thirty years we have been converting America from an industrial giant to a service economy. Service economies don't create wealth, they deplete it. The availability of cheap consumer goods to the middle class is sustained by foreign labor and the likes of Wal-Mart, rather than by the improving circumstances of the working class.

When we were acquiring all these rights, privileges, and expectations, we were not overly concerned about the destruction of our environment, the depletion of our natural resources, the concentration of wealth in the hands of a very few, or our generally declining standard of living. We failed to notice that the mighty U.S. dollar had lost more than 95 percent of its value while under the "protection" of the organization charged with its preservation. We didn't see that we were shifting rapidly from the world's wealthiest nation to the world's greatest debtor nation. We didn't care that high-paying jobs were being sent overseas and those of us who were finding replacement jobs were getting paid 30 percent less than before.

We deliberately blinded ourselves to the truth because we were told that we had rights and that our government would always be there to take care of us. We didn't understand that a people who are completely dependent upon their rulers are little more than slaves because they have willingly sacrificed their own happiness and that of their children and grandchildren.

That is the state in which we find ourselves today, and this is why it *is* different this time. Here are some important facts:

Debt. No nation in the history of the world has ever owed so much per capita to so many, and our debt has been incurred at every level from the individual to the federal government. Increasing our tax rate to 100 percent would not be enough to solve the problem. The only solution is to inflate the dollar, which means completing its destruction. The destruction of the dollar is almost inevitable. How do we prepare for it?

Peak oil. North America passed the peak of its oil discovery more than thirty years ago. Now, as had been predicted, our oil production is in terminal decline. All the improvements in technology for finding and extracting oil have failed to reverse our decline in production. The world is rapidly increasing its consumption of oil, and the supply is rapidly decreasing. The rest of the world will soon hit its all-time peak of production—if it has not already done so. What do we do then, and how do we prepare when alternative technologies are too little, too late?

Pensions and retirement. Governments and corporations are abandoning pension plan obligations like a man fleeing a burning house. Slowly and painfully an awareness is coming that an unfunded indeterminate liability cannot be serviced when the currency is in terminal decline and the demand for increased benefits is unrelenting. The currently popular substitute for a retirement plan funded and guaranteed by government (Social Security) is a plan funded by employers and employees and guaranteed by no one (401(k)s). How do retirees decide on spending their dwindling funds, when they know the money has to last the rest of their lives?

Housing bubble. Residential real estate in many parts of the world and particularly in parts of the U.S. was on a tear for forty years in the longest-running bull market in anything the world has ever seen. This bull market was fed by easy money and relaxed standards, to the point that a homeless person could qualify for a mortgage if he or she asked. Affordability dwindled to its lowest level in history, and we finally found the pin that burst this bubble. What will *you* do when you are "under water" in your mortgages?

Market volatility. Three generations after the Great Depression, we have finally forgotten the horror which resulted from the 89 percent decline in the stock market between 1929 and 1933, which makes it high time for history to repeat itself. The stage was set in late 2007; just as the housing market is full of people who cannot afford the homes they occupy, the stock market was full of companies whose earnings were overstated. Even if those earnings were genuine, the major indexes were still at more than twice the level at which they found themselves during "normal" times. How will we fare when the stock market falls to more appropriate levels? We are just beginning to find out.

Hydrocarbons as fuel and feedstocks. The Industrial Revolution was built upon cheap access to every raw material man might conceivably use, especially energy. Having wasted in fifty years the stored energy it took the earth eons to create, we are also faced with the first-ever loss of commercial deposits of certain essential minerals and raw materials. What will happen when we can no longer manufacture a third of the products we depend upon every day?

Water. Don't look now, but a pint of water in the supermarket costs much more than a pint of gasoline at your local gas station. Aquifers are being depleted, desertification is overcoming much of Northern Africa, and glaciers are shrinking. Cities, counties, farmlands, and more will dry up and blow away in the future as the demand for water outstrips the supply. Who will you hold responsible when you must abandon your home because there is no more city water available?

Shortages. We are entering a world of shortages. We are in a time when much of the third world is elbowing its way into the "first world." There are enough resources on earth today to support a population of perhaps two billion in the style to which Americans have become accustomed. What happens to the additional three billion who feel they have the same right to that lifestyle as we do? And what about the remaining two billion who are completely without hope?

The American "Empire." The end of the Cold War was supposed to bring a "peace dividend," a reallocation of defense spending to much-needed domestic and social spending so that we could eliminate poverty and disease. In Ronald Reagan's day, Americans enjoyed a great deal more respect throughout the world than we do now. Today we are widely hated because of what we represent. We have great enemies because we have created them, and now we spend more on defense than at any time in history. American sons and daughters put their lives on the line every day in more than 120 countries around the world as imperial America pretends it is "the world's last great superpower." What will we do when someone without a country and with no ethnic or religious or political affiliation—an Oklahoma City bomber, for instance—detonates a nuclear weapon or even a cheaper, smaller "dirty bomb" in a major American city? How will we respond?

Stronger central government. The American republic may have run its course. All three branches of government have abandoned the principles upon which they were founded and grabbed power from the others. We can point to the specific "failures to anticipate" on the part of the Founding Fathers and laugh at the things we can see which they, if they were so bright, should have seen as well. What we *cannot* do is reverse the trend of two centuries of stronger and stronger central government dominating every aspect of our lives, creating myriad regulations and punishing us for infractions of rules we never heard of. George Washington was indeed a Federalist, and he had to be; but he also counseled us wisely to avoid entangling alliances, and he was humble enough to retire after two terms and two unanimous elections.

Republics and freedom. The Founding Fathers hoped and prayed that future generations would be as wise as they and as diligent in preserving the liberties so many had fought and died to win. To our shame and sorrow, the Founding Fathers' hopes were in vain. Once we discovered we could "vote ourselves funds from the public purse" our grand Republic was finished.

Those are sobering considerations. Now let's contrast them with what I believe is the true great hope for our world. I hope that Ray Kurzweil[11] is right that we are just at the beginning of the technological revolution. I hope that as the development of technology moves into its exponential growth phase, we will find solutions to all sorts of problems and we will wonder why we hadn't thought of them before.

It *is* different this time. The rules have changed; the playing field is not level. The pendulum has swung far from morality and honesty. The U.S. dollar, upon which all our hopes ride, will shortly disappear, as will the short-lived American "middle class."

How will *you* adapt to these changes?

Chapter Seventeen

Keeping ahead of Inflation

The single greatest investment risk we face is failing to make the purchasing power of our money increase in real terms.

As we have already mentioned, if you are to be successful in managing your personal finances, your investments need to overcome three primary obstacles: *taxes, inflation,* and the *declining dollar.* All three are moving targets, and most of the time we only know whether we have been successful after the fact, when we've had a chance to measure the performance of our investments against the facts of taxes, inflation, and the declining dollar.

Of these three factors, the declining dollar is the most nebulous and the hardest to get our hands around. This is because we have to ask ourselves "The dollar declined—relative to what?" We may not recognize the effects of the dollar's decline until we want to *spend* the money we have invested for the future.

One of the reasons why I like retirement accounts so very much is that I usually don't have to be concerned about taxes until the client starts taking money out. In the case of a Roth IRA, I don't have to worry about them at all, because the account has been funded with after-tax dollars and all withdrawals come out tax free.

This leaves inflation as being the most easily identifiable of the three factors, though not the easiest to quantify. If we know the real rate of inflation, we can use it as a target that we must exceed if our money is to grow.

• • •

The Consumer Price Index Argument

Since so very few people understand and utilize the correct definition of inflation ("falling money"), let's use the widely accepted definition ("rising prices") for the purposes of this chapter. However, the distinction is critical. The first has to do with the rate of money creation relative to the growth of the economy—which helps to explain why most people do not understand it. The other has to do with an issue we face every day: are we paying more for what we buy? Unfortunately, both calculations—growth of the money supply versus economic growth and changes in the consumer price index—are subject to significant manipulation by the government.

Let me try to give you a feel for how price inflation works. By the widely held definition, which I will refer to from now on as the CPI definition, we experience inflation when prices rise. What makes prices rise? Economics 101 says that rising prices are caused by increased demand or decreased supply. This is only a partial definition, one that applies to raw materials and inventories on hand when companies have pricing power. Pricing power means that a company can raise its prices by choice, not because they are forced to by rising costs. If you remember the late seventies, we heard a lot about "inflation profits." These profits came about because companies were free to raise prices on existing inventory. They had raised their prices because their costs had increased, but in the meantime they were able to profit from what they already had on hand.

The rest of the reason why prices rise has to do with increasing costs. When raw materials prices rise, rents increase, or labor rates rise; in order to remain profitable the manufacturer must pass those increased costs on to its customers. There are also the costs of R&D, engineering and design, and actual production costs, and these can increase for various reasons. Some manufacturing firms, for example, have relatively low labor costs because their manufacturing is largely automated, but their R&D and equipment costs can be very high.

The consumer price index is the responsibility of the U.S. Department of Labor, Bureau of Labor Statistics, www.bls.gov. Here's what they say about the CPI:

> The CPI represents changes in prices of all goods and services purchased for consumption by urban households. User fees (such as water and sewer service) and sales and excise taxes paid by the consumer are also included. Income taxes and investment items (like stocks, bonds, and life insurance) are not included.

> There are CPI indexes for the entire U.S., the four census regions, and twenty-six local areas. Indexes are also available for two population groups: all urban consumers (CPI-U) and urban wage earners and clerical workers (CPI-W). [13]

Prices for the goods and services used to calculate the CPI are collected in 87 urban areas throughout the country and from about 23,000 retail and service establishments. Data on rents are collected from about 50,000 landlords or tenants. The weight for an item is derived from reported expenditures on that item as estimated by the Consumer Expenditure Survey. Prices are taken throughout the month.[14] Here's where it becomes important:

> As the most widely used measure of inflation, the CPI is an indicator of the effectiveness of government policy . . .

The CPI and its components are used to adjust other economic series for price change and to translate the series into inflation-free dollars.

Over 2 million workers are covered by collective bargaining agreements which tie wages to the CPI. The index affects the income of almost 80 million people as a result of statutory action: 47.8 million Social Security beneficiaries, about 4.1 million military and Federal civil service retirees and survivors, and about 22.4 million food stamp recipients . . . Since 1985, the CPI has been used to adjust the Federal income tax structure to prevent inflation-induced increases in taxes.[15]

In other words, the CPI does two things; it tells the government how well or poorly they're doing (as "an indicator of the effectiveness of government policy"), and it determines how much of an increase, if any, millions of people will receive to help keep them up with inflation. For both purposes, it is obviously in the government's best interest to report CPI figures as low as possible.

The CPI is very important in many aspects of our economy and our government. Therefore, even though I believe it is the wrong indicator, it is important to understand how the numbers are created and how they are used. The CPI numbers we see from our government generally understate the rate of inflation. Why? Let's look at another portion of the definition of the CPI from the BLS Web site:

"Traditionally, the CPI was considered an upper bound on a cost-of-living index in that the CPI did not reflect the changes in consumption patterns that consumers make in response to changes in relative prices.

"Since January 1999, a geometric mean formula has been used to calculate most basic indexes within the CPI; this formula allows for a modest amount of substitution within item categories as relative price changes.

" . . . The . . . geometric mean formula, though, does not account for consumer substitution taking place between CPI item categories. For example, pork and beef are two separate CPI item categories. If the price of pork increases while the price of beef does not, consumers might shift away from pork to beef. The C-CPI-U is designed to account for this type of consumer substitution between CPI item categories. In this example, the C-CPI-U would rise, but not by as much as an index that was based on fixed purchase patterns."[16]

"With the geometric mean formula in place to account for consumer substitution within item categories, and the C-CPI-U designed to account for consumer substitution between item categories, any remaining substitution bias would be quite small." [17]

I'm not particularly concerned about the use of a geometric mean, but I'm *very* concerned with the way our government decides that consumers have made substitutions. The pork and beef substitution mentioned in the example above is a good one. Think about your own personal consumption. How likely are you, observing that the price of steak has risen in the grocery store, to shift to pork instead? Over the long term you might make such a substitution. I believe, but cannot prove, that American consumer tastes are determined more by issues of health and quality than they are of price.

This may not be a reliable example, but if price or cost were such a vital component in our decisions, why are so many of us consuming so many meals in restaurants when we could save money by eating at home?

I am concerned that the CPI is flawed regarding substitution and productivity. The productivity argument is that a worker's productivity increases just because the clock speed of his computer increases. Once the technology reaches a certain point, the computer is able to function at roughly the same speed that we do, which means that further increases in computer speed will provide only minor, if any, increases in productivity. Yes, the ability to "crunch" larger and larger amounts of data can make us more productive; however, I feel that real productivity must be measured in more and broader terms. For example, we may have access to better computer-generated analyses of more data, but does our ability to make good decisions increase with the availability and quality of data?

Buying a faster computer or obtaining a faster Internet connection may or may not increase your personal productivity. Likewise, just because advances in technology make computers faster and more powerful does not mean that we spend any less on them; we tend to buy the newer and better machine for about the same amount of money we paid for the old one. Your experience may be different, but in my business over twenty years I have seen a decline in the prices paid for my computers followed by an increase, until today I am paying about as much for a new machine as I paid for a much smaller one twenty years ago.

The substitution and productivity arguments are flawed in other ways as well. People who like BMWs may switch to other models of luxury cars, but generally they are not going to downgrade their vehicle because prices have risen. You probably won't trade in your Cadillac for a Chevrolet or your Accord or Camry for a Geo Metro. Instead, we adjust. We find a way to purchase what we want.

• • •

Inflation's Impact upon Families

The price of "starter homes" has risen significantly over the past fifty years. You could buy one of the early tract houses in Levittown, New York, in the 1950s for about $7–8,000. Today, a similar but brand-new "starter home" can sell for up to $225,000. That's an average annual price increase of roughly 7.1 percent; 7.1 percent is significantly greater than the average rate of inflation acknowledged by the government over the past fifty years. Wages have not increased at a rate of 7.1 percent per year either.

You might think of inflation as the additional sacrifice required today to purchase that "starter home" above and beyond the sacrifice necessary to purchase it in the 1950s. If you recall, back in the forties and fifties it was not yet uncommon for the wedding couple to receive their first home as a gift from parents and relatives. The invention and heavy promotion of mortgages allowed the price of homes to rise dramatically, and people's habits changed from thrift and saving to borrowing and spending. That trend continues today, to the extent that Americans now have a negative net savings rate; we spend more than we earn year after year.

The Industrial Revolution preceded the rise of personal debt, but it likewise contributed to the possibility of higher prices. In England, children lived and suffered under appalling conditions in factories and mills, working very long hours in what was ordinarily a very unhealthy environment. Through their efforts, as through slavery in the British Empire and the United States, the cost of producing consumer goods was reduced, but that cost was borne in other ways. When children could bring in more income than it cost to raise and feed them, and families became larger and similar demand for those cheaper consumer goods mushroomed.

In the United States, it was the daughters of rural families who were initially recruited to work in the cotton mills who made significant contributions to their family's income. Working for wages away from one's own home or town was a new concept, and it changed the face of the world. It accelerated a massive movement from rural areas to the industrialized cities.

Once it became an established practice for the children to leave home and find employment, it was only a short step to the development of a consumer economy. The production of low-cost goods was the driver, but it was marketing and advertising that stimulated consumer demand. It took about a century for the cost of living to increase enough to compel mothers to enter the workforce. Consumer goods that had never existed before gradually got moved from the "want" category to the "need" category. In order to maintain the family's standard of living, it was necessary to generate more income, especially once child-labor laws excluded children from most forms of employment.

Unfortunately, consumer prices continued to rise, and over the long term that sounded the death knell for the American ethic of savings and thrift. Today, even with both spouses working, many American families are heavily in debt and will not have enough money to retire.

• • •

What causes inflation?

In the previous several paragraphs, I have described events without precedent in human history. These events caused Americans to fundamentally and permanently change the way they live. My question is this: in the face of such changes, can any government-generated index of economic activity be considered reliable? Even if we could fix what I feel are fundamental flaws in the calculation of CPI, we still would not have a reliable indicator of the actual rate of inflation in the United States.

According to the inflation calculator on the BLS Web site, it costs $21,045.66 in 2007 to purchase what $1,000.00 would have bought in 1913, the year in which the Federal Reserve was created by

Congress to do one thing, to preserve the value of the U.S. dollar. Under the protection of the Federal Reserve, the once-mighty dollar has lost 95.25 percent of its value.

Is this a meaningful number? Well, ninety-plus years is a long time to look at anything. Let's break that down into the annual increases in our cost of living. If you had put $1000 in the bank in 1913 and paid no taxes, you would've had to earn 3.294 percent per year for your money to grow to $21,045.66 in 2007. Now, 3.294 percent doesn't necessarily sound like an awful lot to earn each year; it is less than the average performance of the stock market, but it is more than the average savings or certificate of deposit rates available throughout that same period of time. Most people who had money to set aside put it in the bank rather than the stock market. Today in this country there are hundreds of billions of dollars in non-interest-bearing bank accounts, a practice that goes back decades.

Assume that 3.294 percent was a meaningful and accurate number. The next question would have to be what caused the increases. Why do we have to pay twenty-one times as much for things as our great-grandparents did?

We immediately look beyond in the consumer to the producer, for to a great extent it is the producer and the seller who set prices in the marketplace. What we discover is a "vicious circle" of increases that force other increases. In order to remain profitable, the manufacturer must pass along cost increases to the consumer. We don't think about that very much, but it is a particularly important issue today as we are faced with the prospect of running out of of certain natural resources.

Will we be able to find appropriate substitutes so that the government can use those substitutes in its CPI calculations? Since the beginning of the industrial revolution, technological advances have enabled infinite substitutions, along with a seemingly infinite increase in the availability and variety of consumer goods. One of the greatest examples of all is the substitution of plastics—petroleum-based chemicals—for wood, coal, fabric, and metal. Technology and substitutions are responsible for almost everything that we have today. It was a great substitution when oil was $.10 a barrel and drove whalers out of business. Now that the daily consumption of oil has begun to exceed its daily production, we are ready for the next great substitution; unfortunately, nothing has yet appeared to take the place of oil.

Raw materials are one of the sources of rising costs. As raw materials costs increase, consumer prices increase. What about labor? Would there be any pay raises unless there was inflation? Prior to the Industrial Revolution, people were paid based upon their profession or trade. Pay raises would accompany promotions and would not be given otherwise. The rise of modern industry only increased the number of social strata; it did not advocate pay increases for identical performance. In fact, industry always tries to *reduce* its costs so as to increase its profits, and pay cuts were the rule when management could make unilateral decisions. Only inflation in terms of increased prices would justify a pay raise, and most of the time that pay raise would have to be demanded. That's the primary reason why labor needed to become organized, to avoid exploitation by the owners.

Increases in manufacturing costs would be the next driver of price inflation. We all recognize that technology has dramatically reduced the costs of production, to the extent that with many products there is more value in the intellectual capital than there is in the materials and production. No signs of inflation there; in that regard, technology has made life *less* expensive.

Up until now, we have come up short in our search for the drivers of increased consumer prices. Only the increased costs of raw materials along with the "keeping up with the Joneses" mentality of consumer demand can account for price increases at the store. Let's add one more component, one that dramatically affects our cost of living. In all industrialized societies, government has become one of the greatest costs to the consumer. There are many reasons why this is the case, but let's focus on just two of them: the "legal" redistribution of assets and war.

• • •

The "Legal" Redistribution of Assets

Governments, regardless of their type, are never completely self-sustaining. The royal family in Great Britain may be the biggest single land holder in the British Isles, but their wealth alone surely could not sustain the British government. In most countries, governments meet their costs by some form(s) of taxation. There are certain governmental functions which we deem essential, and they all cost money. At one level or another, we expect our government to provide us with public safety (which includes protection of personal rights and defense from aggressors), highways, primary and secondary education, courts, embassies, and little else. Technology and industrialization have helped to bring about a massive expansion of government. Today most Americans believe that we need government to regulate telecommunications, commerce, food, drugs, education, housing, the interior, the environment and much more. These demands cry out for a bigger and bigger government, and big government has a big price tag.

A major and more recent demand on governments is the responsibility for the public welfare. Everything that government does must be authorized by the people through their legal representatives. That authorization must include taking from the people the anticipated costs of that government action. Therefore, the first and primary "legal" distribution of assets by government is the funding of the government by the people, for the government has no other source of revenue. Much of that revenue will be passed on to others, but much of it will be used to hire and pay government employees. Whatever benefit we may derive from our government, therefore, he has a cost that we must bear. By paying taxes we spend money that might otherwise have been utilized for our own personal gratification.

A strong argument can be made that much of what government does 1) is unnecessary, 2) is done inefficiently, 3) could be done better by the private sector, and 4) constitutes a drag on the economy. Funds that our government distributes as aid or welfare, both domestic and overseas, represent one of the largest categories of waste, for there is little or no control over how those funds are spent by the recipients, and therefore those funds are less likely to provide worthwhile economic stimulus. In other words, by means of reallocation and potential misallocation of funds, the government becomes a significant contributor to the cost of living. Doesn't it make sense that that increase to the cost of living must be reflected in the consumer price index?

• • •

War

Maintaining a large military force these days is terribly expensive, but fighting a war costs even more. The United States maintains military forces in approximately 125 countries all over the world. This is done at tremendous cost; our defense budget over the past fifty years has added greatly to the deficit and our national debt. The U.S. military establishment is the single largest consumer of energy in the world.

In war, equipment and materiel are destroyed and must be replaced; men (and women) are killed or wounded and likewise must be replaced. In general terms, each person who serves in the military forces is a drain on the national economy; if he or she were employed privately he could be a contributor to the economy.

When we employ industry to build weapons and military equipment, we are utilizing talent, industrial capacity, and scarce natural resources to create products that otherwise could be used by consumers in the private sector.

• • •

Comparing The Cost Of Living With The CPI

Clearly, the cost of government increases our cost of living. Can we claim that government expenditures also add to consumer-price increases? It is safe to say that every penny spent by government that could be better spent in the private sector is a penny of waste added to the CPI calculations.

Let's conclude this discussion by attempting to make a comparison. The cost of living is the dollar amount it takes to buy a certain "basket" of commodities, and those commodities can include food, clothing, shelter, and more. We say we have inflation when the dollar cost of that basket increases; we say we have deflation when that cost decreases. It is safe to say that the CPI is the rate of change of the cost of living. At least, that's the way it should be defined.

Money-supply Fluctuations

Now let's look at another way of determining changes in the cost of living. This one ignores consumer prices as a general rule and is primarily concerned with the supply of money. Money is a commodity. The value of money can fluctuate in the same way the value of corn or aluminum can fluctuate. Money, or currency, is not unique among commodities as a medium of exchange, but it is by far the most commonly used today. As we have discussed previously in these pages, the value of money relates directly to its purchasing power but is affected by its abundance or scarcity.

When a government takes upon itself the authority to create money or currency, we would like to believe that that government also takes upon itself the responsibility to preserve the integrity and value of that currency. Unfortunately, that is not the case, for governments throughout history have deliberately debased their currencies. Usually, currencies are debased by governments in order to "keep up appearances," to try to create the impression in the minds of the people that the currency—like the government behind it—is sound and stable.

Money is the only commodity that can be created by government decree. For this reason, it is vitally important that all who participate in that currency have the privilege and opportunity to determine whether its value is to be maintained or debased. When the currency is debased, its value falls relative to other commodities; it takes more money to purchase these commodities than it did previously. When there are too many dollars in circulation, the value of each is diminished.

How much money should be in circulation? The Federal Reserve makes that decision on a daily basis, but is there any relationship between the amount of money they create and the amount our economy needs without igniting inflation? Historically, as I mentioned previously, the amount of money in circulation was in direct proportion to the amount of gold and storage. Only when the currency is debased does a government have the opportunity to create money out of "thin air."

The United States dollar and its predecessors were frequently debased by the means mentioned above. There were moments in history when the expression "sound as any dollar" really meant something, for the dollar was redeemable in gold or silver or both. That ended in 1968, and we are unlikely to see it again during our lifetimes.

• • •

The Dollar Floats—and Sinks—Freely

Today the dollar is allowed to float freely among the world's currencies. Its value changes minute to minute against many of those currencies. Our government has decided on numerous occasions to increase the number of dollars available. This has been done, so the story goes, to avert a "crisis" of one sort or another. The Federal Reserve has seen fit to "add liquidity" to the markets when it looked as if traders and investors might push the markets down significantly. It happened in 1987 when the stock market crashed, and it happened more recently when Long-term Capital Management collapsed. In fact, the money supply has been deliberately expanded far in excess of the actual growth of the economy for many years now. This has been beneficial to the U.S. Government because it has facilitated the greatly increased spending demanded by Congress. When your spending greatly exceeds your income, it's always nice to have a printing press available to print money for you.

Does the general public perceive that there are too many dollars in the world? Does the rest of the world, which holds so many hundreds of billions of those dollars, feel that there are too many of them in circulation? The answer to both questions for now is *no,* but in the last couple of years a general decline of the U.S. dollar has set in. Though this decline cannot be solely attributed to loss of faith in the dollar, that loss of faith is a growing portion of the decline. Remember that every dollar in existence is a promise to pay, and someday it will be redeemed. If we were to allow the value of the dollar to remain strong, the sheer number of dollars in existence could enable the United States to be broken up and sold off to countries all over the world. The process has already begun, as foreigners redeem U.S. Treasury bonds and use the proceeds to buy American real estate and American industry.

• • •

CPI or Money Supply?

I conclude this discussion by asking a question: which measure more accurately determines the value of the U.S. dollar as a commodity, the CPI or the money supply? Our government claims it is the CPI, and there are many on Wall Street who defend that position. To me, the only aspect of that argument that holds water is the part about increased costs that come with increased scarcity of natural resources.

I believe that the best answer to this question is in the money-supply figures. We can accurately estimate the number of dollars that should be in circulation based upon the true growth of the economy as measured by GDP or some other measure. If we then compare the growth of the money supply to the growth of the GDP, we can tell whether there are too many or too few dollars in circulation. If there are too many—and everything I see convinces me that there are—our government is deliberately debasing a fiat currency.

Remember the "vicious circle." When retailers raise prices, buyers must demand wage increases to be able to pay the higher prices. Wages are a significant cost, and higher wages mean higher prices. If we could look at money supply from a historic point of view back to the beginning of the Industrial Revolution, we might get a much better idea of the amount of inflation we have already experienced and how much we ought to expect in the future—if present trends continue.

• • •

The Size of the Problem

If you are going to set money aside for any purpose, you need to make sure that that money grows. As long as we have inflation and taxes, the return on your money must surpass the combination of those two rates, or your purchasing power will decline year after year. Remember, *all* of your money must meet or surpass those rates, not just the portion of it that you choose to put at risk.

What's a good return for 2008 that *might* enable you to break even on the purchasing power of your money? Let's do a quick calculation. The best way to do it is to start with a target return and erode it with inflation, taxes, and the dollar decline. That way, the calculation looks like this:

* Target return   18 percent

- Inflation (my assumption, not the CPI figures)   (8 percent)

- Taxes, 25-percent tax bracket on the target return   (5 percent)

- Decline of the U.S. dollar relative to the euro   *(5 percent)*

- Net return on an 18-percent gain   **0.00 percent**

We can make a small upward adjustment to that net return because some CPI inflation is included in the decline of the dollar relative to foreign currencies; however, to be on the safe side and to break even you really ought to try to make more than 18 percent on your money this year. Will you do that? Only if the *average* return on all your assets (including IRAs) exceeds 18 percent. That's not very likely in a year when the housing market is falling apart, banks are paying nothing on checking accounts, the stock markets are in a topping formation, and oil companies have run out of oil to drill for.

Are these numbers extreme? Not at all. In fact, we have seen them several times in American history, most recently in the late 1970s. Since high inflation is generally bad for the stock market, if history repeats itself you won't be able to depend on the stock market to provide the returns you need to retain your purchasing power.

From the illustration above, you can see why I believe the dollar is being systematically destroyed. You can also see why President Richard Nixon declared inflation "out of control" when it exceeded 4 percent per year. Inflation is a devastating force that destroys everything in its path. There is an inverse correlation between the growth of the money supply as dictated by the Federal Reserve and the value of each dollar in existence. More dollars means that each dollar is worth less. It's almost like a zero-sum game. The inverse relationship would be more apparent if the Federal Reserve and the government were not trying very hard to conceal the truth.

• • •

How to Fight Inflation

What can you do? How can you possibly hope to keep ahead of inflation during periods of high inflation? The simple answer is that you can't. In order to obtain a return sufficient to conquer inflation, taxes, and the declining dollar, you would have to put all of your money at great risk at a time and in investments where such risks simply cannot be expected to do what we need them to do.

Let's complicate the problem a little. In the late 1970s interest rates at least approached the rate of inflation, though they never actually met or exceeded it. For a brief period of time we actually saw money-market funds paying double-digit yields. It's different today, however. The Federal Reserve has created enormous inflation, which is just even now working its way through the system and is about to have a huge impact on our lives, while at the same time they are lowering interest rates to unbelievably low levels.

Artificially low interest rates like those we are seeing today in government, municipal and corporate debt are devastating to those who derive much of their living from interest. In addition, foreigners holding trillions of dollars of U.S. debt cannot be happy as they see the value of their dollars erode against their own currency and receive a rate of interest that is far less than the rate of inflation. If the Federal Reserve wanted to punish the entire world for their foolishness in sustaining the United States dollar as the world's reserve currency, they could hardly have chosen a better way to do it.

What can you do? You can invest a portion of your investment funds into things that will rise in price during inflation. As prices rise you should profit, because the value of the things you have bought will "keep up."

There are other asset classes that are increasing in price not because of inflation but because of their increasing scarcity. When that scarcity is not yet factored into the price, you can buy very cheaply.

We can now make a short list of things you ought to look at now:

- Agricultural commodities–corn, wheat, soybeans, sugar, coffee, cocoa

- Base metals–zinc, aluminum, copper, lead

- Precious metals–gold, silver, platinum, palladium

- Foreign currencies–Australian dollars, Canadian dollars, euros

- Energy–oil, natural gas, coal

How would you invest in these things without opening a commodities account? Buy them in your regular stock brokerage account using the appropriate mutual funds, closed-end funds, ETFs, and stocks.

These days we can utilize leverage in certain mutual funds and ETFs without actually borrowing money to do so. These investments are leveraged by the fund manager, using an amount of debt specified in the prospectus. Such investments are dangerous because they can go against you as quickly as they go in your favor. Let's look at an example that is *only* an example, and not any kind of recommendation:

- Total investment portfolio $100,000

- Portion invested in savings, CDs, and fixed annuities $ 50,000

- Portion invested in commodities as described above $ 50,000

We will assume for this example that half of the $50,000 is invested in unleveraged assets and the remaining half ($25,000) is invested in leveraged assets.

- Target return   18 percent

- Return on Savings portion   5 percent

- Return on unleveraged investment portion   18 percent

- Return on leveraged portion 36 percent

Total return computation:	$50,000 at 5 percent = $2,500
	$25,000 at 18 percent = $4,500
	$25,000 at 36 percent = *$9,000*
Total Gain:	$17,000 or 17 percent

Would I use this strategy with my own money or my client's money? No. I am not willing to subject my clients' money or my own to that much risk. Even if I were not concerned about a leveraged fund going against me, the leveraged mutual funds must make extensive use of derivatives. Derivatives are the primary cause of the subprime mortgage crisis that has infected the entire world. They carry a significant level of risk in and of themselves, almost regardless of the way in which they are used.

I will occasionally place a small amount of my clients' money into a leveraged fund but never a significant portion such as the 25 percent illustrated above.

And what about other leveraged investments that have been used commonly in the past? Real estate is almost always purchased using leverage and until just a couple of years ago people seemed to do pretty well in earning above-average returns. That cycle has ended, and it may not begin again for years. Many investors use the margin available in their stock accounts to borrow as much as half of the purchase price of their investments. Since the U.S. stock market seems to be in the beginning stages of a trend reversal, changing from a lengthy uptrend to a strong correction that may persist for years, that strategy could produce significant losses.

Make sure that you have some of your money in investments that will go up in inflationary times. If you do so, you will help to preserve the purchasing power of some of your money but not all of it by any means. Even in the worst bear market, there are always stocks that are rising, and the tools I have described in these pages can help you to find them.

In the long run, all of us are victims of inflation, especially when we have deliberately brought it upon ourselves. Only governments benefit from it because they can pay their debts with a cheap currency.

Chapter Eighteen

How do you figure out what to buy?

We have come a long way. You now have a better understanding of investments and markets. I hope that by now you have developed a healthy skepticism for the hundreds of thousands who look at you as a commission—or a paycheck.

In this chapter we will address that all-important question of what you should invest in. I have read too many books that try to teach you a methodology or sell you their "black box" but don't give you any idea as to how you find things to buy. Here are some of the places you can find ideas:

- Print media, including the Wall Street Journal, Business Week, Forbes, Barron's, Fortune, the Financial Times, the Wall Street Digest, and many more. Perhaps the best of them is the weekly Economist.

- Print and/or electronic media, including any of the sixteen-thousand-plus financial newsletters currently available.

- Online services, including Yahoo! Finance, Bloomberg, MSNBC, thousands of mutual fund Web sites, and much, much more.

- Database services including Morningstar, Value Line, and others.

- The independent analytical services like Standard and Poor's, Moody's, Fitch, Weiss, and others.

- Financial "professionals" as defined previously.

- Subscription services with e-mail notifications of recommended trades.

These are just a few of the many sources of information available today. Each of them may or may not have any particular value; they may offer information that is incorrect, outdated, or based upon incorrect analyst opinions. Even if you make a career out of trading, you still have to narrow down the sources you rely on, or else you can spend your life doing research instead of trading.

Prior to the development of the Internet, you could find only a small fraction of the information available today. There are probably more people today trying to make themselves heard on the topic of financial advice than at any time in human history. Finding those who know what they are talking about is like shooting at a moving target.

• • •

How will you structure your assets?

By now you have evaluated your current financial situation and come up with some ideas about allocating your current investable funds as well as a portion of your disposable income. Most Americans ought to purchase some additional *life insurance,* a policy that you (or your spouse, which is a better idea) own outright, rather than the life insurance offered by your employer that is canceled when you change jobs or retire.

You may also have decided to establish separate *college funds* for your children, using either a Section 529 plan for each or perhaps the old standby of the UGMA or UTMA account for each of them.

An *emergency fund* should also be in your plans, and that will ordinarily utilize something very conservative and flexible like a money-market fund.

Next on the list, if you have additional discretionary income, you may wish to allocate it toward *a regular-investment account.* Though this account is designed to be long term, since it is not a retirement account the money is available to you without penalty for any purpose prior to age fifty-nine and a half.

Last but not least—and for most people this should be item one—you will probably want to *enhance your retirement* by supplementing Social Security and, if you have one, your 401(k). This can be done through a traditional or Roth IRA or what is called a non-qualified annuity.

• • •

What asset classes should you use?

With this information, you are now ready to select appropriate asset classes for each of these accounts or investment programs. You are not necessarily restricting yourself to one or two particular asset classes in each account, though that might not be a bad idea, but you are trying to narrow the scope of the research that you are going to have to do to come up with good investment ideas.

The investment vehicle you use has certain constraints on what you are allowed to purchase. Some retirement accounts can be very restrictive. For example, most 401(k)s available in the United States today will not allow you to trade stocks, options, or ETFs. Most 401(k)s offer a choice of about fifteen mutual funds. Your research is a lot easier when you only have fifteen investments to choose from. Unfortunately, at any given moment none of those choices may be good ones. Normally those fifteen choices will include several domestic-stock funds, several domestic-bond funds, a money-market fund, a total-return fund, and one or two international-equity funds.

Employer-sponsored 401(k) accounts are generally very restrictive regarding the asset classes available to you. Unfortunately, most Americans have most of their investment money in their 401(k), and it is there simply because it is something of a "forced savings" program. When it comes to selecting asset classes for the remainder of your investment and retirement funds, you will usually choose an account at a firm that specifically offers the asset classes you want.

If you want to trade options in an IRA, you should use a brokerage IRA account. Options have significantly greater profit potential than stocks, but most options strategies are not often available in an IRA account. Most IRA providers permit you to use only one options strategy, the covered-call strategy. That tends to be a very conservative strategy, one that is not particularly profitable over the long term. Why not use the more aggressive options strategy in your non-retirement brokerage account and swing for the fences with your stock picks in your IRA?

"Stocks at a Discount"

You might want to consider using my "Stocks at a Discount" program. In this program, most of your money is kept safe by being invested in the closed-end, high dividend-paying mutual funds you have purchased at a discount to their net asset value (NAV). Some of these funds have options available, meaning that you can employ a covered-call strategy with them. You then use the dividends and interest generated by these closed-end funds to purchase highly speculative, very inexpensive stocks, the ones that you hope will produce huge returns. If you use this strategy in an IRA, you don't have to worry about income taxation until you retire.

Section 529 Plans

If you are saving for your children's education, the Section 529 plan is available. Though I like the tax structure of the 529 plan, most of the plans I have seen do not offer a sufficiently broad range of investment choices. It doesn't matter how much money you save in taxes if you are not *making* any money. If you do not have profitable choices available, you've got the wrong plan. Don't confuse tax strategies and investments.[18]

The most flexible investment program

The most flexible program will be your regular brokerage account. It is also the one most directly and immediately taxable. I used to recommend an online broker for the trading portion of that account and a no-load family of mutual funds for the rest. More recently, I have begun to favor the single account approach utilizing a discount broker that offers its own extensive family of mutual funds. In such an account you can use all the sophisticated options and strategies you wish without restriction, as long as you comply with all the brokerage firm's financial requirements.

• • •

Finding and Choosing Your Investments

Let us say that you have decided to use a money-market fund both as your emergency fund and as the place for you to keep cash in your brokerage account and your IRA. Depending upon your tax bracket, you might want to use a tax-free money-market fund for both your emergency fund and your brokerage account; however, you cannot use a tax-free vehicle of any sort in any type of retirement account.

From this point on you need to have a *methodology* that you will utilize in making all of your investment decisions The first decision to make is whether it will be "top-down" management or "bottom-up" management on your part. This all comes down to how you go about formulating your opinions of the market: do you want to decide upon a market or an economic trend, or would you rather find a particular stock by using a series of screens? With the "top-down" approach, you decide that now is a good time to be buying gold, for example, or real estate, or Japanese technology stocks. You make those decisions because you feel that one currency will fall against another or that interest rates have risen as far as they are going to for now or that inflation is going to return with a vengeance and so on.

How would you arrive at such an opinion? You would have to consider several sources, not all of which are reliable. The same is true of analyzing an individual stock; you never really know whether the information is reliable or relevant, and even if it is you can never really tell what effect making such information more widely known will have on the stock's price.

Because the "top-down" approach is both time-consuming and expensive, it is mostly used by financial institutions rather than individual investors. Some large institutions publish this type of research, and if you can find a reliable source, this could be worthwhile to have. You and I simply cannot do all of the work ourselves. There are only so many investments that you can actively monitor at any given time. Identifying, evaluating and monitoring economic trends simply adds to your burden.

That's not to say that correctly identifying the underlying economic and political trends isn't important. You may recall the old cliché that "a rising tide raises all boats." You can buy a perfectly good investment at what appears to be a very good time for a reasonable price and still get blindsided by that trend or event you failed to predict.

• • •

Example: Government Interference

For example, on October 31, 2006, the Canadian government announced that they were going to close tax loopholes for corporate income trusts. This program had enabled certain Canadian companies to pass on their earnings as dividends tax free. Many people had purchased stocks of these companies in order to enjoy the higher dividends. Governments seem to be a lot like CEOs; if they are not stirring things up all the time, they do not feel like they are justifying their existence.

Few people saw this coming; most of the sources I read that had recommended Canadian dividend-paying stocks were still in. On that day the Toronto Stock Exchange fell more than 2 percent. The popular income trusts fell about 12 percent and months later had not recovered.

That was not the end of the story, however; a quick look at the charts of some of these trusts (AAV, PTH, PVX, and others) shows that they had begun to fall much earlier. Advantage Energy Fund (AAV) fell from a high of $14.56 on October 26 as low as $10.86 the day after the announcement, a decline of about 25 percent. However, it had actually peaked at a price of $21.30 per share, and it may have bottomed at a low of $9.75 during the week of January 5, 2007, a decline of about 54 percent. This decline correlates fairly well with the decline in natural gas. What the announcement did was to kill a possible recovery in the stock's price.

It is obvious that some investors knew enough to sell their shares back in January 2006. Note that trading volume (number of shares traded each day) "spiked" at the peak and did not spike again until the announcement.

● ● ●

The "Needle in a Haystack" Approach

This method has become extremely popular now that we have high-speed computers and high-speed Internet connections, as well as access to enormous amounts of data. Just as Google uses multiple parallel processors to be able to search massive amounts of information in infinitesimally small amounts of time, so investors and traders can "mine" huge databases to try to find the hidden gems. Using a fundamental approach, you can screen for earnings increases or price/earnings ratios or dividend yields or any number of factors or combinations of factors to create a "short list" of stocks or other investments that you want to investigate more thoroughly. Using these tools you can sift through thousands of potential investments in a matter of seconds, freeing you to do other things while selecting for you only those patterns that have the best potential.

Please take a look at Chart 6 in the center section, the Advantage Energy weekly chart.

Using a technical approach, you can search for certain types of patterns such as those we discuss in *Charts and Patterns* in the center photo section. Technical analysis even allows you to backtest your patterns to determine how successful your methodology would have been in the past. There are thousands of people who do exactly that when they look for investments these days. It's very much like panning for gold; every once in a while you come up with a nugget.

• • •

Creating Your Own "System"

I never let myself forget my competition. Most people this business do not believe that you can "time" the market, and therefore they don't even try. To keep my risk level as low as possible, I would rather be forced to wait for something to correct so that I can buy it cheaply rather than pursue a trend already in motion. I would rather have the comfort of having bought something for less than it is actually worth. Finally, I also like to focus on dividends. If the value of my investment declines after I purchase it, I will still get paid for owning it. For the same reason, it's nice to be able to sell options against your stocks to slightly reduce your risk and increase your income.

To invest you must have informed opinions based upon correct information. You form an opinion of the world as it currently exists and make a decision about which investment sectors might do well in the near future. Once I have done that "top-down" analysis, I choose specific stocks or commodities that I will focus on.

I am not a day trader. I want to buy investments that are going to increase my net worth. I base my decisions on my understanding of the world as I see it. Therefore, when I have formed my opinions based upon my fundamental research into the economy, the political environment, and the current state of the various markets I survey, I then look for specific investments in the categories I have decided to put money into.

I strongly recommend this approach. As you gain experience and confidence in your own ability to do research and to formulate useful opinions, you will learn how to filter all the information available to you You will be less prone to panic when the market goes against you for a few days because you have seeing the bigger picture. In fact, you may find as I do that you are taking action in anticipation of a change in trend. That can put you into the best of all worlds, because you will be selling when everyone else is buying and buying when everyone else is selling.

• • •

Putting Your Plan into Action

Lets put together a rough scenario of the world as we understand it today. Here are the assumptions under which I currently labor:

1. The U.S. stock market is, generally speaking, overpriced.

2. Technically, the S&P 500 double-topped in 2000 and 2007 (1552.87 in March 2000 and 1,576.09 in October 2007), creating the possibility that a very long-term bull market was ending.

3. The economies of China and India are growing at a tremendous rate, drawing to them natural resources of every type that decades earlier used to flow to the United States and Japan. This creates relative scarcity, which in some cases can turn into a permanent scarcity and even shortages, with negative effects on every economy dependent upon those commodities.

4. Crude-oil production peaked worldwide in the 1970s, and coal production is about to peak or may already have done so. This is a very inflationary, as shortages always are.

5. The deliberate creation of excessive amounts of dollars will "fill the inflation pipeline" with the effects of inflation to be felt for several years into the future.

6. The "housing bubble" is bursting, which will create a significant drag on the U.S. economy and have consequences for many economies around the world.

7. Interest rates are artificially low, stimulating investment and over-investment in areas that would ordinarily be ignored.

8. Government intervention in the markets is having a significant effect on numerous sectors of the economy, benefiting some and harming others.

This is part of my "worldview." These statements are not really opinions; rather, they are statements of belief drawn from factual evidence. They form the basis of my investment program. What do we do with a worldview like this? What kind of investments do we look for?

From the worldview to the specific investments:

1. An overpriced stock market is always a huge red flag. It indicates that any investment into that market is going to carry an additional burden of risk. I said that the residential real-estate market in the United States was overpriced and acted accordingly. In some areas of the country the residential real-estate market is still overpriced. Regardless, my worldview will not allow me to purchase real estate of any sort at this point in time. Why? That goes right back to Elliott wave analysis. What a trend has changed the previous trend will usually correct itself in a *Fibonacci retracement.* That means that that particular investment or market will give back at least 37.375 percent and as much to 62.625 percent of the entire gain in the previous bull market. Just the opposite is true of a declining market; it will correct to the upside by roughly the same amounts.

Whether Fibonacci relationships work or not, they serve as a very useful guideline when we are looking at reentering the previously "hot" market. Remember, there are three types of trends: rising, falling, and flat. When a rising market ends—and our technical analysis indicates that the trend has indeed been completed—it has less than a 33 percent chance of resuming before it has undergone a complete correction. Elliott always called for a correction in the opposite direction to the primary trend. When something goes flat, it's often hard to tell whether it has changed direction or not. It's always more difficult to make money that way.

2. There are double tops and triple tops and multiple tops, and sometimes we need to listen to what they are telling us. A double top, especially one of the size of that in the S&P between 2000 and 2007, clearly reduces the possibility of further gains in the S&P 500 over the next several years. From the moment of the double top, we need only look for confirmation of a change in trend to give us our signal to exit (or even go short).

3. There are many ramifications to what is happening in China today, not the least of which is the fact that natural resources are dwindling rapidly and their prices are rising dramatically because the world's largest third-world country is doing its best to move into the industrialized world. Several years ago I toured a recently-completed planned community of twenty-five million people. I have seen the kinds of resources required by that type of economic growth. It creates two problems for us and the United States; first, we are forced to pay higher prices for everything and second, we will be required to make massive technological changes in order to compensate for the increasing scarcity of resources upon which we depend.

Think about that. If we have an overpriced stock market, that means that stocks are more expensive than they should be and are not a good investment at this point. If prices rise because of the scarcity of basic commodities, companies possessing inventory can make "inventory profits" up until such time as they run out. After that they have to pass along price increases to their customers.

In general, the stock market does not like inflation because business profits are squeezed. If we are also required to make massive technological changes, that can only cause turmoil in the stock market. This is especially true when we are compelled to switch to new, unproven, untested, and in some cases nonexistent technologies, none of which may ever be profitable.

4. If oil becomes a scarce resource—and it has—we can expect its price to go up until such time as an inexpensive alternative is found—if ever. As of mid-2008, no reliable and less expensive alternatives exist, either for fuel or as industrial feedstock. Wouldn't that make oil a relatively safe bet with high-profit potential?

5. What investments that we can afford kept ahead of inflation the last time around, in the late seventies and early eighties? Back then it was real estate, energy, certain natural resources, and precious metals. We have more than ruled out both residential and commercial real estate for 2008, but what about the others?

6. Now that the housing bubble is bursting, who will be affected by the explosion? Certainly there are many companies to avoid at this moment, but are there also companies that can provide us with profits by shorting them?

7. Historically, most people have been hurt by low interest rates and particularly by artificially low interest rates. This is especially true in inflationary times such as we have right now. It is more difficult

than ever to obtain a positive real rate of return with very little risk, because the safe investments like bonds are paying a rate far below inflation and taxes as we have seen previously.

Is there a way to profit from low interest rates? Rates on government bonds today are much lower than they ought to be. This is good for our government because the cost of servicing our enormous national debt is much lower than it otherwise would be. One thing is certain: artificially low rates will not stay in place forever, particularly in an inflationary environment. Therefore, your best bet might be to bet against government bonds in anticipation of the essential "regression to the mean" that must come.

There is an inverse relationship between interest rates and bond prices: when interest rates rise, bond prices fall. When interest rates fall–and they cannot go much lower than they were in January 2009–bond prices rise. I call this the "seesaw" relationship. If you had been short U.S. government bonds in the late 1970s, you could have made a fortune because of that relationship. Interest rates rose dramatically and Treasury bond prices plummeted. By 1979 new thirty-year Treasury bonds were paying 13 percent, and the value of bonds issued years earlier had fallen dramatically.

Alternatively, might we be better off looking for interest rates on lower-rated securities that have remained high, or perhaps high yields linked to inflationary assets such as oil? Better still, what if we could find a high yield in a currency that was appreciating against the U.S. dollar?

8. You probably know many people who benefit from government intervention in the markets, whether it be from government subsidies to specific industries or government programs mandated by legislation or any of a number of different schemes. Wouldn't you love to be one of those people living in luxury in Manhattan who bought a piece of farmland with government financing and who accepts large payments from the government every year not to farm that land? There are opportunities, and they are not all that hard to find if you know where to look.

A program like this, properly designed and implemented, will enable you to "go with the flow." You will make the trend your friend and not try to carve out your own path through the wilderness. There are risks enough when you latch onto a trend early. Why would you want to subject yourself to all sorts of additional risks by striking out on your own?

• • •

Making the Actual Trades

Once you have gone through all this analysis, you are almost ready to place a trade. I say almost because you only want to trade when the time is right. Many times I have had to wait a day, a week, or a month for something to bottom before I bought it because I didn't want to pay too much. You will do the same.

Based upon the worldview and the decisions that flowed from it, let's create a real portfolio and discuss each of the recommendations. What follows are some of the positions my clients and I held in the first quarter of 2009.

1. Atlas Pipeline (APL)–Atlas is an energy play. It owns several companies and divisions and is involved in both the production and distribution of energy, primarily natural gas. Atlas declined 91% from its 2007 high of over $55 to its 2008 low of $4.68, dragged down by a sinking stock market and plummeting energy prices. Atlas pays a substantial dividend. We started buying it at around $16 and sold covered calls against our positions.

If you don't use covered calls you might want to use trailing stop orders against your APL shares. A trailing stop is an order you place which is GTC or "good-til-cancelled," and you specify a dollar amount as the trigger. With APL I might use a price of $.40. With that trailing stop loss order in place, when the price of APL falls $.40 from its most recent high since the order was placed your stock will be sold.

2. Market Vectors–Gold Miners ETF (GDX)–this ETF hasn't performed all that well in relation to gold or silver in recent months, but it trades like a stock, and it has options. GDX is like a precious-metals mutual fund such as the *Fidelity Select Gold Fund* (FSAGX), but it offers more flexibility. I usually sell covered calls against GDX.

3. Silver Strategic Resources, Inc. (SSRI)–this is a great way to own silver, all other things being equal. If you read what Ted Butler (find his opinions at www.investmentrarities.com) has to say about silver—and I believe his ideas are correct—silver is a classic case of a commodity in diminishing supply and increasing demand. The only thing preventing silver from going to the stratosphere is the immense "short" position held by a few traders.

SSRI recently became very inexpensive. While silver was falling from about $20 to $9, a decline of over 50%, SSRI fell from its peak of over $45 to $5.35, a decline of 88%. You could buy SLV (each share represents 1 ounce of silver; SLV has no options) or DBS (each share represents a fraction of a silver futures contract; DBS has options) but I prefer to buy the cheapest alternative, and at that moment SSRI was it.

4. Currency Share Australian Dollar / Canadian Dollar / Euro (FXA, FXC, and FXE)–these ETFs are the easiest and perhaps least expensive way to purchase foreign currencies and earn interest on them. As the dollar declines, you need someplace to put your money—this is one of them. There are several other currencies available, including the Swiss Franc—all of them have options. As with everything else, you have to buy them at the right time and you should enhance the yield and reduce your risk by selling covered call options.

5. Powershares WilderHill Clean Energy Portfolio (PBW)–this ETF tracks the WilderHill Clean Energy Index of companies that focus on green and renewable sources of energy. Like GDX, this is an easier way to invest in a certain sector. However, remember that this is an ETF and you can perform

technical analysis on it; be sure to buy and sell at optimal times. PBW also offers options. PBW still had not bottomed by late 2008; wait until it does.

6. GDF, EMD, MGB, JGT, MCB, CMK–these are all high-yield closed-end funds. Buy them at the right times, use trailing stops as appropriate, and sell them when they go to a premium over NAV. All of them plummeted in 2008 and we sold them; by early 2009 they were much more attractive. Watch out for high management fees; you can compare them at www.etfconnect.com.

7. AXU, CDE, CFW, CNQ, BHI, LMC, ROY–these are stocks of companies involved in energy and/or basic resources. All of them stand to profit from rising commodity prices. Buy them at the right moment and use options where they are available. This (commodities) is the only area where I am comfortable about "buying on the dips" because of the potential for an extended decline in the overall stock market. Use options or stop loss orders; we moved out of all these stocks in 2008 and are looking for them to bottom before moving back in. Watch the financials on these stocks; some may not have the staying power to weather an extended decline in commodity prices.

8. "Penny" stocks–I always hold one or more "penny" stocks, especially when I have purchased them with the proceeds of one of my high-yielding stocks or ETFs. Some of these stocks do not lend themselves very well to technical analysis because their prices have fallen almost to zero. I buy them because I love a bargain. When a company looks like it will someday become profitable (once again), I don't mind paying less than a penny a share for their stock.

Almost everything my clients and I recently held, except for insurance products like equity-index annuities, was on the list above. The only other notable exception was some regular no-load mutual funds involved in the commodities business.

Is this a non-diversified portfolio? It consists primarily of commodities. It excludes just about everything but energy, mining, precious metals, and foreign currencies. In that sense it is not well diversified. Remember that we are trying to make all of our assets perform well at the same time, not to invest in five different categories in the hope that at least two of them will be rising at any given time.

Let's look at it another way. What could cause some or all of this portfolio to fall and lose money? Here are some of the ways:

- 1. Inflation is conquered, and the dollar strengthens.

- 2. A cheap, abundant substitute is found for fossil fuels and put into immediate use worldwide.

- 3. Technology advances to the point where we no longer need certain commodities that today are become increasingly scarce.

What are the chances of any of those things happening? Slim to none.

Someday, when we have forced the inflation genie back into its bottle and have solved all the world's scarcity problems, I will look at the rest of the stock market and other non-inflation-oriented investments. I look forward to that day, and hope I won't be retired by then.

Chapter Nineteen

Trading and Investing

So far we have discussed *why* every American needs to be an investor. We have talked about the factors that make successful investing difficult and why financial professionals may or may not be of real help. By now you know how to establish a financial plan, how to set aside more money on a regular basis, and how money can grow if invested properly. We also talked about the nature of risk from a unique perspective.

We now arrive at the heart of this book. In this chapter we will pull together all that has been discussed previously and help you devise a strategy—or set of strategies—that you will implement, revise, and adjust to make them personal and effective.

I include trading in the chapter on investing because *trading is a subset of investing*. Trading is generally short term and is inappropriate for most people for reasons already mentioned. That said, each trade is an investment in its own right, and the rules for selecting trades are the same as those for selecting investments.

Most investors don't consider themselves traders. Many people believe that investments should be held onto indefinitely. They think that way because my industry encourages them to do just that. They also think that way because it makes it easier to manage their investment assets.

This book is about creating wealth. It is also about deserving better returns on your money. Intelligent investing takes work. This book will help you work more efficiently, but if you don't do the work properly you will not deserve good results—and you will probably not be successful.

If you are going to be a successful investor, you need to learn how to trade. That doesn't mean that you need to become a day trader; most day traders lose money because day trading is incredibly difficult under the best of circumstances. When I talk about trading, I am simply talking about selecting one investment out of a universe of investment choices. The initial selection is a trade because for some period of time it is a short-term transaction. Selling that investment is another trade. Purchasing a subsequent investment with the proceeds is a third, and so on.

I include those transactions in my definition of trading because the criteria for making investment decisions are almost universally the same. You want to buy something that will increase in value by a certain amount over a certain period of time. Or, if you are shorting an investment, you want it to decrease in value by a certain amount over a certain period of time. Shorting means that you borrow the investment (for example, one hundred shares of Microsoft) and sell it, expecting to buy it back at a lower price. Since this is an investment and carries risk, you want to make sure that the increase you receive exceeds the return available from a "risk-free" investment like U.S. Treasury T-bills.

The Wealth Creation Way goes further than that. I not only want my investments to outperform T-bills, but I want them to beat inflation and taxes. With the once-mighty U.S. dollar in "terminal decline," I also want my investments to offset the decline in the dollar, if any, during the period of time I hold them.

There is another side to this. You will never put all of your investment money into one investment—not if you are smart, anyway—but the investment(s) you chose to buy were selected from some universe of investments defined by you. You made conscious decisions about which groups of investments you would *not* investigate; you decided, for example, that you were not going to purchase stocks of countries outside North America or that you were going to avoid Chinese stocks or technology stocks or homebuilding stocks and so on. You also had to decide which sources of information you would or would not look at to assist you in making your investment decisions. These "top-down" decisions have greatly reduced the size of your "universe" of potential investments. None of us has time to review every possible investment; we can, however, let the technology work for us by establishing certain criteria and allowing the software to scan for investments meeting those criteria.

When you make an investment decision, you are saying that you believe this one investment will outperform everything else in your universe of potential investments, which is why you choose to buy it now. Considered in that light, that is a pretty heady decision. Very few of us are that confident in our own analytical abilities to be able to make that claim, and yet we continue to invest. Obviously, some middle ground must be found, some set of decision criteria that will enable you to invest profitably while managing your time and the risks you have taken on.

• • •

The Trader's Ten "You Have Tos"

You have to:

1. Pick your market (commodities, stocks, bonds, options, real estate, and so on).

2. Pick your time frame (short term, long term, or day trading).

3. Pick an amount of leverage. (How much can you lose and how quickly can you lose it?)

4. Pick an analytical method (technical or fundamental or a combination).

5. Choose your specific analytical tools. (There are literally dozens, with hundreds of minor variations.)

6. Pick your product. (You can buy stocks or their equivalents through ADRs, ETFs, single-stock futures, LEAPs, SPDRs, listed options, closed-end and open-end mutual funds, variable annuities, and more.)

7. Become a jack-of-all-trades and a master of one.

8. Educate yourself in the proper use of the tools you have chosen.

9. Practice, practice, practice.

10. Get good at it and be consistent in applying your method.

• • •

Psychology and Human Nature

Do you remember the leadership academy I discussed in chapter four? There was one session of self-evaluation that I found very interesting. It was the one in which we divided ourselves into four basic groups: controllers, promoters, analysts, and sensitives. There are people in each of those groups who trade stocks and other investments. Members of the various groups approach trading in different ways. The controllers assume that they can bend the markets to their will; the promoters believe they can influence the price of an investment just by "talking it up" among their friends and associates. The analysts think there is an analytical method that will enable them to trade successfully, and the sensitives only buy stocks that they feel good about.

These are oversimplifications, but they make a good point; we all like to think that we have control over our circumstances. Unfortunately, we don't. The markets will do what the markets will do. Unless you have a very large sum of money at your disposal and know exactly what you are doing, you are probably not going to be able to control any particular market for any length of time. All the investments you will ever make have at least a 50 percent chance of being worth less than what you paid for them during the time you own them. How will you respond to the condition of your investments as they fluctuate in price over time? Will you be a "nervous Nellie," taking time from your busy day to check the markets and watch your stocks closely? Will you go into denial when your portfolio's value has fallen and refuse to take appropriate and timely action? Will you respond to that common human tendency to think you're a genius when the market is up and to panic when it's down? Will you question your own judgment and second-guess yourself day after day?

We do these things because we are human. To be successful in trading and investing, you have to develop a mindset that will keep you from sabotaging your own efforts and turning your investment capital into commissions and losses.

For example, let's say that you purchased one hundred shares of Exxon Mobil (XOM) at $75.50 on February 6, 2007. This is the type of trade both an Elliottician and a momentum trader might make.

The Elliottician might think that XOM was going to complete its fifth wave up above its wave-three high of $79.00, while the momentum trader would be expecting the upward trend to continue. Another trader might want to "buy on the dips."

Please take a look at Chart 7 in the color section, the Exxon Mobil daily chart.

You purchased Exxon Mobil as an investment, intending to hold on to it indefinitely. After all, we are using more oil, and finding less oil every day. XOM is very profitable, pays a nice dividend, and has recently declined in price to make the stock more of a bargain. We expect the stock to find support at about $70.50, the low point of its recent decline. We will not be particularly concerned if the stock falls below its ten-day (blue) and twenty-day (red) moving averages, but we will be a little concerned if it moves beneath its fifty-day (green). The stochastics indicate that the stock can continue its upward trend for some time to come.

Notice what happens almost immediately after we make our purchase at $75.50. XOM falls the entire next day and bottoms close to the opening price on the third day. XOM declared a $.32 dividend on February 7, but that event ordinarily has very little effect on the stock price. We know that almost all of our investments will be worth less than what we paid for them at some point in time, so we are not particularly concerned—yet. Did we set a stop loss for this trade? Did we simply set a "mental stop" instead so that we would be forced to make a decision instead of letting the technology protect us from our own emotions? If we did set a stop, what was the price? In other words, at what price would we be feeling enough pain to compel us to sell this stock?

That last question is difficult to answer. Perhaps a good rule of thumb would be to allow our time frame to determine the dollar amount between our purchase price and our stop loss price. XOM is one of the world's largest companies; it is not considered a growth company, nor is it a particularly speculative stock. All other things being equal, it is probably safe to assume that as long as the price of oil is rising, the price of Exxon Mobil will also rise. This is *not* a particularly good assumption if Exxon Mobil is unable to find new sources of relatively inexpensive oil. Since Exxon Mobil pays a regular dividend, we know that the stock price will be adjusted downward each time a dividend is declared.

Since we anticipated holding Exxon Mobil indefinitely, we might set a stop 10 percent away from our purchase price. Because Exxon Mobil is not a particularly volatile stock, a 10 percent stop loss is as good as any. In this instance, that would mean setting our stop-loss price at $67.95 per share. Note that this price is below short-term support, which suits our purposes just fine—or so we think at the time.

Moving ahead a week or so, we see XOM trading up to and slightly above our purchase price, and we feel that we made a good purchase decision—so far. The moving averages, which were inverted when we made our purchase (the fifty-day moving average was above the ten-day and twenty-day moving averages), seem to be realigning themselves, but the stochastics are troubling. What we need to notice here is the formation of a top, which is confirmed on February 14, 2007. XOM did not advance much above our purchase price and soon fell off again. This time it broke all three moving averages, and we should begin to be concerned. The stochastics continue to fall, and we're really not sure what to expect.

On February 26, 2007, we breathe a sigh of relief as XOM trades, albeit briefly, at a new high since we made our purchase. It did fail to break conclusively above that resistance level, and that it a concern. However, we are just as likely to think that "the third time is the charm" and that we can expect Exxon Mobil to resume its uptrend in the next day or so. Besides, why would we think about selling something when "it's just beginning to make money for us"?

February 27, 2007, is the day with that long red candlestick. At the end of that day, if we are watching closely, we realize that XOM has *not* fallen all the way to its support level, neither has it fallen all the way to our stop loss price. It *has,* however, taken some money out of our pocket, and we are inclined to wonder why that happened instead of the move we expected.

If you watched XOM closely, you could second-guess yourself a dozen times on February 27, which could open the door to making a dozen bad decisions. Since stocks rarely fall decisively on one day and resume their uptrend in the next, it is entirely reasonable to expect XOM to continue to slide over the next several days. If you are looking at XOM after the close on February 27, you know this, but will you decide to take action? After all, crude oil traded up today, while XOM "fell out of bed."

Let's conclude our example by moving ahead to the end of the chart. Notice that XOM slid four more days before rebounding and that it broke its support line *and* triggered our stop. Again, if we have been watching XOM closely, we have been on an emotional roller coaster. If we had placed a stop-loss order, we would have been stopped out with about a 10 percent loss. Our judgment and analytical ability have been called into question time after time, and at this moment, now that the stock is rebounding, we are missing out on the rebound and not looking very smart.

This is just a partial description of how an XOM buyer might feel at different points along the way. I hope you get a feel from it as to what most people would think and what they would be concerned about, because it is emotions that make profitable trading—and, for that matter, profitable *investing*—difficult if not impossible. Many of us are subject to the "herd" mentality, which might more accurately be described as the "lemming" mentality, for we tend to run in a pack right over the cliff. The classic recent example occurred in the late 1990s with the dot.com bubble. We like to believe that there is "safety in numbers." After all, we tell ourselves, it *was* recommended by someone we saw on CNBC, or *all* of our friends bought it at the same time we did. When an investment goes against us, few of us are willing to admit that we have been wrong and take the pain of a small loss before it becomes a larger loss.

In short, human nature leads us to sabotage our own analytical skills and talents. Without strong self-discipline, the likelihood of success is small, particularly in a day when there are thousands of people arrayed against you—and most of them have more experience, better training, and access to better technology than you do.

That "iron discipline" must also extend to what you read and listen to. On any day of the year, you can find the complete spectrum of opinions on just about any investment you might want to make. Add to that your own analysis of the investment, and it can be very difficult to make a decision. Once you have created your method, your approach to analyzing potential investments, if your method works to your satisfaction you must not allow others to second-guess you. As you trade, you will discover your own personal strengths and weaknesses, including your analytical abilities and your behavioral traits. You will discover how much capital you are really willing to commit to an investment and your level of risk tolerance. Just about any personality type can develop and implement a successful trading methodology; the trick is to find one that works for you.

Now that we have discussed the fundamentals of trading and investing and have some understanding of the nature of risk, let's look at some specific methods and techniques that you might want to adapt to your own purposes.

• • •

Trading

Trading is a form of investing. Both require us to invest our own money and perform our own analysis. The primary difference between the two is that if we actively trade we don't intend to hold a particular stock or security for an extended period of time. However, we still must allocate a certain portion of our investable funds for the purposes of trading. In other words, our "trading fund" *is* an investment. In fact, it is very much like a mutual fund, but instead of hiring a professional manager we are managing it ourselves. We ordinarily set certain expectations for the return on that investment.

Trading is more difficult than investing. You have to be right about many things, and you have to be right consistently if you are to be successful at trading. You have to be right over a time frame that leaves no room for stocks that decide to move sideways.

Let's look at a practical example:

You allocate $10,000.00 to an account designated for trading, particularly short-term trading. In your first trade, you invest half of your allocation or $5,000.00 into a particular stock. That stock then rises 20 percent, and (ignoring commissions) your $5,000.00 has now grown to $6,000.00.

The first thing we have to look at is what the overall effect of that trade has been on our money. If the remaining $5,000.00 allocated to trading has been sitting in cash, its return is only the T-bill rates or the money-market rates currently in effect. Assuming that our trade made its 20 percent in one month and that money-market rates are 4 percent, here's how the numbers work out:

1. Allocated $10,000.00

2. Trade 1 $5,000.00

3. Cash $5,000.00

After one month:

1. Trade 1 $6,000.00 gain of 20 percent

2. Cash $5,016.67 4 percent annualized for one month

3. Total value $11,016.67 or a gain of 10.17 percent

That's not bad. Suppose, however, that the $5,000.00 that remained in cash in our first example had been invested in something that proceeded to *lose* 10 percent. Here's how the numbers work out now:

Allocated $10,000.00

1. Trade 1 $ 5,000.00

2. Trade 2 $ 5,000.00

After one month:

1. Trade 1 $6,000.00   gain of 20 percent

2. Trade 2 $4,500.00   10 percent loss in one month

3. Total value $10,500.00   or a gain of 5 percent

This is all reasonably intuitive. It would be very nice if we could simply extrapolate a 5 percent gain in one month indefinitely into the future, but we can't. There are several subjective issues we need to think about as we ponder our next move.

Assume we kept all of our money in cash for the second month and just watched the markets. If the stock we had purchased in Trade 1 continues to rise after we sold it, we can say that we made a mistake in selling it with "only" a 20 percent profit. If 20 percent was our original target, we did just fine and can't complain about money that we left on the table. We can question our strategy of simply selling the stock when it achieves a certain percentage gain. It might have been more appropriate to set a trailing stop, if this is a security that permits that type of order. With an appropriate stop-limit order, we could have remained in the stock indefinitely as long as its price continued to rise. We would only have been taken out once the stock fell enough to trigger our stop.

On the other hand, if Trade 2 had rebounded after we took a loss on it and risen beyond our original purchase price, we would have felt foolish at having "dumped" it.

As I mentioned previously, you must have a system, the right methods, and sufficient discipline to maintain the system in accordance the rules you have established. There's nothing wrong with taking profits when they reach 20 percent or taking losses when they reach 10 percent. In fact, with such a strategy, you don't even have to be right 50 percent of the time to make money. We all strive to be right more than 50 percent of the time, and once you factor in slippage[19], commissions, and other transaction costs, you begin to understand why that 50-percent number is so important. Just because we have established a stop-loss position does not mean that we will be filled at that price. If the stock is falling rapidly we can get filled at a lower price. If we have set a stop-limit order, we might not get filled at all.

Establishing a strategy that works for you is something that takes time. Fortunately, there are numerous software packages that enable us to test strategies on paper without putting any of our own money at risk. We do this through "back testing," which shows how much money we would have made or lost by pursuing a particular strategy. Most strategies have no valid premise but are based upon statistical studies. This means, among other things, that a strategy that works well in back testing may never work in real life.

I have found that trading can be as much a matter of luck as anything else. I trade options more than stocks, and I sell options rather than buy options, because I don't have to be right about the exact tops and bottoms of anything. Many people prefer the actual day-to-day trading of stocks, and a small percentage of them are actually successful.

In the 1990s many people, particularly those who had been laid off, were attracted to what we call "day trading." The technology was available to trade almost anywhere one had access to a computer and the Internet, though when day trading first began to be popular, Internet trading was not yet available. In those days you could do some of your analysis on the computer, but you still might have to phone in your trades.

Why were people attracted to day trading? They had time on their hands. For some it was time stolen from their employer; others were trying to turn their 401(k) to riches. The suddenly unemployed had money to invest, either from their severance package or from their regular salary. Trading commissions and brokerage fees had been slashed with the advent of discount brokers and, later, Internet brokers.

None of this, of course, meant that anyone would be able to be more successful in trading than he would have been in any other period of history. There simply were more people available with more tools at their disposal who were willing to watch their hard-earned money go down the drain. As is so often the case with gambling, day trading produced its own crop of "addicts," people whose habits resulted in divorce, loss of their home, loss of other personal possessions, and, in some cases, even crime.

Once the market began to turn down in earnest early in 2000, even those few day traders who had been successful up to that point began to struggle. It's just too difficult to anticipate very short-term fluctuations in value. With all the tools at my disposal, I rarely day trade; the odds are simply not in my favor.

Having said that, let's look at a meaningful form of trading. This type of trading is not the one where you are looking to eke out an additional twelve cents; rather, we're looking at potential investments we expect to hold for a relatively short period of time and from which we hope to receive a return within a predicted range. In this type of trading, we have a timeframe in mind. We're interested primarily in the increase (or the decrease, if we are selling short) in value of that particular security. Dividends are usually of little concern to us. We might use options exclusively, or we might use them to hedge or to enhance the trading position.

• • •

Stock Trading

The simplest example is a stock that you expect to rise in value. Since I like beaten-down stocks, let's look at one that has fallen out of favor. Since Microsoft is such a popular issue and a company so many of us love to hate, let's use it for an example. Please take a look at Chart 8 in the color section, the Microsoft monthly chart.

On August 23, 2006, Microsoft (MSFT) was selling in a range between $25.52 and $25.95. We all think we know lots of things about Microsoft. The conventional wisdom is that this company is a "cash cow," one that generates huge amounts of cash it can either distribute to its shareholders, perform research and development, or use to purchase other companies. Fundamentally, the company looks sound and stable. It holds a near-monopoly position in its market, having bought out or suppressed most of its competition. The company is a household name, and most people believe it is a growth stock and therefore a candidate for trading.

Those who hold to the conventional wisdom, however, were disappointed for about six years. Microsoft peaked in the last week of December 1999 at $53.25 per share. By the end of the next year, it had fallen as low as $17.87, down 66 percent. Since then it has remained "dead money," trading between that low and a 2001 high of $33.81. The only exception is the short-lived "breakout" in late 2007.

Still, there have been a few opportunities for trading along the way. At the end of April, 2006, Microsoft broke out of a slow and gentle uptrend and dropped overnight from $27.25 to $24.00. That's a gap, and many traders will tell you that gaps are usually "filled," meaning that the stock will trade in the range between the high and low of the gap. Microsoft did just that, and within three months it had "closed the gap."

How would you trade the gap? Of course, hindsight is twenty/twenty, but there are several fairly simple ways to trade gaps. The first thing you need to know when something gaps down like Microsoft did is whether the initial low of the gap is the low or whether there will be further selling that will further depress the price of the stock. After the gap occurs, the first thing you do is review the fundamentals. See whether anything significant has changed in the company's financial structure, markets, products, patents, and so on. A gap of this sort means that the company's P/E ratio has just improved, making it something of a bargain—all other things being equal.

Now consider the new, lower stock prices and corresponding new, lower P/E ratio in comparison with Microsoft's industry peers, technology stocks in general, and the average P/E ratio of all industrial stocks. We must make a subjective judgment as to whether the market will like the new price enough to buy the stock. After all, the stock is still in its narrow trading range of six years, but it has now broken out of a trend. Such breaks are almost always significant.

Now let's assume that we have decided that there may be additional selling in Microsoft. We figure that investors and traders may be scared off from the stock for a while, and there is always a possibility that the gap occurred for reasons as yet not publicly disclosed. We can initiate a trade at this point. What we might do is issue a simple *buy-stop* order and buy the stock when it has traded above a certain price above the initial low of the gap. That way, if there is to be further selling, we simply will not be filled.

The second way to approach this is to use a *trailing stop*. We believe that Microsoft has now become a bargain because it has gapped down, and we're willing to invest in it as soon as it turns up again. We don't know how far it will fall, and a trailing stop will enable us to capture the first upward movement. Trailing stops must be set carefully to be effective; otherwise, we can simply catch a slight rebound prior to the next wave down.

In both cases we would have a *target price*. Once we had made our purchase, we would establish a limit order at which we would sell our shares and take our profit. The obvious price at which to take our profit would be the point at which the gap was filled. In this case the gap would be filled at $26.94, and it would probably be safe to set our limit order at $27.00.

Let's see how these two different orders would have worked. If we had set a buy stop at a price like fifty cents above the initial gap down, we would have placed an order to buy at about $24.60. We would probably have been filled on July 27 when Microsoft just touched our price. In this instance we could have used a *stop-market* order, meaning that our purchase would be made at the next available price, and we might have gotten the stock for slightly less than $24.60. That's hindsight, however. We might have been a little bit uncomfortable with any fill price in that range because that happened to be the high of the day. In fact, as you can see from the chart, Microsoft did not manage to move above $24.60 in any meaningful way until three weeks later when it *gapped* up on August 18. (A gap occurs when something does not trade during the current period in any of the previous period's range.) From that point on, we would have been in a profitable trade, and it would have been prudent to protect our profits. More on that later.

The trailing stop, properly placed, would have been more successful but only if we had actively managed the trade on a day to day basis. Microsoft proceeded to fall another $3.00, and of course we would have loved to catch the bottom. If we had looked at a weekly chart we might have gotten a clue as to where the bottom might be, because in March of 2004 Microsoft bottomed at $21.32. In June of 2003 Microsoft had bottomed at $20.96. I'm not convinced that support and resistance last that long, but with a stock like Microsoft it is entirely possible.

If we were actually fishing for $21.50 or so, we could have used a $.75 trailing stop to make our purchase, but it would not have worked. On two occasions prior to bottoming, Microsoft rose more than seventy-five cents in a week or less. Even a $1.00 stop would have failed us in the second of those two occasions.

Where do we set the stops? With any relatively volatile stock like MSFT, we need to place our stops carefully. The initial gap was about $2.50; we could have set our stop at half that and still had a potentially profitable trade. In hindsight, that was the perfect number; we would have been filled at around $1.25 above the low of $21.46, or at $22.71. When the stock then hit $26.00, we would have a profit of $3.29, or 14 percent. That assumes, of course, that we used no additional stop loss trades, and that takes some courage.

Additional technical analysis might have helped. The methods I would've used here include Fibonacci retracement, stochastics, and Elliott wave. As it turned out, the Refined Elliott Trader software gave us a better answer.

How do we make these subjective judgments without the benefit of hindsight? Traders may claim to rely on "gut feel," "instinct," or "intuition," but those are little more than luck.

I usually don't trade gaps such as the one described above in the discussion about Microsoft, but I certainly enjoy them when a position I hold gaps up, as did DKHR a couple of years ago. DKHR was a stock I found on *Yahoo! Finance*. It was obviously an undervalued situation, and I liked it enough to recommend it to my clients. We had an average cost of about $7.00 per share, and I was thrilled when one particular day it gapped up to $14.00 per share. Things like that happen all the time, but you often have to prepare for them and then wait patiently until they take place. I did not expect DKHR to gap up; I expected the stock to rise by 40 to 50 percent. That's one of the few occasions when a stock has exceeded my expectations.

I generally do not trade stocks that sell for more than $10.00 per share. If you buy a $50.00 stock and it goes up $5.00, you have made 10 percent. If you buy a $7.00 stock and it goes up $5.00, you have made 71 percent. Having made the unfortunate mistake of putting a client into Lucent (LU) several years ago at $60.00 per share, the client and I both soon became painfully aware that it's a long way down from $60.00. It's not nearly as far from $5.00 or from $1.00. Of course, you might own many more shares of an inexpensive stock, but with proper stops or "mental stops" you try to buy as cheaply as possible and protect your principal.

I do a lot of work with stock options and options on futures. I like not having to pick the exact top or bottom of a market but rather having the leeway of one or two standard deviations before I am proven completely wrong. Before we turn to options, however, let's look at one more example of a stock trade. This one will utilize both technical and fundamental analysis and in this case the Elliottician RET software gave us the trading points.

• • •

Example: XsunX

XsunX (XSNX) is an interesting technology company. From a fundamental standpoint, there is almost no data on which it may be evaluated. The company has never sold anything, and its primary asset is the license to a patent. However, that particular patent holds great potential for XsunX.

XsunX is attempting to produce a certain type of transparent film that, when applied to a window, can generate electricity just like a regular solar cell. Because it employs an advanced technology and uses less hardware than conventional solar cells, the company claims that it is about four times as cost effective as conventional solar cells. Their film costs half as much and generates twice as much electricity.

Since the company has no sales and when I first bought it had not so much as a marketing agreement with anyone, the company had to be evaluated solely on the merits of the license. I was willing to take the gamble that 1) the company would be able to manufacture the product, 2) the company would be able to find glass manufacturers willing to enter into an agreement, and 3) the company would actually be able to sell its products to developers and contractors. I will admit that my judgment was swayed somewhat by examining the chart of the company's stock. XsunX came out as an IPO in 2003 at $2.00 per share. In September 2005 the stock was selling for as little as a penny ($.013), and those who bought the stock at the IPO had lost about 99.5 percent of their money—on paper, at least. Please take a look at Chart 9 in the color section, the XsunX monthly chart.

I first heard of the stock later in 2005 when it had risen to about 40¢ per share. I felt that if people had been willing to pay $2.00 per share initially, and if the company had a viable product, 40¢ per share was an acceptable risk. From experience I was reasonably certain that those remaining initial shareholders were probably going to hang on until they got back at least what they had put in. That turned out to be the case.

I began buying XsunX, and recommended it in the next issue of my newsletter *Wealth Creation and Preservation.* By the time that issue came out, the price had already risen to 80¢ per share. The RET software was key to my making that recommendation, for it indicated that the stock should soon go to at least $2.00.

When the stock hit $2.00 per share, I was convinced that many of the initial shareholders would bail out. We sold and took huge profits. Following the recommendations of the RET software, we then proceeded to buy back shares when the stock fell to $1.60. The stock then soared all the way up to $2.91 per share. (We got out before it peaked.) Once again we took a significant profit, and we bailed out because the software indicated that the next wave would end somewhere between 40¢ and $1.00 per share. That's exactly what XsunX proceeded to do. We kept small positions that we purchased at around $1.60 just in case the stock continued to rise, and we placed limit orders to buy significant positions in the stock at 75¢ per share or better. Shortly thereafter the stock fell to $.30 and stayed in a narrow range since then. We should have sold our entire position and not gotten back in. With penny stocks you may only see one money-making rally.

Why did I hold on to half positions, and why did I buy again now that the stock is below the price at which I first recommended it to my clients? The answer to that comes from the fundamental side of the story. To this day, to my knowledge, XsunX has yet to sell anything. When it does, I still believe that they will have a terrific product and the stock might be worth holding for several years after they began to show a profit.

XsunX, then, is one of those "triple threats," a stock with a strong fundamental story and a strong technical position and a stock whose trading pattern fits the Elliott wave. As good as Elliott wave analysis is, there are many securities and commodities whose trading histories do not fit Elliott wave patterns.

Before we leave XsunX, that's take a look at how much we were willing to accept in losses. XsunX is a "bulletin board" stock, one that is ordinarily thinly traded and one issued by an "unseasoned" company. You cannot use stop-limit orders or "good-til'-canceled" orders with bulletin-board stocks; it is simply not permitted. Bulletin board stocks also do not have options, which makes it impossible to hedge in that manner.

When I first bought XsunX at 40¢ per share and my clients first bought it at 80 to 90¢ per share, I was well aware that our risk was 100 percent. I was willing to make the recommendation because of the strong technical story and the strong fundamental story. XsunX is one of those stocks you hold onto no matter what, if you have purchased it at a good price. We were fortunate to have target prices at which to trade. We knew when to sell and take profits initially, when to repurchase, and when to take profits the second time. Because of the software, we not only knew when to sell the second time, but we knew that we had to sell because the stock was going to fall so significantly.

If you had looked at XsunX when it was $2.91 per share and you did not utilize Elliott wave analysis, you might have held on to the stock. Depending upon your strategy, you might have held on until it fell below its fifty-day or even its two-hundred-day moving average before you sold it, and you might even have taken a loss. Because of the analysis, the only move in which I do not have a high degree of confidence is the current one, where we have purchased at 75¢ per share or less. My confidence is lessened because of trading psychology. I know that there are some who have now been burned a second time in the stock, who will not return to get burned a third time. The stock was very heavily traded when it was moving upward, and that usually means that there are more participants than usual. Certainly the daily trading volume was well above the normal level. That means that more people may have had a less-than-satisfactory experience with the stock and they too may not return.

In fact, at this point XsunX looks a lot like one of the old "dot.com" stocks. It made a huge run-up in price at a time when the company had no sales. When the "bubble" burst, the stock proceeded to lose 80 percent of its value. XsunX still has no sales and no profits. We must have a compelling reason to buy it at this point, and because of its technological potential, I believe we do.

• • •

Options Trading

Now let's look at an options trade. This time we will look at futures instead of stock options. Futures are different than stocks for one very simple reason: there are very few commodities that are no longer used. The exceptions are the currencies and the stock market indices, but I can't name any *commodity* used by consumers or industry on a daily basis that has ever become obsolete.

Commodities include:

- Wheat, corn, and soybeans

- Silver, gold, and platinum

- Live hogs, live cattle, and pork bellies

- Cocoa, coffee, and sugar

- Financials (Treasury bonds, stock indices, and currencies)

- and more

• • •

Treasury Bond Commodity Futures

Let's take a look at U.S. Treasury bonds, which are available on the futures market. One Treasury bond contract is worth about $100,000.00 and in many cases is leveraged as much as 90 percent or more. That's a lot of leverage, and it can work for you or against you. If you buy a Treasury bond futures contract, you may only pay the minimum margin requirement of about $2,500.00, but you are liable for the entire value of the contract.

As I mentioned previously, I'm not particularly good at picking precise tops and bottoms of markets, nor do I know anyone who is. That's one reason why "momentum investing" has become so popular in recent years; all you have to do is to follow the trend. To me, following a trend is very much like a game of musical chairs; you need to keep a chair close by at every moment because the music might stop. Since I am not a momentum player and I'm not good at picking tops and bottoms, I prefer to have some leeway, some "wiggle room," so that I don't really have to worry as long as I am right about the primary trend. To do this I use options contracts.

What I'm trying to do is to find a commodity that is moving within a trading range. If through my analysis I determine that that trading range is going to continue, I am willing to bet that the price of the commodity will not go above a certain price or below another one. I can use statistical analysis to determine those prices, restricting myself to trades outside one or even two standard deviations. In fact I recommend such a technique, because options, like baseball, easily lend themselves to the statistical analysis.

If we look at Chart 10 in the color section, the monthly chart of U.S. Treasury bond futures, we see that thirty-year Treasuries peaked in June of 2003 at a price of over 124. They then fell sharply, hitting a low of just under 104 in August of that year. Since then, for the most part, they have been in a fairly wide trading range. We use the monthly charge initially to determine whether there is a trading range or not. Once we determine that there is some sort of a range, we can then move to the weekly and to the daily charts to see whether we have a viable trade. In my trading I use only medium-term contracts;

there tends to be too little value remaining in the short-term contracts, and I avoid the long-term contract because I like to get paid once in a while.

Looking at Chart 11, the eSignal T-Bond futures weekly chart, we see what appears to be a five-wave Elliott impulse wave down. Wave four is forming and can carry as far up as 113 16'. The 16' refers to 16/32, which reduces to .50 or half a point. before wave five down begins. On the weekly chart the stochastics don't really bear out this analysis because wave four has not caused them to rise into the 80 percent range or even above 50 percent, as they often will before a change of trend.

The RET software had something else to say, as did Bill Gross, who manages more bonds of all types than perhaps anyone in the world. Bill believed that Treasury bonds have entered a new bull market. Just making that statement on CNBC and in a few financial publications was enough to stall the trend, at least temporarily.

In fact, that is exactly what happened. The trend was stalled briefly, but within a few weeks completed a normal wave five down at 105 13/32. In fact, bonds tested that level several times before the trend changed and they rallied sharply.

Let's look closely at Chart 12, the Refined Elliott Trader (RET) chart of Daily U.S. Treasury bonds. The software found a trend that had begun much earlier, on 17 June 2003. That trend was a CT, or contracting triangle. You can see how the straight lines drawn from (ct) past (b) and from (a) past (c) will eventually converge. If indeed this was a contracting triangle, bond prices must stay at or below the upper straight line and at or above the lower straight line, which is exactly what they did. Notice that bonds entered the 60 percent box and peaked in December 2006, ending for the moment the rally Bill Gross had called for. After leaving the 60 percent box the trend turns gray, but you can see that bonds remained within the triangle for several more months.

Long term, Bill Gross turned out to be right, for T-bonds double-topped at much higher levels in 2008. On the basis of fundamental analysis such an event would occur only if interest rates were to fall significantly, an event that would only take place if all risk disappeared from the system or if a serious bout of deflation were to occur. It looks like we are getting that deflation despite the tremendous amount of money creation taking place at the Federal Reserve.

You can draw this chart a little differently by trying to make the straight lines touch the trend in more places, but the point is well taken. No matter what you may have thought was going to happen based upon your fundamental or technical analysis, the contracting triangle seems to be holding sway as the most favored scenario.

Now let's look at Chart 13, the eSignal Daily chart of U.S. Treasury bonds. This chart initially appears to confirm what we saw on the weekly chart, though in this case the indication is that wave four cannot go any higher than 111 16' (111 and 16/32, or 111.50) or so. What we *think* we know at this point, then, is that the trading range for Treasury bonds is between 113 24/32 on the upside (the low of wave one, for wave four cannot enter wave one's territory) and about 106 00' on the downside; 106 would be an appropriate place for a wave five to end. There are calculations that may be performed to come up with a more accurate figure.

Options on Treasury Bond Futures

Let's look at some options. We first want to look at *short-call options,* since our premise is that Treasury bonds are about to peak and a fifth wave down will begin. If we believe that bonds will go no higher than 113 24/32, we will probably be comfortable selling the Dec 2006 112 call, which last traded for 42/64, or $656.25. Remember, a call option gives the buyer the right to buy the underlying security or commodity at a specified price on or before a specified date. People buy call options when they think the security or commodity is going to rise in value; if we sell a call short, we believe it is going to fall or stay the same. All other things being equal, we have a 67 percent chance of being right, for we are covered on at least two of the three possible outcomes.

By selling this option "naked," we received the premium of $656.25, which is ours to keep on the day the option expires, which is November 21, 2006. We have to meet the margin requirements to make this trade, and those requirements can range from $1,000.00 to more than $3,000.00. We also have the obligation to sell one Dec 2006 Treasury bond contract at the price of 112 if the market goes against us and bonds continue to rise. In a "naked" call our risk is unlimited, which is why there are margin requirements.

Now let's look at doing the second side of the trade, selling a put option. A put is the opposite of a call; by selling a put you receive a premium as you did with a call option. When you *sell* a put option you give someone else the right to sell you one Treasury bond contract. You want to sell a put option with a strike price lower than you expect Treasury bonds to fall to. We're looking at a trading range where bonds can go as low as 104 16' If you sell a December 2006 104 put option, you have half a point between the option's strike price and the lowest price you expect to see for Treasuries. These puts are far out of the money, which means that they won't be worth much to us. Since we believe that wave-five down is going to begin soon, it would not be a good idea to sell a put now for very little money only to see it increase in value as bonds fall.

The "spread" strategy of using a short put and a short call (selling one of each and collecting the option premiums) has one significant advantage: you are guaranteed to make 100 percent on one side of the transaction. If you have done your analysis properly, you also have a good chance of making 100 percent on the other side of the transaction. As time goes on, Treasury bonds may move in price. If they go up, the value of your short call will go up against you, while the value of your short put will decline in your favor. If the market decides to move strongly in one direction or the other, you'll find yourself "underwater" on the spread because the increase in value of one leg of the spread will be greater than the decline in value of the other leg. The spread then becomes a waiting game and a trial of your patience, for the value of the losing position can quickly rise 100 percent or more. As is true with any other trade, you have to decide when you are wrong and act accordingly.

In this example I have sold one DEC 2006 112 call and am waiting for the price of the Dec 2006 Treasury bond contract to decline to a point where I anticipate it will be profitable to sell the 104 put. Most books on trading will tell you that you should enter both legs of the position simultaneously. They tell you to do so because it is generally believed that you cannot time the market or accurately predict what will happen to the particular commodity underlying your spread. I believe that my analysis can come up with a better prediction so that I can "leg in" to the spread as described above.

Once I have entered any trading position, I watch it. Since options are generally more volatile than stocks, it is not uncommon to see a gain of 50 percent in just a week or two. I am a firm believer in the old adage "You can never get hurt taking a profit." I like taking profits. I enjoy doing so as often as possible. Realized gains are "money in the bank" and, unlike "paper profits," cannot be taken away from you. When I have a significant paper profit of about 40 percent or more, I have to reevaluate my strategy. Usually when something has moved that far that quickly, we're going to see a correction, and a correction means giving back some of your paper profits.

In a spread, if one leg is up 40 percent, the other leg is probably down at least that much. Though it may be tempting to take the profits, I have to remind myself that I will earn the remaining value of that option if I wait. Options are wasting assets, and most of the time they expire worthless. Since my other position has gone against me, it is generally in my best interest to keep the profitable position on so that I may minimize my ultimate loss, if any.

If I am profitable in a long or short stock position, however, I will also reevaluate. If I have made good progress toward my price target and I believe that the target will yet be achieved in my time frame despite what I suspect will be a correction in the near future, I might want to sell a call option against my stock position—if options are available for that stock. If the strike price of the "covered" call option is at or above my target price, I will still end up selling the stock at my target price should it rise that far, and I will always be able to keep the premium I received from the sale of the option.

• • •

Short Selling

Let's look at one other example of stock trading, a "short sale." I rarely sell stock short because you have almost unlimited risk, while the maximum return you can make will be 100 percent if the stock goes to zero.

Short selling often requires you to borrow stock from your broker and sell it. You must meet the margin requirements for short selling. If you could just sell a stock short, take the money, and run, everybody would be short sellers. Instead, most securities firms require you to keep the amount you received from the sale plus the amount required to meet the margin requirements in the account at all times.

There may be some stocks that trade in a "channel." There are three types of channels: rising, falling, and flat. Their definitions are quite simple; rising channels have higher highs and higher lows. Falling channels have lower highs and lower lows. Flat channels have roughly identical highs and roughly identical lows. The theory behind trading channels is simply that you can extrapolate a trend into the future. In other words, what has happened in the past is going to continue for an indefinite period of time, and you can profit from repeating actions that would have been appropriate previously.

This approach is dangerous for several reasons. First, it is unusual for anything to stay within a channel for any great length of time. Elliott wave analysis calls for trends that rise or fall, though the Elliottician people have identified "flats" that really are, which in theory makes channel trading possible. If you are a "support and resistance" trader, you can make a case for things moving in a flat channel.

Since you expose yourself to so much risk and because it is so difficult to determine when a trend has completely run its course, finding a stock that has hit the top of its (flat) channel is one way of identifying a potential short sale. A stock that has hit the top of a *falling* channel has a greater likelihood of breaking out through the top of the channel. A stock that hits the top of a *rising* channel could be poised for a breakout or a blowoff, either of which would move the stock out of its channel.

• • •

Investing for Tax-free Income

There is a class of securities that offer tax-free interest. Some of them offer interest free from income taxation in a specific state as well as free from Federal income tax. These securities are offered by governments, usually states, counties, cities, airports, toll roads, and other entities. Because of their nature, the Congress has seen fit to allow them to compete for capital with the distinct advantage of tax-free interest, which reduces the yield the issuing entity must pay.

In other words, if you can purchase a AAA-rated thirty-year U.S. government bond today at par that will pay 5.00 percent per year, you would only receive about 3.75 percent in tax-free interest from a municipal bond.

• • •

"Rules" for Successful Investing

1. The best time to take a profit is when you have a profit.

2. Don't fall in love with your stock; it doesn't know that you own it.

3. A trend will always continue—until it ends.

4. Successful investing requires a combination of fundamental and technical analysis.

5. Opinions are worth no more than what you pay for them and often much less.

6. Your investments are your responsibility; you cannot afford to rely solely upon the advice of others.

7. Any stock can go to zero; very few commodities will ever go to zero.

8. There is probably an element of luck, however small, in any successful investment.

9. Successful investing requires you to tilt the odds slightly in your favor.

10. An investment's price can go in any of three directions: up, down, or sideways.

11. To be useful, a technical indicator must have a valid premise.

12. The Elliott wave may be the best tool ever devised for technical analysis, because it may most closely measure human behavior.

13. As good a tool as Elliott wave analysis may be, there are many investments whose price patterns do not conform to Elliott wave structures.

14. An investment with absolutely wonderful fundamentals does not "have to" go up.

15. You will probably never buy at the exact bottom or sell at the exact top. You need to identify the trend, not the absolutes.

16. If you lose just a little bit on each trade, you're never going to make up for it by making lots of trades.

17. Don't try to catch a falling knife. Don't fight the trend. Use it to your advantage.

18. Don't believe everything you read. In fact, don't believe most of what you read.

• • •

When will you sell your investments?

The time to sell is when:

1. You need the money for a planned expense.

2. You need the money for an unplanned expense.

3. The investment has done poorly and you decide it's time to "pull the plug."

4. The investment has done well or reached your target and it is time to sell.

5. You feel this investment will not perform as well in the future as another you have in mind and wish to purchase now.

6. You feel that changes in the market, the economy, or this company's industry will negatively impact the stock in the [near] future.

Notice that I have said nothing about the influence of taxes on your investments. I never hold on to an investment so that I can change it from a short-term gain to a long-term gain for tax purposes. I also won't buy an investment solely because of its tax benefits.

Chapter Twenty

Tax Avoidance Is Legal; Tax Evasion Is Not

Death and taxes, the only certainties in life. Would it surprise you to learn that as an American citizen you have the privilege of paying taxes on your income regardless of where you live and work? It shouldn't. Ever since the passage of the Sixteenth Amendment in 1913, Americans have been paying more and more in taxes to all levels of government. Income taxes were not the first to be passed into law; there were numerous excise taxes in place on certain products and economic activities, and property taxes existed in many jurisdictions; but these were not sufficient to fund a growing federal government.

Since the federal income tax became law, the floodgates have been open for additional taxation of Americans. Most states have state income taxes, most have state sales taxes, most employees are subject to Social Security and Medicare taxes, our employers pay unemployment taxes, and businesses bear an enormous tax burden.

Many Americans pay nothing in income taxes; they get a full refund each year. Some of them actually get an additional check from the IRS called the earned income credit, which is a fancy way to disguise what amounts to nothing more than a transfer of wealth from the haves to the have nots. However, those who work and do not earn enough to pay income taxes still pay Medicare and Social Security (FICA) taxes, and these are substantial and growing.

There is even double taxation of dividends in the United States. Businesses pay dividends out of what is left after they pay income taxes, and then the recipient of those dividends is taxed on them as personal income. We also tax capital gains, which is a very bad idea for a country wishing to attract investment dollars.

If you were to compare two individuals, an American living in the U.S. and a Chinese living in Hong Kong (prior to the expiration of the lease when Hong Kong was controlled by the British), you would find amazing differences. If each were making U.S. $100,000 per year, after thirty years of investing the same portion of their income after taxes, the American would have $250,000 in his investments, but the Hong Kong resident would be a multimillionaire. The sole difference is taxes. In the U.S., government is your silent partner, albeit one that contributes neither capital nor expertise. Government takes its share of your profits right off the top, but if you have losses it doesn't give any back. Government takes money from your business in property taxes, unemployment taxes, the employer's portion of Social Security and Medicare taxes, license fees, and much, much more.

Government is beginning to sound a lot like Wall Street, isn't it? Think about it. Wall Street makes money whether you do or not. Government makes money whether you do or not. Neither of them necessarily provides any benefit to your business; in fact, both may harm your business through anti-competitive measures or in many other ways. Neither has any interest in your success, except that they will take more from you if you are successful.

My advice is simply this: make your money first and worry about taxes later. Tax rates are low enough (compared to where they were in the 1960s, for example) to make them a nuisance rather than a disaster. Using your retirement account(s) appropriately and funding them up to legal limits is one way of legally reducing your tax bite. Talk to a competent financial advisor about other methods.

Above all, when you have done everything you can to legally reduce your taxes, pay your taxes. Penalties and interest are very expensive and unnecessary. There is usually very little to be gained by fighting the IRS; they can keep paying their lawyers' salaries long after you have run out of money. Don't get too excited about moving your money offshore, either; most of the useful loopholes have been closed, and the costs of moving yourself and assets out of the country are often greater than the potential benefit.

If you are ever audited, most of the time you will want to have an attorney working for you. Most audits are "fishing expeditions"; the IRS suspects they can get additional revenue out of you and will do everything they can to make a legitimate demand for it. IRS agents are fair, and they act within the law; but they are also professionals, and you are not—at least, not insofar as your taxes are concerned.

Be sure to bring only what you are asked to bring to the hearing or meeting with the IRS people; many people have hurt their case when they volunteered unnecessary information either by bringing along supporting documentation that was not requested or by saying something in the interview.

I also recommend that most people produce their own tax returns. The software packages sold online or in the office-supply superstores enable you to grasp the basics of taxation. Most of them utilize a question and answer format. The way you respond to those questions determines which will be asked subsequently.

By preparing your own tax return, you begin to understand how incredibly arcane our tax code realy is. You also get ideas about how you might legally reduce your tax bill next year. Most important, you will probably discover that you really are paying taxes, not just "getting a refund."

Chapter Twenty-One

Protecting Yourself

The risks associated with living in this great country have increased dramatically in recent years. We are the most litigious society in history; far more people are sued than are hospitalized each year. We have liabilities our predecessors never dreamed of as the courts and Congress have created "rights" the Founding Fathers deliberately excluded from the Constitution and the Bill of Rights.

- There are massive volumes of laws we must obey, and even if we obey them to the letter, some smart lawyer can twist the intent of the law to our detriment.[20]

- If your house is broken into, you can be sued and lose if the thief is injured while engaged in the commission of the crime.

- If the heating oil tank in your basement springs a leak, you can be sued for the environmental damage. If you break one of those high-efficiency fluorescent bulbs that are becoming so popular, it can costs thousands of dollars to remove the hazardous materials the tube contains.

- Property laws are being ignored in favor of eminent domain by many communities around the country. The way it is being used today, eminent domain is nothing more than legalized theft.

- If your neighbor holds a grudge against you, all he has to do is call the police and give an anonymous tip about how he saw a drug deal go down on your front lawn. Your house, cars, bank accounts, and all your possessions can be seized by law-enforcement officials. Since you are not charged with a crime, you have no legal recourse. The only way to recover your property is to buy it back at the sheriff's auction.

- A thief can steal your identity in seconds when you hand over your credit card to pay for a regular transaction.

- When your identity is stolen, you can be held responsible for acts committed by the person or persons who impersonate you.

There are many ways in which you can be left without legal recourse in your own defense. The First Amendment has been trampled as political correctness replaces free speech. You can lose your job and your career for a sentence you speak that offends another. You can be accused of sexual harrassment and lose without being aware that you had done anything wrong.

You can become the scapegoat when something goes wrong at work and lose your job, your pension plan, and more, so that the guilty party may unjustly shift blame away from him or herself.

You can be found guilty of a crime that was not a crime when you committed it.

You can be spied upon, imprisoned, and held without trial by our government without ever being charged with a crime.

Your phone and all your personal communications can be listened in on by others without a warrant and all without your knowledge.

You could contract a serious, even fatal illness while hospitalized for something completely unrelated. Some medical procedures can be dangerous by their nature. Thousands of medical mistakes are made each year by otherwise competent physicians.

Your life is an open book to all who know how to access your information and use it.

• • •

How can you protect yourself?

This issue has become so complex that books have been written on regaining some semblance of privacy in your personal affairs. My approach is a simple one, but it can be very helpful in keeping you from becoming a victim.

1. Purchase insurance protection against identity theft. This protection should cover all aspects of your personal information including your medical records, your Social Security number, and your driver's license in addition to protection of your financial information.[21]

2. Purchase legal insurance. This coverage gives you access to attorneys in your area who are on call at all times to answer legal questions, review contracts, advise you on the legal options available to you, and come to your defense when needed.

3. Maintain a low profile. Keep your home comfortable but unpretentious. Your cars should also not mark you as a potential target. Don't throw money around or engage in conspicuous consumption. Keep as many of your assets private as possible. Give as little indication as possible that you would be a good target for a criminal.

4. Consider a personal liability policy, either as a rider to your homeowner's insurance or as a separate policy. That may help to protect you when someone slips on your icy walkway. The problem with that

idea is that when people are sued the plaintiff's lawyer has usually examined your financial situation and demanded a sum exactly equal to your liability coverage.

Your other insurance coverages should be appropriate and affordable. As we discussed previously, it is up to you to decide how much life, supplemental health, disability and long-term-care insurance is right for you—and how much you can actually afford.

5. Maintain your health with exercise, adequate rest, and good nutrition. Seek natural and holistic alternative approaches to prescription medications and life-altering surgical procedures. Hospitals can be dangerous; avoid hospitalization whenever possible. It is all too easy to pick up some of the horrific infections you can only get in a hospital.

Understand fully the risks and objectives of every medical procedure and medication prescribed for you. Do your homework and learn about various options in the treatment of illnesses you or your loved ones may have. Get a second and even a third opinion whenever it is appropriate.

6. Establish and maintain cordial relationships with your neighbors whenever possible. The concepts of neighborhood and community may have all but disappeared in most parts of this country, but that doesn't mean they should have. In the next few years as energy soars in price, we will tend to become less mobile. We will stay in place longer than we used to, especially when we can't afford to move because our house won't sell. Neighborhood Watch groups can be helpful in building relationships, as is participation in PTA and community activities.

Being a good neighbor can place a burden upon you when people look to you for help, but you will find that in times of trouble those who know and have come to trust you will come to your aid when the need arises.

We don't see much in terms of common beliefs in many communities today except possibly Amish or predominantly Mormon communities. Diversity within a neighborhood can be a source of friction and mistrust, much of it based upon differences in culture, upbringing, religion, and money. I believe that people become what we expect them to become when we have a good relationship with them. I also believe that most people genuinely want to be happy, to live useful lives, and to be good citizens. We just don't know how to do it sometimes because we don't have good role models.

7. Be the best employee you can be. Earn your keep; be loyal to your employer. If you find that your employer is doing things you do not agree with, find other employment as quickly as possible.

These things are not suggested in the spirit of sage advice or preaching, nor are they given solely to put you into a position where you are less likely to defend yourself, your family, your home, your career, or your livelihood. These suggestions are given because following them will help you to become the kind of citizen our Constitution requires if it is to survive. We must be a moral and an ethical people, holding to high standards of integrity and contributing in many ways to our community. If we had that type of society, we wouldn't see 1 percent of the adult population of the United States in prison, as we do in early 2008.

John F. Kennedy famously said, "Ask not what your country can do for you. Ask what you can do for your country." Some pundits have construed *country* to mean *government*. I like to think that President Kennedy was referring to our obligation to be good citizens, steeped in a great knowledge of and respect for our great Constitution, and deserving of the rights and privileges we enjoy because we have not surrendered them to our government. I also like the statement "America is great because America is good," incorrectly attributed to Alexis de Tocqueville.

America has seen great days and may yet see them again, though I can foresee some dark times ahead as America redefines itself. Americans have gone through tough times and come out better for it. Our problem, like that of humankind throughout its history, is of surviving the good times. For better or worse, the good times are rapidly coming to an end.

Part V

Creating a Brighter Future

Under any reasonable set of expectations about future spending and revenues, the risks posed to the Nation's future financial condition are too high to be acceptable.

–The Nation's Long-term Fiscal Outlook, September 2006 Update, U.S. Government Accountability Office (GAO)

What, then, is the Singularity? It's a future period during which the pace of technological change will be so rapid, its impact so deep, that human life will be irreversibly transformed. Although neither utopian nor dystopian, this epoch will transform the concepts that we rely on to give meaning to our lives, from our business models to the cycle of human life, including death itself.

–Ray Kurzweil, *The Singularity is Near,* p. 7

Chapter Twenty-Two

Participating in the Global Economy

Earlier you may have taken issue with my discussion about taking care of your own needs before you develop a social conscience. That is not my belief at all, for I believe in developing some sort of harmony with this beautiful world we call our home. I made that statement because, as I will discuss below, I believe it is more difficult than ever to obtain that harmony.

Many years ago a new client came on board who had just accepted an assistant professor position in a component of the University of Texas (UT) system. We discussed his impending once-in-a-lifetime choice of Teacher Retirement System (TRS), which is a defined benefit program, and the Optional Retirement Program (ORP), which is a defined contribution program. Back then I was recommending ORP; financial professionals cannot work with TRS because contributions are mandated and performance is governed by the state. In his case, he would also be contributing to Social Security, though with no real money in the Social Security trust fund it is dangerous to rely on the Federal government for a retirement income.

The reasons why I recommended ORP were, aside from the possibility of compensation for me, 1) the importance of complete control over your account (after a vesting period of one year and one day) and 2) the value of not being subject to the whims of the state, for the state can alter retirement benefits at will. At the time I was genuinely concerned that TRS was paying out more than it could afford, because payouts were being based upon recent and above-average performance in their investment portfolio. I believed that such a level was unsustainable. As was demonstrated by the severe market decline of 2000, I was right; continued poor performance would prohibit states and other governmental entities from paying promised benefits.

You may recall that in recent years several governmental entities have flirted with or even declared bankruptcy. New York City was one of them, as was Cleveland, Ohio; Orange County, California; the western counties of New York State, and several others. I believed that the possibility existed for almost any governmental entity to be forced into bankruptcy if its leaders did not practice fiscal responsibility. The only exception is the Federal government, which alone has the power to print money—as if that meant that it had the right to do so to finance a profligate and wasteful government.

My concern about bankruptcy was the real reason I was so much in favor of ORP. I felt it was important for my clients to have as much control over their money as possible. Participating in TRS or the state-run system meant surrendering all of your contributions and the state's in exchange for a promise to pay.

Looking back fifteen years later and seeing how poorly many ORP investors have done with their accounts, my clients might have been better off participating in TRS. Better a fixed and guaranteed payment from the state instead of having to take a monthly withdrawal when you could well be eroding your principal. Better, of course, unless inflation is eroding the value of those fixed and guaranteed payments and neither choice will provide an adequate living.

My clients did not do poorly. I managed to produce an average return of about 10 percent for more than a dozen years as I actively managed hundreds of ORP accounts, and my clients had minimal exposure to the stock market. Those others whose ORPs did poorly generally were too heavily invested in tech stocks as the year 2000 came and went, or their timing was poor, or they simply took too much risk. I know of one individual (not a client) who watched in dismay as his million dollars in ORP became half a million. Many people did worse than that.

I made my recommendation to this prospective client and he agreed with me that ORP was the way to go. He then said something I hear very seldom. He said he wanted to invest in a socially conscious manner. He felt it was important to make a statement in each aspect of his life to demonstrate his commitment to certain principles and beliefs he held dear. I acknowledged his wishes and concerns and expressed a similar desire and proceeded to do the only thing I could do, which ended up losing the client and his account. The only socially conscious choice was a family of funds with a poor track record, one I had available to me in the UT system but never used because it did not make good money for the client.

In that day and this, a "socially-conscious" investor wants to avoid hypocrisy in every aspect of his life as best he can. Ralph Nader, it is said, doesn't own a car, but he rides buses. Each of us has beliefs and notions about the world in which we live, and we seek meaningful ways to make our voices heard. Sometimes our feelings are expressed in a reverse manner as we boycott or refuse to invest in certain industries we find objectionable. For some people, liquor is evil; for others, gambling, or pornography are evils from which they do not want to profit. Many people, like this client, believe that the oil companies are exploiting the world for profit and destroying the environment in the process; others feel that nuclear power is absolutely unacceptable, whether in their backyard or anyone else's. Many of those who are paid handsomely to preach the "gospel" of global warming are themselves significant contributors to the problem.

The mutual funds responded to this wish by creating various "social" funds. The fund's prospectus would specifically state the industries the fund would avoid and those it would promote. The fund manager might invest in "environmentally-friendly" companies and avoid the "sin" companies.

There are two fundamental problems with this type of investing:

1. 1. By excluding certain companies because of a negative personal bias or by overemphasizing others

because of a positive bias, investment returns can be skewed significantly—usually to the lower end of the scale, as it has turned out.

2. 2. Although there are numerous "green" or "social" funds to choose from, it is unlikely that any will meet any one investor's specific criteria as to what is good and what is bad.

The latter point is what cost me a client. If energy is one of a very few market sectors in an upward trend, if you just won't own the big oil companies you will cut your investment returns.

To this day I have never adequately addressed his worthwhile objectives, but I will attempt to do so in these pages. In addition, I would like to address some of the significant issues facing all of us as investors or just as inhabitants of this small planet.

• • •

The Economics of Scarcity

Our world today faces unprecedented challenges. The "carrying capacity" of planet Earth, as Jared Diamond[22] tells us, is as little as two billion people once we run out of available hydrocarbons, including oil and natural gas. The earth's current population is more than three times that, somewhere in the range of 6.6 billion. Absent revolutionary new technology—and that technology is clearly absent today—more than two-thirds of the world's population would not be able to live without hydrocarbons.

Our planet is consuming ever-greater amounts of crude oil and natural gas, but our capacity to produce, refine, and deliver these products and their derivatives is not keeping pace. According to the theory proposed by M. King Hubbert[23], we will have reached a worldwide peak of production about the time you read this, if not earlier. In fact, peak oil may have been attained in late 2006. If so, all we are doing now is concealing the truth to avoid a panic.

How is this possible if the world is indeed "awash in oil," as many would have us believe? Simply put, we have used about half of all the oil ever found, and much of what is left is unrecoverable by current or prospective technologies. The methods used to produce oil today are generally very expensive, and some of them would not be employed if crude oil were selling for under $30 to $50 per barrel. The remaining oil is increasingly concentrated in parts of the world where Americans are mistrusted and disliked.

As for our old, reliable sources, most of them are being depleted rapidly and are headed for terminal decline. The North Slope, the North Sea, the largest Mexican field, and many others have been producing for decades and now are ready to head into steep production declines. No longer, according to Matthew Simmons[24], can Saudi Arabia "open the spigot" when someone asks them to flood the world with oil as Ronald Reagan did many years ago. It simply cannot be done any more. In fact, overproduction for many oil fields means being forced to leave a much higher percentage of the oil in the ground than would otherwise be the case if we were not using enhanced recovery techniques to force the field to produce beyond its normal capacity. An oilfield that would have produced 25–30 percent of its oil will, utilizing enhanced techniques like gas or brine injection, go into terminal decline when only 15–20 percent of its oil has been extracted. For a ten-billion-barrel field, a difference of 10 percent means an additional billion barrels—enough to keep our world going for about eleven days at current consumption rates—left in the ground, forever unavailable.

What will a world without oil look like? Stick around and find out. Ray Kurzweil talks about developing technologies that will, in time, enable us to accomplish everything we wish without resorting to hydrocarbons pumped out of the ground, but for the forseeable future oil and natural gas are every bit as precious as pure water—and becoming just as scarce.

There are many other things in short supply these days, and not all of them as obvious as you might think. Historically, when a substance utilized in industry or agriculture was facing increased demand, means would have been created to make more of it available. Many of the world's greatest technological advances have come about to enable us to take more of the earth's treasures for our own use. All of those technologies have made it possible for more people to live on the earth.

Now, for the first time in human history, we are facing the likelihood of running out of all available sources of certain minerals, not the least of which is crude oil and natural gas. However, the list of projected shortages is very long and includes basics like uranium, silver, cobalt, chromium, zinc, and copper. Sometimes there are available substitutes; sometimes there are none. In some cases the mines have petered out, and none have been found to replace them; or those that have been found have poorer-quality ore bodies or may be much more difficult to reach. As is the case with oil and gas, as their prices increase more and more low-yield sources will become commercially viable, but even the continued availability of a substance at a higher, demand-driven price leads to real price inflation and increases everyone's cost of living.

• • •

Government Interference

One of my biggest concerns these days is government interference in the markets. Many governments of all political persuasions believe that they are powerful enough and wise enough to control the economy and thus prevent recessions and depressions. I will let you in on a little secret: *no government in human history has ever succeeded in controlling the economy and enabling all its citizens to live well.* That communism has failed everywhere it was attempted is not adequate testimony to this statement; communism, based upon everything I have seen in my research, was always designed to bring the masses under subjection.

Socialism too has failed because it too seeks more and more authority to deal with more and greater problems. Once "compassion" gets into the equation, any remnants of common sense, morality, and intelligence quickly go out the window, and are replaced by mindless and enslaving bureaucracy.

No, the true test of economic control must be found in a society that considers itself free. For centuries Americans have surrendered their freedom a little at a time to a central, federal government that has replaced those freedoms with handouts. We in America today enjoy a social safety net of enormous proportions, designed to prevent us from stubbing our toes while allowing us the freedom to destroy ourselves through partaking of the vast expanse of human follies and foibles. The United States today is strangling itself in red tape, and most of us have been conditioned to think this is a natural consequence of receiving all those wonderful government benefits.

How will we extricate ourselves as a nation from our ever-growing government that intrudes into every aspect of our lives? From reading this book you know, if you didn't know previously, that things happen in cycles. Government intervention interrupts cycles, but it seldom eliminates them. It seems to be a natural tendency of people in our day to make their lives easier by asking their government to help them. If so, this tendency must be reversed before government interference can be reduced.

I watch some of what goes on in politics because political events have a significant effect on my clients and myself. Much of what I do as an investment adviser reflects my understanding of the current political environment and the changes I anticipate in that environment over the next several years. Like anyone else, I want to be able to extrapolate trends indefinitely, but long experience with markets and trading has shown me that this is not the case. I never lose hope for this great country of ours because I know that people can and will change when they need to.

What to do

In the meantime, I will continue to practice what I preach. I try to be fair and honest in all of my dealings with my fellow man. I encourage others to do the same.

Whenever I introduce a problem or crisis to my clients and readers, I try to offer useful solutions as well. We, the inhabitants of this beautiful planet, can become better educated and more capable of ordering our lives and making life freer and more comfortable for all. There will be difficult and controversial decisions to be made every step of the way.

Humankind needs a "mission statement" similar to that employed by organizations, a document that would summarize our desire as a species to make ourselves better. Perhaps a growing awareness of the fragility of our environment—and by that I mean our economic environment as well as the natural one—will impel us to band together in a common cause and set aside selfishness, distrust and fear. This we will do by improving our own knowledge and understanding of the world in which we live, and by exercising more compassion as we lift our less-fortunate brothers and sisters around the world. After all, we *are* our brothers' keepers.

Gallery

Dow Jones Industrial Average Historic Returns

Chart 1

Dow Jones Industrial Average, 1928-2008

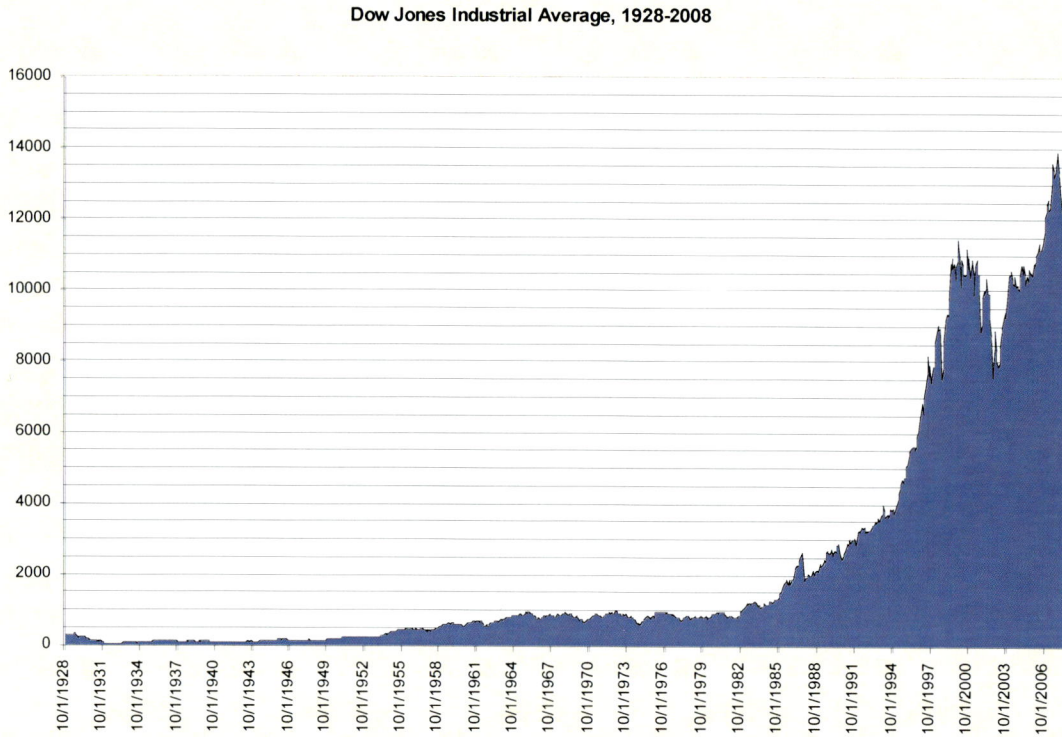

Figure 1. Note that after making several unsuccessful attempts to break above 1,000 the DJIA finally did so in 1982 and never looked back.

Table 1. Dow Jones Industrial Average 1928-2008

This chart shows the rise of the Dow Jones Industrial Average (DJIA) from 1928 through late 2008. Notice that the DJIA closed above 1,000 for the first time in about 1972, after which it remained in a fairly tight trading range until 1983. The increase from 1,000 to 14,000 took only 24 years, a 13,000% gain at an annual rate of about 11.6% per year.

This chart does not demonstrate a perfect exponential curve upward because of the break from March 2000 to October 2002, when the DJIA lost 39% of its total value.

Chart 2. BHP Billiton

This is BHP Billiton, the huge mining firm with operations in many parts of the world. Again, notice the volatility once a peak is reached.

Image 1.
The 1776 Dollar was designed by Benjamin Franklin and nicknamed the "Continental." This 1778 $8 Continental is part of that series.
(Photo Courtesy of The Early American History Store.)

Image 2.
The first "greenback", issued during the Civil War in an attempt
to createconfidence in paper currency. It didn't work.
Source: Federal Reserve Bank of San Francisco

Image 3.
Germany's hyperinflation money: RM 20,000 issued on
20 Feb 1923

Image 4.
Germany's hyperinflation money: RM 1,000,000 issued
25 Jul 1923

Image 5.
Germany's hyperinflation money: RM 1,000,000,000 (1 billion Reichsmarks) issued 20 Oct 1923.

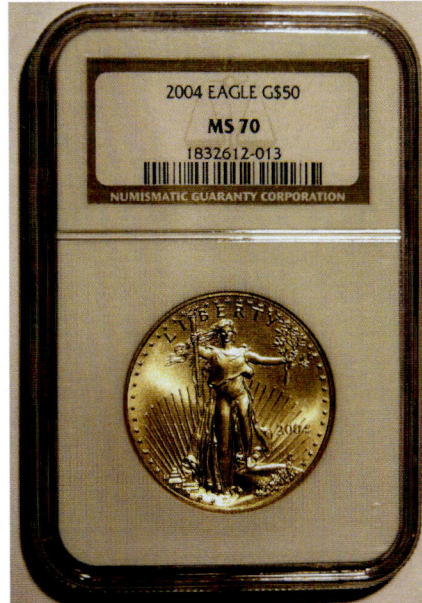

Image 6.
A 1924 $20 St Gaudens Double Eagle and a 2004 1-ounce
Gold Eagle.

Image 7.
1982 South African Krugerrand.

Image 8.
US "junk" (non-collectible) Silver Coins minted before 1965 are 90% silver.

Image 9.
1921 Morgan Silver Dollar.

Image 10.
2007 One-ounce Silver Eagle

Chart 3.

General Motors, Monthly Chart. Each red or green bar represents one month of trading. This chart shows a massive decline in value for one of the industrial giants. Note that the Stochastics are sharply oversold at the right end of the chart.

CWK Adv Chart.ach - ©2008 eSignal, Inc.

Chart 4.

Crude Oil, Monthly chart. Note that on all "candlestick" charts like this the green bar shows a trading month that ended higher than it began, not higher than the previous month. The opposite is true for the red bars.

Chart 5.

ExxonMobil, Monthly chart. Note that the Stochastics indicate XOM is oversold after its sharp decline. Note too that XOM has not yet broken it 50-month moving average (green line).

Chart 6.

Advantage Energy, Weekly chart. I added Bollinger bands (blue lines above and below the data) to show one additional method of Technical Analysis. Also, Volume (number of shares traded per week) is indicated at the bottom instead of Stochastics. The Data Box (left) is a helpful feature available with eSignal.

Chart 7.

ExxonMobil, Daily Chart. Note how the Bollinger Bands can be helpful in determining where a stock can go. The bands attempt to predict the future trading range of a stock or future.

Chart 8.

Microsoft, Monthly chart. Notice where the Stochastics bottom out at four different times, and how MSFT is still really in a long and narrow trading range from which it escaped only once, and temporarily, in 2007–2008.

Chart 9.

XsunX Monthly chart. Note how the stock came out as an IPO at $2.00 per share and plummeted within days to just over $.50. This obviously was not a "hot issue." This chart includes Bollinger bands (relatively useless with so little trading data).

Chart 10.

U.S. Treasury Bonds, Monthly chart. Note how well the Bollinger bands fit. The moves portrayed on this chart are extraordinary in their volatility for bonds as conservative and safe as Treasuries.

Chart 11.

U.S. Treasury Bond futures, Weekly chart. The numbers 1,2,3, and 4 accompanying the candlesticks refer to Elliott Wave designations of a 5-wave downward Impulse move.

Chart # 12. RET software representation of a Daily U.S. Treasury bond chart.

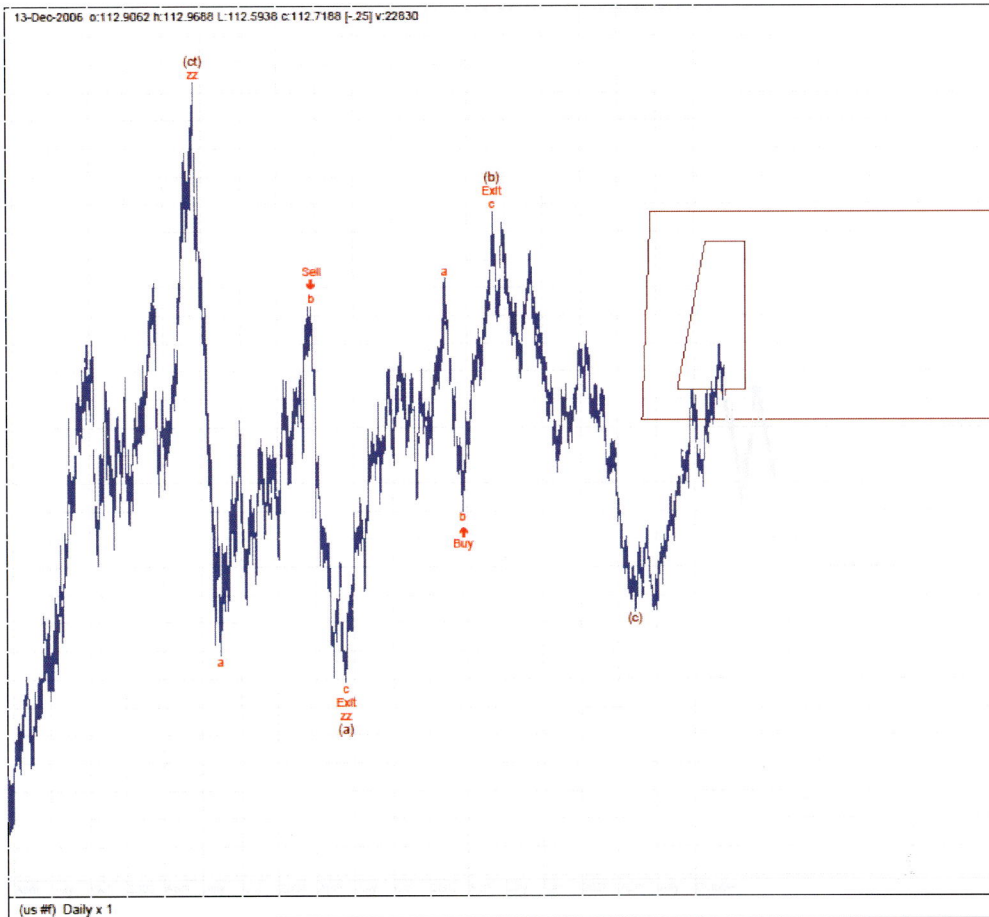

Figure 1. RET software representation of a Daily U.S. Treasury bond chart. Note how T-bond futures have entered the red 60 percent target box, completing a contracting triangle formation and indicating a change of trend.

Chart 12.

RET software representation of a Daily U.S. Treasury Bond chart. Note how T-bond futures have entered the red 605 target box, completing a Contracting Triangle formation and indicating a change of trend.

Chart 13.

U.S. Treasury bonds, Daily Chart. Note that Elliott Wave numbers have been inserted along the candlesticks indicating a 5-wave declining impulse wave that is not complete.

Charts and Patterns

For those of you who are unfamiliar with charts, I wanted to show you what they look like and give you some ideas about how to read them. In addition I thought it would be appropriate to have a brief discussion of chart patterns, particularly Elliott wave patterns.

The charts in the following pages are used with permission of eSignal; the Refined Elliott Trader (RET) charts used to demonstrate Elliott patterns are provided courtesy of Elliottician.com.

• • •

Silver Futures

Please take a look at Chart 14, the silver futures daily chart. This is a candlestick chart, meaning that each individual bar looks something like a candle with a wick. Notice that some of them have "wicks" at both ends. Candlestick charts are very similar to the "Open-High-Low-Close" (OHLC) charts and use exactly the same information, but a candlestick chart makes the data more useful.

Chart 14.

Silver futures, Daily chart. It's not too difficult to spot a trend here, is it?

Both types of charts use five pieces of data: the open, high, low, and closing prices for the period of time represented by the bar or candle as well as the volume for the period. The volume is the number of shares or contracts traded. All technical analysis is based upon these five pieces of information. Moving averages are among the simplest indicators and use only one piece. The closing price; some of the more sophisticated techniques use all five.

Let's take a closer look at this chart of silver. The body of the candle, in red or green, indicates the opening and closing prices of that trading period. The trading period is named on every chart. On a 1-minute chart each bar or candle represents one minute of trading; on a Weekly chart each bar or candle represents one week.

A green bar is used when the stock or commodity closed higher than it opened *for that period,* and a red bar is used when the stock or commodity closed lower than it opened. That's why you may see a red bar on a day when silver was up or a green bar when it was down; it's all a matter of where it opened, not where it closed the previous period.

A candle with no "wicks" shows a stock or commodity that opened and closed at the high and low points of the day's trading. We can say that each candle incorporates four pieces of information: open, high, low, and close. If we chart the volume along the bottom (we did not on this particular chart), we can look at all five pieces of information generated in trading.

The red and green colors make candlesticks very useful. You have an immediate graphic representation of the period's trading that almost jumps out at you. With an OHLC bar chart you have to examine each bar relative to those before and after it.

The box in the upper left with a black background gives the statistics pertaining to the bar where the cursor is located. The three lines that appear to flow along with the candles are moving averages (MAs). Moving averages are very simple to calculate and have been used for many years as a predictive tool. In this case the blue line represents the average closing price of the previous ten periods, which in this case are days. The red line shows the previous twenty periods, and the green line shows the previous fifty. Moving averages are usually calculated based upon closing prices. As each candle completes, its closing value is added to the moving average calculation, and the earliest one is subtracted.

The eSignal software is very sophisticated and makes dozens of technical tools available in conjunction with these charts. The only one I have chosen to show here he is *stochastics,* the red and blue lines you will see at the bottom of the chart. When those red and blue lines are between zero and twenty, the security or commodity is said to be *oversold;* when they are in the eighty to one hundred area it is said to be *overbought.* As I mentioned, stochastics may no longer be a viable method of technical analysis.

• • •

Apple Computer Stock

Now let's take a look at Chart 15 in the center section, a weekly chart of Apple Computer (AAPL). Each candle now represents one week of trading, so the chart shows much more history. Note Apple's tremendous rise since July 2006, followed by an even swifter decline. Stocks, commodities, and markets tend to do that; they often fall faster than they rose.

Chart 15.

Apple (AAPL) stock, Weekly chart. Note how the Stochastics fall each time the stock does, and that the stochastics can remain oversold (below 20) for a long time.

Charts like these provide a powerful and valuable visual representation of what is going on in an investment. Even without training in technical analysis, you can instantly see significant moves and make at least a preliminary determination as to whether you are interested in the investment.

Notice in this chart that the stock bottomed three times, and each time the stochastics were in the oversold territory. This is no coincidence, and it can be useful information in helping us find a place to buy. On the upside, you can see that AAPL was "overbought" for long periods of time, though it continued to rise much of that time.

Ask yourself these questions: Does this chart give you enough information to make a decision about buying or selling Apple? Based upon the stochastics and the actual trading history, do you think Apple is a "buy" at current levels?

I try not to make investment decisions solely upon technical indicators, though many people do and some have been quite successful at it. If I am relying solely on technicals I would add Elliott Wave analysis before reaching any decision. This chart tells us only that Apple has fallen significantly and may be forming a bottom here. That bottom might be considered a "support level"; note that Apple bottomed at approximately the same $120 level back in August 2007. If this is support, we might expect Apple to test the lows once more and then move up again.

We will look at an Elliott Wave chart next, but keep in mind that we should also consider the fundamentals behind Apple before making any investment decisions. There are many reasons why a stock will fall like this, and only some of them are directly related to the company itself. Bad earnings can bring a stock down just as fast as a bad market can.

• • •

Refined Elliot Trader (RET) Software Charts

Finally, let's look at Chart 16, an RET hourly software chart of Enerplus (ERF). I have mentioned the RET software several times in this book.

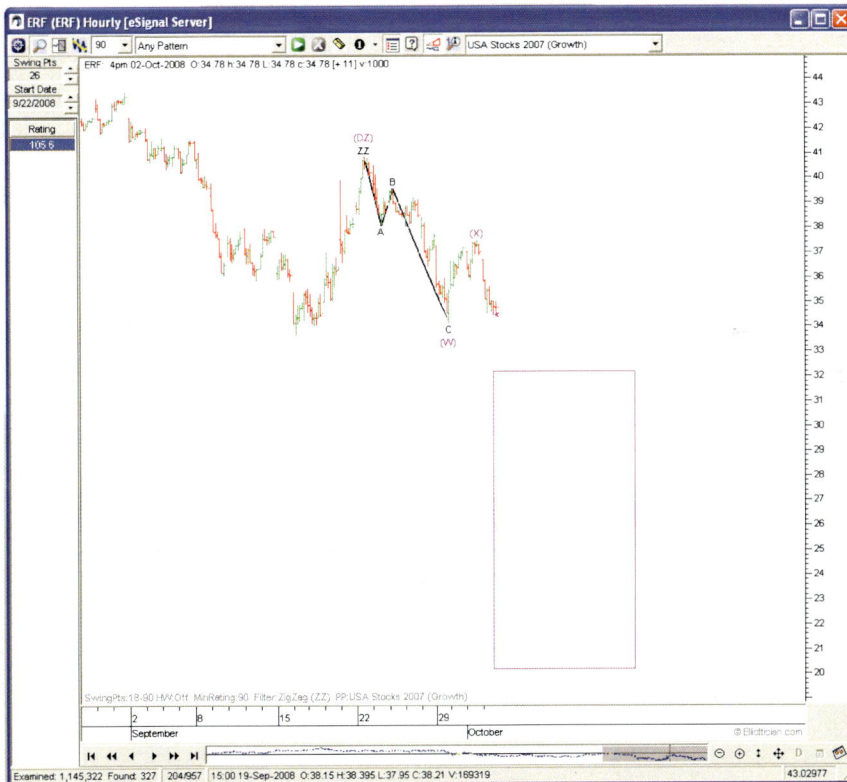

Chart 16.

Enerplus (ERF) Hourly chart. Note how the Double Zigzag (DZ) has already completed the first two portions (W and X) with one full Zigzag (A-B-C). The pink box is the target where the second Zigzag should end.

This is an hourly chart; the data spans about one month. The RET software has identified a formation called a double zigzag (DZ) and given it a rating of 105.6. Any rating above one hundred is worth looking at, especially if it is a zigzag or double zigzag. The first half of the double zigzag is indicated in black as a regular zigzag (ZZ) labeled A, B, and C. C of the zigzag is also W of the double zigzag. Double zigzags are labeled W, X, and Y. The figure bounced up to X and is beginning to form Y, which should be another zigzag.

Note the pink box. This is the target area, the place where this double zigzag is expected to end. If it actually works out that way, the RET software is a better-than-average tool for predicting markets.

Note also on the lower left of the box. The RET software in just seconds analyzed 1,145,322 possible patterns in this chart and found 327 "possibles." Only the double zigzag indicated here passed all the screens.

Why are zigzags so important? The people at www.elliottician.com have spent years researching the various Elliott patterns and discovered that statistically the zigzag is the most reliable. You can see the completed zigzag and observe its formation with two waves in the direction of the primary trend and one counter to the primary direction. A double zigzag is the same except that each major wave is a zigzag in itself.

How accurate is the RET software in identifying patterns? You could have argued for many different patterns to form based upon the information you see in this chart. However, by November 2008 Enerplus had fallen to a low of $17.07, even lower that that predicted by the software. It seemed almost impossible at the time, but the software called the move very accurately. If you had owned ERF you should have sold it as soon as you saw this chart. This chart shows how valuable the right kind of technical analysis can be.

Appendix

Links

If you visit www.wcandp.com you will find numerous links to products and services I believe are worthwhile. Since links and websites change constantly it is more appropriate to reference them where they can be updated constantly.

A Brief History of Money

What is money?

Money is a commodity. It is a tool we use to facilitate economic transactions. Many things have been used as money: seashells, carved stones of various sizes, salt, precious metals, and many other things. Through trial and error we have discovered that whatever we use for money must be practical; it should be portable, easily divisible, and difficult to counterfeit. Until the time of the Industrial Revolution, it was generally believed that money also ought to have an intrinsic value.

Throughout human history people have recognized the value of gold. It is beautiful, useful, impossible to counterfeit, and scarce. Gold has been used as a store of value for millennia. In most respects it is an ideal medium of exchange. However, it is heavy and difficult to carry about in large quantities. That difficulty led to the creation of paper money and opened up a whole new way to steal the wealth of nations.

Paper money is the invention of the earliest "bankers," whose job it was in times past to store gold and issue receipts for it. Since the banker held the gold on deposit, anyone who held a valid receipt for that gold could exchange it for the gold whenever the bank was open. Obviously it was easier (and probably safer) for people to carry around the receipts than it was for them to carry the physical metal. Over time the receipts rather than the gold became the medium of exchange.

It probably didn't take long for the bankers to discover that on a given day no one would present receipts for all the gold they had on deposit in their bank. Based on that knowledge, they could then issue additional receipts for gold in excess of the actual amount of gold on deposit. These could be issued in the form of loans to the bank's customers, for new money is not created from nothing[25]. There has to be a corresponding item on the opposite side of the balance sheet.

A "banker" who issued additional receipts, regardless of the form, would incur a significant risk. There was always the possibility that more gold would be demanded by customers than was available in the bank. If you remember the movie *It's a Wonderful Life*, you know what a run on the bank looks like. Any bank that offers "demand deposits" must be able to meet its customers' demands. When the bank is unable to do so, it is insolvent and is headed for failure unless it can find additional cash somewhere. Prior to the creation of the Federal Deposit Insurance Corp. (FDIC), bank runs were fairly common, and hundreds of banks failed, particularly during the Great Depression.

This type of money creation, where the bank is leveraging its assets, is a form of what is called fractional reserve banking: money is created as an offset to loans. This "money" might or might not be backed by any of the gold held by the bank; today it is backed by the full faith and credit of the issuing institution.

Over a period of many years, banks became much larger and powerful. Central banks, like our own Federal Reserve Bank and the European Central Bank, were formed in the twentieth century by governments in order to give them better control over the currency and the economy. Fractional reserve banking became more and more important to industrialized societies; however, banks did not have the authority to remove the precious metals backing from the currency. That task was left up to the government. Under the rules set down by the Federal Reserve, most banks do not need to hold gold at all. The backing for their assets is the "full faith and credit" of the Federal Reserve.

Economics 102: Central banks and inflation

In our day the Federal Reserve sets the rate the fraction at which money may be limited by banks. It used to be a percent, such as 10 percent. At 10 percent the bank is permitted to lend nine times as much money (or gold) as they have on deposit. More recently, the Federal Reserve has permitted banks to lend money on an "infinite" basis, meaning that they basically are free to lend almost as much as they wish. Reducing the reserve requirements is a tool utilized by the central bank to make more money and credit available; the intent is that loose credit is a stimulus to the economy.

Our current fractional reserve banking system, as I understand it, is inherently inflationary. The use of fractional reserves enables the creation of money above and beyond the available supply authorized by the government. This money is added to the existing money supply and joins in chasing the same number of goods—which allows the price of those goods to rise.

Many economists believe that fractional reserve banking is essential if we are to have economic growth. The argument is made that without fractional reserve banking economic growth is limited to the size of the money supply or, during those times when we were under a gold standard, limited to the amount of gold held by banks. The most compelling argument against fractional reserve banking is its inflationary consequences. Through its actions the Federal Reserve has created far too much money and it has allowed banks to create too much money. Each new dollar debases the value of every dollar already in circulation. Since its creation the Federal Reserve has managed to decrease the value of the dollar by more than 95 percent.

The farmer and the carpenter

Let's say you are a farmer and I am a carpenter. Neither of us has the ability to create money; instead, we produce goods and services that have a money value.

I wish to purchase some of your produce and you wish to purchase my services. If we do not have a medium of exchange, we must engage in *barter*. Barter has been conducted in many societies in many periods of history, but the invention of money greatly simplified the conduct of business. Using money or currency as a medium of exchange, both the farmer and I can value our products and services in terms of that medium. We can establish prices for our goods or services. When our money has a specific value, albeit an arbitrary one established by the government, creating prices is relatively easy. The laws of supply and demand are in effect and we (the market) determine the value of each product or service in terms of the currency. Since we also use money as a store of value (remember, it used to represent gold on deposit) it needs to have an intrinsic value. Today's paper money has no value except the confidence its users place in it.

If the government wants to purchase wheat from the farmer and homes from the carpenter it can print money and buy those things. However, that means that there is more money in circulation even though the number of goods available (the size of the economy) remains the same. This is printing press inflation, when too many dollars are chasing the same number of goods. Prices rise to offset the additional number of dollars.

When a currency is debased by diluting or entirely removing its precious metals backing, or simply by printing money with no backing, those who use the currency as their medium of exchange soon realize that it is not worth what it was. Governments love this type of inflation because they control the printing press and the mint, and can create enough new money to enable them to pay off their debts and to buy votes.

Between the reign of the Claudio-Julian emporers and the 3rd Century AD the size of the Roman denarius and the amount of silver it contained was reduced several times. The percentage of silver in the coins decreased to about 2%. As the amount of silver declined, so did the real value of the currency. The coins were still used as a medium of exchange because even a debased currency is more workable than barter, but it took more money to buy the same goods.

The future of the dollar

In 2009 we are in a world where the once-mighty U.S. dollar is rapidly losing its status. Its usefulness as the world's reserve currency is waning as our government spends money with reckless abandon and the Federal Reserve runs its printing presses at top speed. The day will come when the dollar will collapse and be replaced, causing a tremendous amount of pain and suffering all over the world. There is no way for us to rescue the dollar in its current state; all we can do is to diversify out of the dollar and hold assets that will not be subject to the dollar's demise.

Bibliography

Achelis, Steven B., *Technical Analysis from A to Z*, Irwin Professional Publishing, 1995

American Numismatic Association, *Official A.N.A. Grading Standards for United States Coins*, St. Martin's Press, 1996

Bernstein, Jake, *New Facts on Futures: Insights and Strategies for Winning in the Futures Markets*, Probus Professional Pub, 1992

Bernstein, Peter L., *Against the Gods: The Remarkable Story of Risk*, Wiley, 1998

Blue, Ron, *Storm Shelter: Protecting Your Personal Finances*, Thomas Nelson Publishers, 1994

Bonner, William and Addison Wiggin, Empire of Debt: The Rise of an Epic Financial Crisis, Wiley, 2006

Bonner, William and Addison Wiggin, *Financial Reckoning Day: Surviving the Soft Depression of the Twenty-first Century*, Wiley, 2004

Condon, Gerald M. and Jeffrey L. Condon, *Beyond the Grave: The Right Way and the Wrong Way of Leaving Money to Your Children (and Others)*, HarperBusiness, 2001

Deffeyes, Kenneth S., *Beyond Oil: The View from Hubbert's Peak*, Hill and Wang, 2006

Diamond, Jared, *Collapse: How Societies Choose to Fail or Succeed*, Penguin (Non-Classics), 2005

Diamond, Jared, *Guns, Germs, and Steel: The Fates of Human Societies*, W.W. Norton, 2005

Duncan, Richard, *The Dollar Crisis: Causes, Consequences, Cures*, Revised and Updated, Wiley, 2005

Greider, William, *Secrets of the Temple: How the Federal Reserve Runs the Country*, Simon & Schuster, 1989

Hardy, Dorcas R. and C. Colburn, *Social Insecurity: The Crisis in America's Social Security System and How to Plan Now for Your Own Financial Survival*, Villard Books, 1991

Hartmann, Thom, *The Last Hours of Ancient Sunlight: The Fate of the World and What We Can Do Before It's Too Late*, Three Rivers Press, 2004

Heinberg, Richard, *PowerDown: Options and Actions for a Post-Carbon World*, New Society Publishers, 2004

Heinberg, Richard, *The Party's Over: Oil, War, and the Fate of Industrial Societies*, New Society Publishers, 2005

Huber, Peter W., and Mark P. Mills, *The Bottomless Well: The Twilight of Fuel, the Virtue of Waste, and Why We Will Never Run Out of Energy*, Basic Books, 2005

Jardine, Michael, *New Frontiers in Fibonacci Trading: Charting Techniques, Strategies, and Simple Applications*, Marketplace Books, 2003

Kaplan, Ben, *How to Go to College Almost for Free*, Collins, 2001

Karpel, Craig S., *The Retirement Myth: What You Must Know Now to Prosper in the Coming Meltdown of Job Security, Pension Plans, Social Security, the Stock Market, Housing Prices, and More*, Harpercollins, 1996

Klare, Michael T., *Resource Wars: The New Landscape of Global Conflict with a New Introduction by the Author*, Holt Paperbacks, 2002

Kurzweil, Ray, *The Singularity Is Near: When Humans Transcend Biology*, Penguin (Non-Classics), 2006

Kunstler, James Howard, *The Long Emergency: Surviving the End of Oil, Climate Change, and Other Converging Catastrophes of the Twenty-first Century*, Grove Press, 2006

Leeb, Stephen, *The Coming Economic Collapse: How You Can Thrive When Oil Costs $200 a Barrel*, Business Plus, 2007

Leeb, Stephen, *The Oil Factor: Protect Yourself and Profit from the Coming Energy Crisis*, Business Plus, 2005

MacKay, Charles, *Extraordinary Popular Delusions and the Madness of Crowds*, Harriman House, 2003

Malabre, Alfred L., Jr., *Beyond Our Means: How America's Long Years of Debt, Deficits, and Reckless Borrowing Now Threaten to Overwhelm Us*, Random House, 1987

Morris, Virginia and Robert M. Butler, *How to Care for Aging Parents*, Workman Publishing Company, 2004

Nasser, David and William S. Lupien, *Market Evaluation and Analysis for Swing Trading: Timeless Methods and Strategies for an Ever-changing Market*, McGraw-Hill, 2005

Posamentier, Alfred S., and Ingmar Lehmann, *The Fabulous Fibonacci Numbers*, Prometheus Books, 2007

Prechter, Robert R., Jr., *At the Crest of the Tidal Wave*, New Classics Library, 2002

Prechter, Robert R., Jr., *Conquer the Crash: You Can Survive and Prosper in a Deflationary Depression*, Wiley, 2002

Prechter, Robert R., Jr., *Socionomics: The Science of History and Social Prediction*, New Classics Library, 2002

Rogers, Jim, *Hot Commodities: How Anyone Can Invest Profitably in the World's Best Market*, Random House Trade Paperbacks, 2007

Rubino, John and James Turk, *The Collapse of the Dollar and How to Profit from It: Make a Fortune by Investing in Gold and Other Hard Assets*, Currency (Reprint), 2008

Rutner, Richard, *The Trouble with Mutual Funds*, Financial Press, 2003

Simmons, Matthew R., *Twilight in the Desert: The Coming Saudi Oil Shock and the World Economy*, Wiley, 2006

Slott, Ed, *Parlay your IRA into a Family Fortune: Three Easy Steps for Creating a Lifetime Supply of Tax-deferred, Even Tax-free, Wealth for You and Your Family*, Penguin Books, 2005

Slott, Ed, *The Retirement Savings Time Bomb . . . and How to Defuse It: A Five-step Action Plan for*

Protecting Your IRAs, 401(k)s, and Other Retirement Plans from Near Annihilation by the Taxman, Penguin (Non-Classics), 2007

Stein, Matthew, *When Technology Fails: A Manual for Self-reliance and Planetary Survival*, Chelsea Green Publishing, 2007

Swanson, Gerald J., *America the Broke: How the Reckless Spending of the White House and Congress Is Bankrupting Our Country and Destroying Our Children's Future*, Currency, 2004

Taleb, Nassim Nicholas, *The Black Swan: The Impact of the Highly Improbable*, Random House, 2007

Talbott, John R., *The Coming Crash in the Housing Market: Ten Things You Can Do Now to Protect Your Most Valuable Investment*, McGraw-Hill, 2003

Weber, Jack, *Honey I've Shrunk the Bills: Save $5,000 to $10,000 Every Year* (Capital Ideas for Business and Personal Development), Capital Books, 2000

Weiss, Martin D., *The Ultimate Safe Money Guide: How Everyone Fifty and Over Can Protect, Save, and Grow Their Money*, Wiley, 2003

Wiggin, Addison, *The Demise of the Dollar . . . and Why It's Great for Your Investments*, Wiley, 2005

Recommended Reading

Most of us are very busy and don't take the time to read. We should. I have always encouraged my clients to educate themselves about personal finance and to get involved in the important issues. These books will help you understand not only my point of view but some of the great and troubling issues facing us today.

Bernstein, Peter L., *Against the Gods: The Remarkable Story of Risk,* Wiley, 1998. This very readable book helps you understand how probability and statistics developed over the centuries.

Bonner, William and Addison Wiggin, *Empire of Debt: The Rise of an Epic Financial Crisis,* Wiley, 2006. A very quick read with some good insights.

Deffeyes, Kenneth S., *Beyond Oil: The View from Hubbert's Peak,* Hill and Wang, 2006. One of the best books on peak oil.

Diamond, Jared, *Collapse: How Societies Choose to Fail or Succeed,* Penguin (Non-Classics), 2005. A new "classic" and very interesting reading. What *were* the inhabitants of Easter Island thinking when they cut down the last tree?

Hartmann, Thom, *The Last Hours of Ancient Sunlight: The Fate of the World and What We Can Do Before It's Too Late,* Three Rivers Press, 2004. This very readable book may have an incorrect premise if petroleum is not a true "fossil fuel," but at present the effects of running out of oil will affect us just the same.

Heinberg, Richard, *PowerDown: Options and Actions for a Post-carbon World,* New Society Publishers, 2004. This was my first exposure to peak oil. If you read this book, you also ought to read the next book on the list.

Heinberg, Richard, *The Party's Over: Oil, War, and the Fate of Industrial Societies,* New Society Publishers, 2005. Heinberg tries to grapple with problems everyone should be considering but almost no one knows about.

Kaplan, Ben, *How to Go to College Almost for Free,* Collins, 2001. This will help you obtain scholarships and grants for your children's education.

Klare, Michael T., *Resource Wars: The New Landscape of Global Conflict with a New Introduction by the Author,* Holt Paperbacks, 2002. Klare is right on the money. There are ongoing disputes over water in the U.S. even now, though none have turned into violent conflict—yet.

Klein, Naomi, *The Shock Doctrine: The Rise of Disaster Capitalism,* Picador, 2007. Reading this bestseller is easier if you have taken Economics 101 and 102, but the basic story line can be readily understood. This book is a powerful condemnation of a famous Nobel Prize winner. You won't want to believe what Naomi says, but almost daily a story in the news confirms what she has written.

Kunstler, James Howard, *The Long Emergency: Surviving the End of Oil, Climate Change, and Other Converging Catastrophes of the Twenty-first Century,* Grove Press, 2006. Many people dismiss Kunstler for being overdramatic in his assessment and predictions. This is a depressing book, but you ought to know what he has to say.

Leeb, Stephen, *The Coming Economic Collapse: How You Can Thrive When Oil Costs $200 a Barrel,* Business Plus, 2007. Good discussion, but I'm not sure his recommendations will be effective or comprehensive.

Leeb, Stephen, *The Oil Factor: Protect Yourself and Profit from the Coming Energy Crisis,* Business Plus, 2005. Ditto Leeb's other book, above.

MacKay, Charles, *Extraordinary Popular Delusions and the Madness of Crowds,* Harriman House, 2003. Another recent "classic." Everyone ought to understand how manias begin and end.

Rubino, John and James Turk, *The Collapse of the Dollar and How to Profit from It: Make a Fortune by Investing in Gold and Other Hard Assets,* Currency (Reprint), 2008. Like many other books, this one sets up a problem well but has a hard time solving it.

Rutner, Richard, *The Trouble with Mutual Funds,* Financial Press, 2003. This book is a quick read with good information about classic mutual funds. Probably written to direct people toward ETFs.

Simmons, Matthew R., *Twilight in the Desert: The Coming Saudi Oil Shock and the World Economy,* Wiley, 2006. Heavily researched and very authoritative; we can only hope that Matthew Simmons is wrong about the Arabian oil fields. I think he knows what he is talking about.

Slott, Ed, *The Retirement Savings Time Bomb . . . and How to Defuse It: A Five-step Action Plan for Protecting Your IRAs, 401(k)s, and Other Retirement Plans from Near Annihilation by the Taxman,* Penguin (Non-Classics), 2007. Another readable "problem" book offering some good suggestions.

Stein, Matthew, *When Technology Fails: A Manual for Self-reliance and Planetary Survival,* Chelsea Green Publishing, 2007. So, how big is *your* carbon footprint, and what will you do when the lights go out?

Swanson, Gerald J., *America the Broke: How the Reckless Spending of the White House and Congress Is Bankrupting Our Country and Destroying Our Children's Future,* Currency, 2004.

Weber, Jack, *Honey I've Shrunk the Bills: Save $5,000 to $10,000 Every Year* (Capital Ideas for Business and Personal Development), Capital Books, 2000. This is a little out of date by now, but if you are struggling to make ends meet this book can certainly help.

Weiss, Martin D., *The Ultimate Safe Money Guide: How Everyone Fifty and Over Can Protect, Save, and Grow Their Money,* Wiley, 2003. Weiss runs an independent rating service. He has been right many times when the major ratings services were wrong. He is no technical analyst, however.

Wiggin, Addison and Kate Incontrera, *I.O.U.S.A.: One Nation. Under Stress. In Debt.,* Wiley, 2008. The book has much more information than the movie of the same name; after after two stimulus packages both are sadly out of date. The situation is now much worse than what they describe.

Index

Symbols

"black box" software packages

Numerics

1913- 9, 35, 47, 203, 204, 245, 290
401(k)- 26, 33, 38, 82, 92, 93, 94, 96, 106, 171, 173, 197, 214, 232
44 Wall- Street Fund, 128

A

accountability- 162
adjustable-rate loans- 85, 90, 91
Advantage Energy- 160, 217
agricultural products- 143
Alternative energy- 144
alternative technologies- 158
American Dream- 196
American Stock Exchange-73
Amish- 249
amortization- 91, 185
annuities-37, 51, 68, 85, 170, 172, 180, 210, 223, 227
antiques- 21, 85, 165
Antiques Roadshow- 165
apartment complexes- 162
Apple Computer- 281
aquifers- 197
art- 21, 147, 164
Athabasca- 159
Austrian Philharmonic- 150

B

baby boomers- 165
back testing- 232
back-end load- 126
balance sheet- 84, 93
bankruptcy- 118, 138, 183, 253

Barron's- 75, 213

barter- 152, 156, 291

behavior- 66, 82, 188, 193, 230, 243

big-ticket items- 112

Bill of Rights- 247

bitumen- 160

blind men and the elephant- 194

Bloomberg- 55, 122, 213

blowoff- 242

bonds- 13, 38, 40, 51, 53, 67, 68, 71, 77, 85, 94, 115, 118, 124, 126, 180, 200, 208, 221, 226, 238, 240

bottom-up management- 122, 216

Bowser Report

breakout- 233, 242

British Empire- 203

British Isles- 205

bubble- 10, 31, 161, 197, 220, 229

Buffett, Warren- 124

bulletin-board stock- 237

bullion- 70, 148, 152, 156

Bureau of Labor Statistics- 200

Business Week- 73, 213

buy stop- 243

C

cable TV- 75, 162

California- 59, 109, 253

call option- 21, 134, 153, 222, 240

Canadian Maple Leaf- 150, 154

cancer- 52, 82, 177

candlestick chart- 269, 279

capital gains- 37, 40, 77, 96, 118, 245

captive agent- 49

car insurance- 112

career advancement- 103

cash cow- 233

casino- 68

cattle feeding- 164

central government- 198

certificates of deposit- 37, 68, 93, 169, 171

channels- 242, 152

Chesapeake Energy

China- 62, 77, 190, 220

Chinese pandas- 150

Chinese porcelain- 14, 68

Class-A shares- 49

Class-B shares- 49

Class-C shares- 49

climate- 158, 189, 194

closed-end funds- 22, 55, 126, 173, 186, 210, 215, 223, 227

CNBC- 75

cocoa- 78, 143, 152, 210, 238

coffee- 78, 143, 210, 238

cognitive dissonance- 21, 115

collectibles- 21, 68, 147, 165, 167

collective bargaining agreements- 201

college education- 12, 113

Colorado Springs- 195

comforts of life- 11

commercial real estate- 180, 220

commissions- 20,46, 47, 50, 72, 109, 118, 123, 137, 160, 171, 188, 227, 230

commodities- 22, 53, 67, 77, 124, 143, 189, 194, 206, 223, 243, 281, 153

commodities trading- 153

commodity-trading advisor

community- 47, 59, 220

concentration of wealth- 196

condominium- 110

conflicts of interest- 77

conformity- 115

Congress- 9, 13, 26, 36, 62, 63, 172, 204, 207, 242, 247, 250

conspicuous consumption- 248

Constitution- 10, 76, 247

consumer expenditure survey- 200

consumer price index- 199, 34, 206

contingent deferred sales charge- 171

continuation contract

contract sizes- 143

contracting triangle- 239

convertible bonds- 124

corn/wheat spread

cotton mills- 203

covered calls- 137, 140, 222

crude oil- 219

currencies- 36, 143, 207, 223, 238

Currency Share Australian dollar- 222

cycles- 165, 184, 194, 257

D

daily chart- 228, 238, 272

day trading- 71, 118, 225, 232

de Tocqueville, Alexis- 250

dealers- 69, 112, 150, 156, 166

death and taxes- 245

debt- 12, 13, 33, 36, 84, 90, 118, 124, 161, 195, 206, 221, 291

debt service- 91

debtor nation- 196

decimal pricing- 69

Declaration of Independence- 165

declining dollar- 19, 37, 73, 98, 117, 170, 199, 209

deep-discount brokers- 69

Deffeyes, Kenneth S.- 158

defined-benefit plans- 26, 253

defined-contribution plans- 26, 253

deflation- 20, 36, 206, 239

democracy- 34, 198

denial- 227

Department of Labor- 200

depreciating liability- 109

depreciation-185

derivatives- 131, 211, 255

desertification- 10, 197

diamonds- 109

diamonds, colorless

dirty bomb- 197

disability income insurance- 27, 51, 55, 82, 177, 249

discount brokerage- 94, 173

discretionary spending- 109

diversity- 115

dividend yields- 217

DKHR- 235

dollar float- 207

dot.com bubble- 31, 237, 229

Double Eagles- 149, 155, 166

double taxation of dividends- 245

double tops- 220

downturns- 70

dual passports- 50

E

Eagle coins-152

earned income credit- 245

EBITDA- 185

economic activity- 194, 203

economic stimulus- 205

economist- 71, 77, 290

economists, The- 213

electronic media- 71, 213

Elliott wave- 188, 220, 237, 243, 279, 284

Elliott Wave International- 188

Elliott, Ralph- 188

Elliottician- 235, 165, 227, 242, 279

emergency fund- 90, 170, 214, 216

eminent domain- 247

energy- 22, 27, 31, 59, 110, 143, 158, 189, 207, 210, 220, 255

energy trusts- 22, 173

England- 164, 203

environmental damage- 247

equity-index annuities- 85, 121, 223

equity-index annuity

eSignal- 239, 240, 279

estate planners- 45

estate planning- 50, 13, 53

ETFConnect- 223

ETF- 13, 21, 68, 78, 115, 128, 138, 148, 153, 173, 180, 183, 186, 210, 222, 223
ethanol- 159
exchange-traded funds- 13, 128
expiration date- 131, 134
exponential- 70, 119, 190, 198
extended warranties- 112
Exxon Mobil- 144, 228, 272

F

FDIC- 170
Federal Reserve- 13, 9, 20, 35, 64, 68, 77, 106, 147, 204, 207, 239, 290
Federalist- 198
Fibonacci- 219
Fibonacci retracement- 219, 235
Fidelity- 121, 128, 222
Fidelity Magellan Fund-121, 128
financial advisors- 45, 51
financial plan- 13, 17, 25, 45, 48, 60, 84, 8, 171, 177, 225
financial planners- 52, 45
financial professionals- 45, 79, 55, 177, 183, 190, 171, 225
financial services industry- 17, 45, 51, 56, 116, 190
Financial Times- 213
financial worksheet- 84
First Amendment- 247
Fitch- 213
fixed annuities- 37, 52, 85, 88, 170, 172, 180, 210
flats- 242
Forbes- 213
foreign currencies- 209, 222
foreign government bonds
foreign labor- 196
Fortune- 213, 75
Fortune 500- 162
Founding Fathers- 198, 247
fractional pricing- 69
Frankin, Benjamin- 195, 262
Franklin D. Roosevelt- 148
FranklinTempleton- 129
front-end load- 126

full-service broker- 123, 125

fundamental analysis- 62, 78, 183, 230, 243, 283

fundamental research- 218

fundamentals- 121, 123, 184, 189, 230, 243, 238

futures contract- 135, 144, 152, 223, 238

G

Gap- 32, 166, 234

General Electric- 133

General Motors- 75

generator- 111

glaciers-197

global warming- 10, 189, 115, 254

gold- 22, 35, 67, 70, 128, 135, 143, 147, 150, 153, 216, 217, 289

gold bars- 154

gold certificates- 154

gold confiscation- 151

gold dust

gold jewelry- 154

gold/silver spread

good neighbor- 249

Google- 184, 217

government accountability office- 251

government intervention

government intervention-184, 219, 257

grade expansion- 166

grading services- 149

Graham, Benjamin- 124

Great Britain- 205

greater-fool theory- 69

Greenspan, Alan

Gross, Bill- 239

guarantees- 53, 58, 76, 82, 117, 159, 173, 178

H

hazardous materials-247

heating oil- 247

hedge funds- 53, 190

herd mentality- 66, 121

high-efficiency fluorescent bulbs- 247
higher highs- 241
higher lows- 241
high-yield bond funds- 173
hindsight forecasting- 117
home equity- 10, 90, 97, 111
home mortgage- 97, 90
Hong Kong- 245, 62
hospitalization- 249
hot tip- 122, 80
house hunting- 134
housing bubble- 220, 197
Hulbert Financial Digest- 78
human nature- 193, 227, 66
hydrocarbons- 159, 197, 255
hydroelectric- 159
hydrogen- 159

I

identity theft- 248
illegal drugs- 178
illiquid- 94, 160
impulse waves- 53
incentive fees- 122
income portfolio- 85, 95
income statement- 96, 180, 200, 245
income taxes- 96, 180, 200, 245
India- 62
Industrial Revolution- 197, 203, 209, 289
inflation- 209
inflation profits- 200
infrastructure- 77, 103
initial public offerings- 64, 72
insurance agent- 47, 51, 81
interest rates- 71, 77, 91, 103, 110, 122, 173, 178, 210, 217, 219
interest -only- 91
Internet- 9, 19, 33, 52, 71, 75, 97, 11, 122, 151, 186, 202, 213, 218, 233
Internet trading- 233

interurban rail lines- 159

intrinsic value- 22, 35, 145, 165, 258, 291

inverse correlations- 187, 210

investment advisers- 39, 53

investment bankers- 64

investment mania- 165

investment vehicles- 62

IPO- 64, 72, 235

IRA- 27, 57, 87, 93, 108, 131, 169, 172, 180, 199, 209, 214

J

Japan- 62, 219

junk-bond funds- 126

junk-silver coins- 156

K

keeping up with the Joneses- 195, 205

Kennedy, John F.- 249

King Farouk- 149

Kurzweil, Ray- 198, 251

L

Lane, George- 188, 193,

learning curve- 143

leasing- 91, 122, 164,

legal insurance- 248

level load- 126

level playing field

leverage- 153, 161, 210, 212, 238, 131

Levittown, New York- 202

life insurance- 13, 47, 50, 106, 173, 176, 200, 215

limit orders- 129, 237

limited partnership

limited partnerships- 13, 49, 61, 89, 161, 180

limited partnerships

liquidity- 69, 181, 184

litigious society- 247

long calls- 134

LONG-TERM CAPITAL MANAGEMENT- 207

Lucent Technologies- 235

luxuries- 10, 33, 98

Lynch, Peter- 121

M

Madison Avenue- 11

major automakers- 159

management fees- 47, 53, 63, 128, 223

Manhattan- 221

manipulation- 64, 155, 199

margin- 69, 73, 112, 123, 128, 133, 211

margin account- 73, 112

margin requirements- 144, 240, 242

market return- 70

Market Vectors–Gold Miners ETF- 222

marketability- 22, 69, 163

meats- 143

medical mistakes- 248

Medicare- 13

Medicare taxes- 245, 96, 105

mental stop- 228, 235

Merrill Lynch- 65

metals- 22, 31, 39, 59, 68, 94, 128, 143, 147, 210, 220, 289

methodology- 71, 179, 187, 191, 218

Microsoft- 226, 233

Microsoft Money- 97

middle-class- 195, 32, 50, 57, 61, 103

millionaires- 10

Ming Dynasty porcelain- 165

momentum- 185, 195, 239, 124, 67

momentum trader- 185, 227

money creation- 199, 240, 290

money-market funds- 170

money supply- 200, 208, 290

monosodium glutamate

Moody's- 213

Morningstar- 213

mortgage brokers- 91

motels-162

moving average- 228

MSNBC- 213, 185

municipal bonds- 124

mutual funds- 13, 22, 37, 49, 59, 69, 82, 115, 125, 172, 181, 190, 211, 223, 254,

N

naked call

NASDAQ- 31

natural gas-67, 110, 143, 159, 217, 222

natural resources- 10, 21, 31, 59, 103, 119, 204, 207, 219

necessities- 26, 33, 82

needle in a haystack- 217

negative amortization- 91

neighborhood- 109, 249

nervous Nellie- 227

Nestlé- 152

net asset value- 93, 125, 186

net return- 71, 209

net worth- 10, 94, 99, 162, 181, 218

NGC- 22, 149, 154

Nixon, Richard- 210

no-load mutual funds- 70, 126, 172, 223

non-qualified annuity- 214

non-recourse loans

number crunching- 187

numismatic- 149, 154, 166

numismatic coins- 150, 166

O

objectives- 83, 122, 176, 249, 255

objectivity- 71, 179

offshore banking- 51

oil- 10, 41, 67, 111, 143, 158, 171, 184, 189, 205, 210, 219, 227, 254, 256

oil exploration- 159

Oklahoma City- 198

open-end mutual funds- 173, 126, 226

opinions- 19, 60, 71, 115, 163, 179, 213, 229, 243

options- 131

ORP- 171, 253

overbought- 188, 281

oversold- 188, 281

P

P/E ratio- 184, 194, 234

panning for gold- 217

paper assets- 67

paper profits- 241

paradigm shift- 190

PCGS- 22, 149, 154

peace dividend- 197

peak coal- 158

peak oil- 158, 219, 144, 189, 196, 255

penny stocks- 237

pension plan obligations- 196

perceived risk- 68, 169, 172

personal debt- 203

personal financial management- 17, 32, 57, 81

personal liability policy- 248

Perth Mint- 154

physical delivery- 144, 152

Ponzi schemes- 165

pork bellies- 143, 194, 238

postage stamps- 166

Powershares Wilder Hill Clean Energy Portfolio- 222

Prechter, Robert- 188

precious metals- 22, 39, 59, 96, 94, 127, 145, 223, 258, 290

precious stones- 156

preferred stocks- 118

price inflation- 35, 199, 256

price/earnings ratio- 184, 194, 234, 218

pricing power- 200

principal- 20, 37, 40, 68, 92, 104, 117, 124, 169, 171, 178, 254

prison- 66, 127, 250

private equity- 65

procrastination- 82

professionalism- 48, 51

proof coins- 149

propane- 111

property laws- 247

property/casualty insurance- 47, 51, 56

prospectus- 37, 124, 254

prudent man- 108

PTA- 82, 249

public welfare- 205

publicly traded- 118

purchasing power- 20, 31, 37, 105, 108, 117, 172, 199, 207

put option- 138, 240

Q

Quicken- 97

R

R&D- 184, 200

rags to riches- 67

rare books- 68

rare coins- 13, 85, 155, 158, 166, 68

rare stamps- 68, 166

rate of return- 9, 105, 112, 121, 178, 179, 221

rationalizations- 82

Reagan, Ronald- 197, 225

real estate- 10, 13, 31, 68, 85, 92, 104, 134, 147, 158, 160, 166, 189, 197, 208, 212, 217, 226

real-estate investment trusts- 161

real-estate tax-credit programs- 163, 171

real risk- 69

rebound- 141, 229

redistribution of assets- 205

Refined Elliott Trader- 235, 284, 189, 279

registered investment adviser- 53

regression to the mean- 221

regular strike coins- 149

regulations- 19, 50, 51, 128, 143, 185, 198

Reichsmarks- 35, 264

repeating events- 195

republic- 10, 195, 198

required minimum distributions- 57

residential real estate- 13, 104, 110, 148, 160, 197

Rick Santelli- 71

risk- 11, 17, 22, 28, 36, 37, 59, 66, 79, 117, 130, 143, 163, 169, 175, 176, 178, 189, 209, 220, 242, 251

Roth 401(k)- 106

Roth IRA- 106

royalty trusts- 160

Russia- 62

S

S&P 500- 31, 118, 144, 188, 219

safe harbor- 117

safety deposit box- 71

Saudi Arabia- 158, 255

Savings accounts- 68, 93, 169, 180

Scarcity- 35, 149, 151, 158, 166, 207, 211, 219, 224, 255

scrimping and saving- 113

Section 529 plan- 182, 215, 216

sector funds- 40, 126

securities industry- 49, 57

self-discipline- 229

self-sufficiency- 110

selling when everyone else is buying- 219

service economy- 196

sexual harrassment- 248

shopping channel- 82, 152

short call- 241

short-call options

short put- 241

short sale- 242

shortages- 190, 197, 219, 256

silver- 67, 128, 143, 147

silver jewelry- 156

Singapore- 191

Singularity- 251

Sixteenth Amendment- 245

slippage- 231

smoking- 98

Social Security- 13, 26, 105, 245,

softs- 143

solar array- 111

South African Krugerrand- 150

special situation

Spitzer, Elliott- 72

spread- 131, 73

St. Gaudens- 149, 166

Standard and Poor's- 213

standard of living- 10, 13, 34, 195, 203

starter homes- 202

state income taxes- 245

statistical studies- 231

stochastics- 193, 281, 188

stock certificates- 122

stock indexes- 131, 143

stock market- 122, 16, 21, 31, 38, 59, 67, 78, 95, 118, 133, 180, 197, 210, 219, 238

stock option- 131, 143

stockbroker- 15, 45, 51, 127, 189

stocks- 13, 38, 51, 67, 78, 118, 143, 160, 180, 183, 186, 192, 200, 214, 215, 217, 227

stocks at a discount- 173, 215

stop limit- 146

stop loss- 145, 222, 228

storage units- 112, 161

stretch IRA- 58

strike price- 136, 240

strip malls- 161

structural deficit- 155

student loans- 91

subjective information- 90

subprime mortgage crisis- 211

subsidies- 159, 194, 221

substitution- 201

superpower- 197

surrender charges- 59, 170

Swiss franc- 171, 223

synthetic stock

T

Tamper evident- 149

target price- 185, 234, 237, 242

tariffs- 194

tax avoidance- 245

tax benefits- 162, 164, 173, 244

tax evasion- 245

taxes- 10, 70, 78, 98, 122, 245, 148, 172, 189, 200, 205

tax-free interest- 124, 242

T-bills- 170, 225

technical analysis- 39, 60, 79, 123, 183, 187, 218, 235, 279, 280

technical research

technological revolution- 198

terminal decline- 158, 196, 226, 255

the Wall Street Journal- 56, 75, 213

thinly traded securities- 131, 163, 237

third world- 10, 197

three types of trends- 220

timing the market- 121

top-down approach- 216

topping formation- 209

Toronto Stock Exchange- 217

total return funds- 126

trade execution- 123

trading- 21, 25, 53, 66, 71, 118, 143, 152, 183, 213, 225, 233

trailing stop- 145, 222, 231, 234

transaction costs- 129, 166, 231

Treasury bonds-180, 221, 238, 240

Treasury Department- 124, 149

trend reversal- 211

triple threat- 18, 237

troy ounce- 135, 149

TRS- 253

Turkish stock market- 77

U

U.S. debt- 210

U.S. dollar- 9, 148, 169, 171, 204, 291

U.S. government- 124, 149, 170, 173, 208, 221, 251
UGMA- 214
undervalued- 67, 137, 159, 170, 173, 208, 221, 251
unemployment taxes- 245
University of Texas- 253
unlimited opportunity- 195
unmarketable- 161, 162
USA Today- 72
UTMA- 214

V

Vacation time-shares- 164
valid premise- 78, 187, 231, 243
Value Line- 213
Vanguard
variable annuities- 51, 226
vicious circle- 204, 209
volatility- 40, 73, 120, 143, 197
vultures- 63, 163,

W

Wall Street- 9, 17, 46, 51, 58, 62, 63, 72, 183, 209, 245
Wall Street Digest- 213
Wall Street Journal- 75
Wal-Mart-196
Washington, George- 198
waste- 13, 197, 206, 207
wasting assets- 241
wealth creation and preservation- 236
weather patterns- 193
weekly chart- 218, 235, 239, 279
Weiss- 213
welfare- 10, 26, 63, 205
wheat- 135, 143, 211, 238
window dressing- 188
working class- 196
worldview- 219, 222

X

XsunX- 235

Y

Yahoo! Finance- 213,235

Z

zigzags- 284
zinc- 153, 211, 256

Endnotes

1. If you are contributing to a 401(k) or other employer-sponsored retirement plan, you are investing—though you still may not have enough disposable income to do so if you are not paying off your credit cards each month. Do you think your 401(k) will earn more than the 18 percent-plus interest rates your credit cards are charging? Even with its tax advantages, a 401(k) must perform extremely well to beat credit-card interest.

2. Source: Wikipedia, *Fiat currency*

3. The greater fool theory says that you would buy something hoping that someone even more foolish than you will take it off your hands at a higher price.

4. Under the now-prevalent decimal pricing system, most securities trade in dollars and cents. They used to trade in a eighths or larger fractions, and an eighth is twelve and a half cents. That meant that your Bid could be $10 and your ask could be $10 1/8, or $10.125. Today the spread is often as little as a penny, even for the more expensive stocks.

5. *Scandal sullies mutual funds,* USA Today, September 3, 2003

6. *The American Stock Exchange: Scandal on Wall Street*, Business Week, April 26, 1999

7. Net cost of ownership for your owner-occupied dwelling is its full monthly cost minus the cost of renting or buying a different home, one that is as comfortable but less expensive. You're just going to have to guess at how much a different home might cost.

8. "Servicing" a debt means making the regular, required interest-only or principal and interest payments.

9. "Prudent man" refers to the Prudent Man Rule based on common law stemming from an 1830 Massachusetts court decision. Judge Samuel Putnam stated "Those with responsibility to invest money for others should act with prudence, discretion, intelligence, and regard for the safety of capital as well as income." Harvard College v. Amory, 9 Pick. (26 Mass.) 446, 461 (1830)

10. Lydon, Tom, "ETFs and Closed End Funds–Know the Difference," www.etftrends.com, February 21, 2006.

11. Ray Kurzweil, *The Singularity Is Near*, Viking Penguin, 2005

12. *Consumer Price Index Overview*, www.bls.gov/cpi/cpiovrvw.htm, October 16, 2001

13. Ibid , *Data Available*.

14. Ibid, *Coverage*.

15. Ibid, *Uses*.

16. *Frequently Asked Questions: Is the Consumer Price Index (CPI) a cost-of-living index?*, www.bls.gov. dolfaq/bls_ques2.htm.

17. *Frequently Asked Questions: What is substitution and substitution bias? And how does the C-CPI-U eliminate it?*, www.bls.gov/cpi/cpiuspqa.htm

18. The world is finally catching on to this idea. See *The great college savings fiasco* for the latest on 529 plans, http://articles.moneycentral.msn.com/learn-how-to-invest/the-great-college-savings-fiasco. aspx

19. "Slippage" refers to the difference between your purchase or sale price and the price you hoped to receive but could not because of timing and market movement.

20. Take a look at the current bestseller *The Little Pink House* written by my associate Jeff Benedict for a classic example.

21. You might want to look at *It's all Your Fault! A Basic Guide to Personal Liability and Protecting Yourself in a Litigious World*, Silver Lake Publishing, 2001

22. Diamond, Jared, Collapse*: How Societies Choose to Fail or Succeed*, Viking Penguin, 2005

23. Deffeyes, *Beyond Oil: The View from Hubbert's Peak*, Hill and Wang, 2005

24. Simmons, Matthew, *Twilight in the Desert: the Coming Saudi Oil Shock and the World Economy*, John Wiley & Sons, 2005.

25. Counterfeiting probably comes closest to a way to create money from nothing.